After the Flood

Bogdan Denitch

After the Flood

World Politics and Democracy in the Wake of Communism

Wesleyan University Press
Published by University Press of New England
Hanover and London

Wesleyan University Press

Published by University Press of New England

Hanover, NH 03755

Printed in the United States of America

5 4 3 2 1

Library of Congress Cataloging-in-Publication Data

Denitch, Bogdan Denis.
After the flood : world politics and democracy in the
wake of communism / Bogdan Denitch.
p. cm.
Includes index.
ISBN 0–8195–5248–8 (cl).—ISBN 0–8195–6256–4 (pa)
1. World politics—1989– 2. Post-communism. I. Title.
D860.D46 1992
320'.09'04—dc20 92–53858
∞

Contents

Preface

> . . . and so there were many that began to cry out that the days of darkness had lasted too long . . . And they said, "Come let us build our homes around this bush that has burned throughout the ages."
>
> Now it happened that one by one the branches were consumed and fell in ashes to the ground. Even the roots were burned out and became cold cinders. And once again there was darkness and cold.
>
> Then voices were raised, crying: . . .
>
> "We must start again even if we have to plant a new bush."
>
> Blessed be those who speak such words! May the stones be not too cruel to their feet; may their courage equal our suffering . . .
>
> —From *The Burned Bramble*, by Manes Sperber[1]

Experts Agreed: Communism Was the Wave of the Future

My epigraph is drawn from the preface to a significant political novel written at a time which was probably the nadir of hope for democratic radicals, one of whom was Manes Sperber. *The Burned Bramble* was one of many contemporary doomsday works written in the late 1940s and early 1950s, although, unlike most, its author had retained at least a conditional hope and a general left orientation. Other major books in that now all but forgotten intellectual wave included Arthur Koestler's *The Age of Longing*, the edited volume, *The God that Failed*, and George Orwell's *1984*. These writers shared a vision of the Stalinist totalitarianism that seemed then to be triumphant and invincible, vastly more efficient and ruthless than the flabby liberal democracies and social democratic movements of the West. Capitalism was discredited in part because conservative political and economic elites in the West had been compromised by large scale concessions and collaboration with fascism and Nazism. The rich in France, Belgium, Holland, and even to some extent in Britain had preferred to do business with Hitler, Mussolini and Franco than with their own mild reformist labor and socialist parties. Whatever else capitalism seemed to be at the end of World War II, it was not seen as a defender of democracy or equality. For that matter it was not even particularly efficient as a system. The relative inefficiency of capitalism, particularly one untrammeled with Keynesian state interventionism, was readily conceded by a great many social theorists and most political economists. The necessity of certain forms of state intervention and planning was by then taken for granted everywhere, except perhaps in the United States. Some kind of more or less centralized collectivist state seemed to be the wave of the future right after the Second World War. The most dynamic, brutal, and well organized of these collectivist systems was the Soviet one, which had just played the major role in smashing Hitler's armies and had thereby established hegemony over half of Europe. After a devastating decade of fascist ascendance in the advanced industrial societies of Europe and a World War that had introduced weapons of such mass destruction as to place the continued existence of humankind in question, Stalinism appeared both monstrously efficient and irresistible. For the time being, Stalinism seemed to have either effectively absorbed or displaced the international mass left.

At the point in time, and for four decades to come, the abject defeat and total disappearance within forty years of official Communism as a significant world movement, system of state power, and international force was unimaginable. This was an outcome that was completely unpredictable, as even a more modest internal evolution from totalitarianism to authoritarianism was not considered possible by most Western scholars and policy makers for decades after Stalin's death. After all, that particular rhetorical distinction between totalitarian and authoritarian was used by inveterate cold-warriors to justify backing pro-American dictators in the struggle which was defined as a global contest between two incompatible world systems, a struggle that included a number of local, sometimes extremely nasty, little wars against popular, communist-led insurgents around the world.

Authoritarianism, the queasy Western and American political publics were told, *could* change into parliamentary democracy, and was therefore, despite all of the atrocities of any specific authoritarian regime, the lesser evil. On the other hand, popular movements against these admittedly authoritarian, American-backed dictators were more often than not under the leadership of open or covert Marxist-Leninists, who would inevitably (how ideologues loved that word!) attempt to set up totalitarian systems. As a notable Secretary of State once said, the United States was not about to allow a people, through their own stupidity, to democratically vote in a communist regime. Excessive humanitarian softness and liberalism were, we were told, the cardinal weaknesses of Western democracies, though these were qualities that may have been less than obvious in Vietnam, Cambodia, Algeria, and the many squalid dictatorial regimes in the third world that were staunch allies of the West in the battle against communism.

Totalitarianism was supposed to be immutable and was expected to triumph over a self-indulgently tolerant and very imperfect West. That triumph was not set in some impossibly distant future either, but loomed before the end on this century. As late as a decade ago communist totalitarianism was seen by some as inherently the stronger and more vital of the two contending blocs. Books such as Jean-François Revel's *How Democracies Perish*,[2] which argued that thesis, were bestsellers on both sides of the Atlantic. There were countless books, novels, and spy stories repeating the same message of the greater viciousness and efficiency of communism in the grand world conflict, compared to the soft, capitalist rival bloc led by the United States. Instead, it turned out that the long, dull Brezhnev era represented the high water mark of communism as a world system. Those were, perversely as it may now seem, the good old days of communism, when the Soviet Union became a world-class super power, projecting its power globally, and when the living standards at home were rising, modestly but steadily. There even seemed to be developing some kind of a grudging truce between populations and regimes within the East European Soviet alliance; both began to believe reluctantly that they were fated to coexist, and that they might as well make coexistence as tolerable as possible.

There were repeated rumblings from below in the communist bloc, to be sure,[3] in recent years mostly in Poland, where Solidarity began its long, and then seemingly doomed, struggle against its own communist regime in 1980. Early on, most friendly observers in and out of Poland believed that it was conceivable Solidarity might gain some minor economic concessions, that it might even win begrudging recognition as an independent trade union, strictly bound to an economic role. Only wild-eyed utopians believed that Solidarity could topple the Polish regime. These utopians believed in the ability of people to transform their systems with massive pressure and organization from below, and believed that common struggles and experiences would develop leaders and organizations; such visionaries were and are scarce, in the East and the West. Any robust concept of democracy must necessarily be based precisely on that belief in the abilities of broad layers of the people, citizens and workers, to transform politics through self-mobilization. And yet, alas, genuine belief in substantive democracy is rare in real life, East or West.

By the late 1980s, an irresistible wave of unexpected and unprecedented upheavals from below, throughout the region, had culminated symbolically in 1989 with the toppling of the Berlin Wall. This was followed by the swift, complete, and abject collapse of all Communist regimes in Eastern Europe and the former Soviet Union. By 1991 the Soviet Union itself had ceased to exist, replaced by an unstable, visibly fragile, and obviously temporary Commonwealth of Independent States (CIS). Despite desperate efforts to reform and change, the communist parties throughout the region faced dissolution, confiscation of their property, and in some cases even banishment and persecution. Above all these parties faced the rejection and contempt of most voters. How long this will last is another story, but for the time being most communist parties, no matter how genuinely transformed they might actually be, are at the very least in purgatory.

Gross mismanagement of the economies in the new post-communist states, as well as sharp increases in differences between the small number of those well off and the large number of poor, may lead to some kind of revival of communist parties. However, I believe that while there might be some "hard" left communist parties on the scene in Eastern Europe and the states of the former Soviet Union, they will be relatively marginal. Parties dealing with social issues, unemployment, and egalitarianism will be either nationalist-populist, a sort of East European "Peronism" combining nationalism and social demagoguery, or will be, in the best case, social democratic and allied with the social democratic and labor parties of Western Europe. In any case new and morally (or at least politically) uncompromised people will have to emerge to play a role on the new political scene.

How the mighty are fallen! Relative unknowns and sometimes formerly marginal oppositions are now heads of governments. East European states and states from the new Independent Commonwealth that has so unceremoniously replaced the Soviet Union now petition for acceptance into NATO! Who could have predicted any of this a mere three short years ago?

And yet in the triumphalism in the West that has followed the collapse of communism lies a very dangerous potential blind spot: the assumption that *present* political trends, fashions, and balance of forces are now irreversible—that is, that exclusivist nationalism, anti-communism, and devotion to the absolutes of an untrammeled market and private property shall be with us forever. It is useful to remember the certainty of conventional wisdom that communist totalitarianism would be the irreversible wave of the future. Is it not also dangerous to assume that the current dominant trends in Eastern Europe and the new Independent Commonwealth have a long or even modestly medium range future? There are many reasons to believe that new political arrangements and power relations are shakier and even less secure than the old ones were.

The economies of the post-communist states are uniformly worse at providing necessities, not to speak of luxuries, for their populations as a whole, than the regimes they have replaced. This is something which will get even worse before it gets better. Without massive aid some of these countries face something unheard-of for decades in that part of the world, famines. That is the consensus among the same foreign experts who hail the experimental restructuring of the economies of formerly communist-run states. How long this dismal economic situation will continue is anyone's guess. In the meantime, placing many bets on the sustained popularity of post-communist political leaders does not seem all that safe; popular expectations are high and realistic prospects are low. That dichotomy does not augur a rosy future, and certainly does not present a terrain where democracy and tolerance can be expected to flourish.

Ethnic Nationalism Is Only One Possible Future

Unless one believes that the mass media are capable of manipulating the general public endlessly, one cannot expect that the hollow promises of nationalist politics, and of an idealized market economy, will postpone urgent social and economic issues forever. While nationalism and ethnic autonomy will inevitably be back on the political agenda, there is nothing whatsoever inevitable about the outcomes of new political conflicts. There are many unpleasant possible outcomes: repressive nationalist authoritarianism being one, and thinly disguised restoration of unreconstructed communist elites, bloody intra-tribal conflicts, and chaos for a prolonged period another. Or one can imagine combinations of nasty outcomes, authoritarian nationalist regimes in the major cities and chaotic political banditry in the remote rural areas. We have already witnessed that particular combination in parts of the former Yugoslavia and the Transcaucasian republics of the CIS. Furthermore, nationalist disputes between Czechs and Slovaks, Ukrainians and Russians, and Russians and Tartars, for starters, are on the political horizon. Mechanisms for dealing with these disputes are being painfully built despite the general refusal of the richer countries, above all the United States, to shoulder their share of the costs. A historic chance to establish democracy and a world peace intervention force may be frittered away by the mediocrities who hold the U.S. presidency and top senate and congressional posts, for the sake of cheap domestic politics. That would be a major tragedy and those responsible for it will unfortunately not pay the proper penalty.

Democracy and egalitarianism are also among the possible—and I would argue most desirable—outcomes. Those particular outcomes, however, will require a great deal of courage from the decent democrats in the region, and intelligent and sustained support and aid from abroad. That is, massive aid from the European Community and the United States will be needed, over a prolonged period of time. Provision of such aid would also, to no small extent, serve the purposes of enlightened self-interest. It is in the self-interest of the European Community to assure that repressive regimes on their Eastern frontiers do not let loose a massive flood of desperate refugees. It is in the self-interest of the Western labor movements to assure that Eastern Europe and the independent Commonwealth do not become a repressive "union free" environment for desperately cheap labor, which would threaten their own living and social standards. That self-interest should include at least among trade unionists and the broad-based parties of the democratic left in Western Europe and the United States, an awareness that just as the collapse of communism has quite unfairly hurt the Western democratic socialist project, the development of a decent and viable democratic left in Eastern Europe will help Western counterparts.

But egalitarian democracy is in great danger throughout the region; its vulnerability is a part of the historical price being paid for decades of communist rule and the systematic depoliticization of the broad public. Public opinion has been better prepared, both by the communists and by much of their opposition, to accept the easy politics of identity, exclusivist ethnic nationalism, and social demagoguery than the long and difficult task of building a civil society and tolerant pluralist democracy. These East European states as well as the states emerging from the former Soviet Union are ethnically heterogeneous societies, and the politics of identity, posed in terms of ethnic separatism, cannot coexist with any form of pluralist democracy. As Yugoslavia and the Transcaucasian republics of the CIS show all too clearly, a state identified as a national state automatically creates separate classes of citizens: the majority, who form the *political nation,* and the minorities, who even if tolerated have fewer rights. The rights of a minority depend on the continued tolerance of the majority, and minorities are told quite clearly that the state is not their state, that they are there on sufferance of the "real" citizens. Such fragmentation insures that minority peoples who have lived in the same location for centuries do not have even the option of a melting pot! One reason why a melting pot is hard to imagine is that in a number of cases the majority "ethnic" nation is also identified with a specific religious conviction. Thus, to become a member of a dominant nation, one must not only adopt the language of that group but also its religion.

That notion of the "nation" as a pure ethnic and religious domain brings us back to the religious wars of reconquest in Spain or the Thirty Years' War in the Germanies. Those were wars, let us remember, characterized by great brutality and by attempts at forcible conversion and the expulsion of the unconverted. Ethnic nationalism potentially represents this kind of step backwards into a bloody future. Taming and civilizing that newly reborn nationalism is the most urgent task for those who would attempt to build democratic societies. The former Yugoslavia is an almost ready-made laboratory for the interaction of nationalism and democracy in a post-communist society.

I, for one, remain firmly convinced that the continual line of expansion of democratic rights and participation, from the great French Revolution to our own era, has not ended. The democratic project is very far from completion. And history has not come to a stop. Liberty, equality and fraternity (or as one would probably say today, community) still seem more inspiring, and congruent with a decent civilized society, than the defense of one's own tribe and the right to grab an unfair economic share.

In attempting to explain modern nationalism one has to deal with the stuff of myths and legends as well as history and modern politics. That means getting specific and tearing apart a number of commonly held beliefs created and spread by the media. The most pernicious of these beliefs is that there is something almost biological about the peoples of Yugoslavia, or Eastern Europe and the former Soviet Union, that makes them more prone to kill each other than other peoples of the world. Somehow the latest conflicts in the new Europe are more visible, closer to home, perhaps because they are more European. Otherwise public opinion in the West would have been more concerned with the murderous war against non-Moslems in the south of Sudan, the continuing wars in Burma, India, Afghanistan, Northern Iraq and many other spots where people relentlessly keep fighting and dying. In all of these countries the formal reason why people die in large numbers is nationalism, sometimes the repression of nationalism. In many of these places nationalism is inseparably wrapped in religion.

Everywhere one sees the all too familiar pictures: young men (more rarely women) strutting around with automatic weapons, political leaders posing in notable comfort, and huge numbers of miserable non-combatant civilian refugees. One also sees international observers trying to lower the number of dead and injured and wringing their hands in despair. Hopefully there will be a time when the international community will be able to do a great deal more. New initiatives in forming long-range peacekeeping missions under the aegis of the United Nations may at last provide a peace force with sufficient teeth to make a difference. Such a force will of necessity begin on a relatively small scale but holds promise for a new world order which is more than merely a *Pax Americana* or a *Pax Germanica.* There may well be a time when this genuine peacekeeping activity will be coupled with an internationally enforced Bill of Human Rights. That would be a Bill of Rights for all citizens, for the majorities and above all for the minorities. It would defend individual rights and the right of people to organize collectively to defend their rights. Until that exists the world public will only be able to wring its hands in pity and condemn those most guilty.

Modern nationalism, whatever its positive historical role, is the great misfortune of our era in so many parts of the world. And yet, as is argued cogently by Benjamin Barber in "Jihad Against McWorld" in the March 1992 *Atlantic Monthly*, nationalist particularism is in good part a reaction against the alienating forces of an increasingly supra-national economy and a consumerist civilization that is uncontrollable through any democratic mechanisms by the citizenry of even the most powerful states. *Both* of these forces, nationalist particularism expressed as a politics of identity *and* supra-national economic and cultural alienation, threaten democracy and citizenship today. For democracy to be meaningful, politics has to have a meaning and a purpose. Citizens have to believe, and that belief has to be based on some approximation in reality that their activities and choices can affect their societies, that they matter.

I am deeply grateful to the Michael Harrington Institute for Social Values at Queens College of the City University of New York, for generously helping me conduct the research for this book. Colleagues like Francis Fox Piven and Joseph Murphy and Stanley Aronowitz have been trying to help me refine and improve my analysis for years. Irving Howe has all but given up trying to improve my writing, although he still reads my manuscripts. His criticism has been of great value. My research assistants have read and critiqued early drafts. The errors of fact and judgment in the book are, of course, all mine.

B. D.

New York, New York
June, 1992

1

European Unity, Neocorporatism, and the Post-Cold War World

The pace of historical change in Europe, east and west, began accelerating at a breathtaking pace in 1989. Three years later, political leaders, public intellectuals, and the media were still trying to catch up as the processes continued. General public opinion lags ever farther behind the ongoing changes, although there is a widespread general sense that the familiar world we have known since 1945 is changing in quite fundamental ways and quite irreversibly. The world order created by the Yalta, Teheran, and Potsdam treaties, which enshrined the bipolar division of the world between the Western and Communist blocs that with some minor modifications would last for almost half a century, has come to an unlamented end.

Although the old world order has died, the "new world order" has remained a mere slogan of the Bush administration. It is popular in Washington as a substitute for any kind of vision of a world that might include the notion that international affairs consist of more than problems in communicating the desires of Washington with a proper "spin" to make them more palatable. It has been given no substance because it is not based on any multilateral agreements and reflects no broad consensus. The "new world order" slogan merely serves as a rather small fig leaf to hide U.S. post–Gulf War aspirations to undivided world hegemony. It is a hegemony wielded without any responsibility. As in the war against Iraq in 1991, this hegemony is not a convincing instrument of any coherent policy. And just as in the war in the Persian Gulf, it will probably get a great number of people, primarily in the third world and in countries that had been run by Communist parties, killed directly, and even more indirectly. But such casualties are hardly ever counted[1] and almost never count when it comes to the all-important U.S. domestic debates about international questions. All too often, international questions are resolved by what advantage can be obtained from them in domestic political rivalry. Thus, international issues in the United States are very often reduced to slogans, and opponents are demonized, everything being fitted to the notorious two-minute sound bite for television. This may be a reason the U.S. allies are so uneasy whenever they detect greater American policy assertiveness on international issues. It can lead almost anywhere.

Three major developments, each of which would by itself have represented a major historical breakthrough, have continued to unfold at a rapid tempo. They represent dramatic changes, which have fundamentally transformed the world political and social order established at the end of World War II. The three interrelated developments are the collapse of the Communist ideological and political hegemony in Eastern Europe, effectively removing that alternative as a global force and movement from the political scene as an effective contender; the consequent end of the cold war between the Communist states and Western capitalist blocs led by the United States of America and the Soviet Union; and last, but by no means least, the approaching economic, social, political, and cultural integration of Western Europe. European unification, even at its earlier stages (which are limited to the present European Community), leads to the emergence of a new economic superpower, whose strength is not based on military force, as has been the case with the Soviet Union and the United States.

These developments also have accelerated the relative decline in importance of both established superpowers. The Soviet Union, which today increasingly means the Russian Republic with whatever allies it keeps, hardly qualifies for that term except through courtesy. This decline is occurring if only because military power alone will tend to have less and less importance in the new international relationships of strength that are emerging. Less importance does not mean no importance at all. It does, however, mean that the futility of sheer military power for the achievement of policy goals will become increasingly evident. That power is now mostly negative: it can delay and postpone developments such as the disintegration of multinational states, but it remains a very crude instrument for achieving specific positive goals, such as establishing stability in a region. The short-lived euphoric triumphalism in the United States that followed the massive military victory of the U.S.-led UN coalition in the Gulf War only temporarily postponed the visible decline in relative power and influence of the United States. It could not even shape to its satisfaction the nature of a postwar regime of an abjectly defeated Iraq. The fate of the Kurds in Iraq remains problematic despite the engagement of the European Community and the United States on their behalf. The ability of the United States and the "new world order" to achieve a Middle East settlement, the peaceful transition of a multiethnic Soviet Union into component democratic states, and a decent and democratic settlement of the bloody breakdown of Yugoslavia is very ephemeral.

With the ending of an era comes a change in paradigms. More modestly, at least there will be a change in descriptive labels and names. The old ones have been worn out while the new ones are still struggling to be born, and politics will for a while continue to be described in terms whose values have perhaps shifted beyond utility. A few examples should suffice: the Soviet *Union* is not even a question today; it is not a usefully descriptive term, and the North Atlantic Alliance is given all of the respect the terminally ill deserve. Eastern Europe has always been a problem where terminological clarity was involved, with Greece, for example, being out of Eastern Europe since World War II, whereas East Germany was in. German unification has changed that particular anomaly, of course.

What is one to make out of terms like "socialism" or "communism" today? My own convention is using the uppercase form to refer to official movements; lowercase forms refer to the doctrines.

This is still begging the question. What was the real name and, more to the point, the nature of the political, social, and economic systems that have collapsed in what used to be the Soviet Union and its alliance?[2] That is not at all a pedantic question limited to those interested in arcane theories. If the Soviet and Eastern European regimes were some kind of *socialism*—that is, if socialism of any variant is likely to lead to the stagnation and authoritarianism that characterized those societies—then socialism itself will remain too dangerous a gamble with democracy and liberty to ever have a chance to revive. If, on the other hand, these were some other types of societies, neither socialist nor capitalist, then the verdict on socialism is not yet in. It may revive in popularity and attraction as a program, even perhaps under a different name, just as free-market liberalism did after being marginalized for decades following World War II. It is clear that perhaps for the rest of the decade the term *socialist* will remain suspect in former Communist-ruled countries.[3] Quite apart from that question, to what extent are more innocent "socialisms" like Western European social democrats, or democratic socialists, implicated in the debacle of Communist regimes that held power for almost half a century?

On the other hand, there is a dangerous tendency for political analysts to consider recent developments as setting a new world trend, or even perhaps a new order, that is set in stone and will last forever. We should be more cautious. The twentieth century is strewn with new developments that were going to last, if not forever, at least for very long. The Versailles settlement following the war to end all wars, the thousand-year reich, the irreversible tide of Communist totalitarianism with its famous dominoes, the Keynseyan revolution solving forever (remember?) the cycles of recession, and the short-lived American Century should all warn us to be cautious. My suspicion is that the new world order will be a particularly short-lived era, and I believe that the era of triumphant capitalist celebration of the death of socialism will not last much longer. Although major new developments have transformed the Old World arrangements dramatically, the contours of the new era have not yet stabilized.

Neocorporatism: The Pattern of Contemporary European Capitalism

These radical transformations have unfolded within a world economy that remains firmly capitalist. To be sure, this is a highly modified capitalism, unrecognizable to those who would rely on simplified and essentially ideological descriptions of a system as a free market economy or other similarly naive understandings. To the contrary, *really* existing capitalism, in most advanced industrial societies, represents an economy and society much modified by national and international state and transnational financial institutions and monopolies' continual interference in the working of competition or a free market. It is a system that is, in most nation states and now increasingly within the European Common Market as a whole, also modified by widespread and broadly accepted welfare state measures, social programs, and trade unions. It is a system heavily dependent on state institutions for financial support and for its continued existence and stability. These institutions provide a plethora of services, protection, regulations, and direct and indirect subsidies, without which modern capitalism is unimaginable. In practice, outside the relatively more primitive and confrontational capitalist states, notably the United States and Great Britain (the so-called Anglo-Saxon powers), this system can be fairly described as neocorporatist far more accurately than as simply capitalist.[4] Even in less advanced capitalist states, the business community is ever ready to turn to the state for loans, support, protective legislation, and, ultimately, for the use of laws and force to combat internal and external enemies. That is why it is more appropriate to think in terms of capitalist systems, rather than a capitalist economy.

It is nevertheless a system that, with all of its modifications, perpetuates domination over the economy and, most of the time, the state and society by the class owning or controlling the key concentrations of capital. That is why neocorporatism is clearly a variant of capitalism. The state and society may develop more or less autonomy from the class that dominates the economy. The fit between the overall interests of such a system and the interests of individuals or sectors of the capitalist class may be more or less imperfect. What capitalists do retain in these societies is at least veto power over measures that threaten their continued economic domination. Within these parameters, however, a wide variety of arrangements are possible.

Three are typical. The first I will call the Anglo-Saxon model, whose form has emerged with greater clarity in the United States since the Reagan administration and in Great Britain since Thatcher held power. Reagan and Thatcher developed the model by leading the first massive attacks on the welfare state since World War II in advanced industrial democracies; their paler successors continue this model in a somewhat lower key that lacks the conviction of the founders. Despite the strident antistatist rhetoric, it has been characterized by a great deal of obvious tilting of state power on direct behalf of the industrial and financial elites. This variant of capitalism is crudely confrontational in dealing with trade unions and ideologically hostile to the welfare state as a matter of principle. It is also, in part for the reason stated above, the less efficient model of capitalism.

The second, and more widespread, variant of modern capitalism is neocorporatism. In this system *both* labor and capital wield de facto ability to veto measures that they regard as threatening their basic interests. This variant is most common throughout continental Europe and Japan. It is in part the reflection of the impact of cultural factors on political culture, stressing the virtues of cooperation and collective effort as against the extreme U.S. emphasis on individualism and competition. The European Community is dominated by this variant of capitalism. Sometimes neocorporatist capitalism is administered by Labor or Social Democratic parties, in which case the arrangement is tilted in favor of egalitarianism and generous social provisions. Sweden has been the best example, over time, of this third model. It is shaped by a powerful Social Democratic party backed up by well-organized unions that organize the large majority of the work force; one could call this the Scandinavian model. Even an occasional electoral defeat does not affect the fundamental nature of Swedish society. This is in no way any kind of socialism. It is still a form of capitalism but one stretched into an unfamiliar shape because of the great power of the labor movement and the consequent relative autonomy of the state. The Scandinavian model is a subvariant of neocorporatism.

Neocorporatism is a response to an old problem; capitalism is a very peculiar system: "No other ruling class is so profusely criss-crossed internally with competing and conflicting interest groups, each at the other's throat—the dog-eat-dog pattern. Competing national groups are split by regional group interests, different industrial interests, antagonisms within an industry, rivalry between producers of consumers' and producers' goods, light and heavy industry, and so on, aside from religious, political or other ideological differences. Internally capitalism is a snake pit."[5] Such a system has to be protected from itself if it is to survive when there are external competitors. These can be external in that they represent rival nation-states or, even worse, potential rival contenders for economic and political power, the organized parties and unions of a socialist-oriented working class. That last threat, real or imagined in 1938, drove substantial parts of an otherwise reasonably patriotic French bourgeoisie to prefer even Hitler's victory to as mild a French Socialist as Léon Blum. In less extreme cases the choice is a class compromise known as neocorporatism.

Corporatism and neocorporatism are terms that have been popularized by a younger generation of political theorists during the past three decades to describe the economic and political order that developed as a result of an implicit or explicit class and political compromise within advanced welfare state capitalist democracies. In effect, this compromise comes about between increasingly centrist capitalist parties and the increasingly moderate parties of the traditional broad Left. The compromise consists of an implicit agreement or, better yet, understanding that neither the business elite nor the labor movement is to attempt to eliminate the other as an active force. To the contrary, there is an agreement that what is at stake in politics will not be the existential questions affecting the survival of the major players. Both agree to accept the state and the existing political system, with a powerful and relatively autonomous civil service bureaucracy, as a mediator that both attempt to influence within essentially accepted and agreed upon parameters. Otherwise stated, "periods occur in which the warring classes balance each other so neatly that state power, as ostensible mediator, acquires for the moment a certain degree of independence of both."[6] Just so. I would add that such periods of stalemate can last for long "moments" and that they generate ideological and political support as against the uncertainty of social transformation on one hand or social Darwinian assaults on the welfare state on the other. It is also the case that within the broad parameters of such a compromise a wide political battlefield does exist. The compromise may tilt more in one direction or the other, be more prolabor or more procapital. That depends on the actual relations of political, social, and class forces. It also depends to an ever greater degree on the international scene.

The parameters of neocorporatism in parliamentary democracies are those of what is known as a *Rechtstaat*, that is, a state that abides by its own laws and constitutional order. Thus, whereas a welfare state may be made more economical or generous, its essential shape will not be in jeopardy. It is part of an implied social contract, not subject to political bargaining any more than parliamentary democracy itself is. Unions may get a little more or less influence in decision making but will not threaten the existence of private property or "legitimate" managerial prerogatives. That is the other part of the social contract. Moreover, management does not actively threaten the existence, prerogatives, and power of "responsible" trade unions but regards them as partners (junior, to be sure). In short, both unions and management are seen as valid and necessary, even essential, parts of a social order assuring the common good through social harmony. Similar toleration is extended to other important social actors, such as the much-coddled private farmers or the secure civil servants.

That description of neocorporatism is, to be sure, an idealized and somewhat sanitized picture of actual existing power relationships, which are often far crasser in real life. Neocorporatist arrangements have existed under a highly limited pluralism, even under openly authoritarian regimes like those of Perón and Franco, where the state was considerably more than a mere umpire. It certainly was neither neutral nor subject to legal and constitutional limits. However, neocorporatism has also been a term far more accurately describing the relationships that have developed in most of the countries of the European Community. The welfare state is too widely popular to be in real danger. The broad social democratic, labor-based Left is today too legitimate a part of the political and social scene to get less than a third of the electorate in most of Europe, which makes it either the governing party, with or without coalition partners, or the major opposition and thus the alternative government. On the other hand, the much-modified capitalist system that now exists has had too many of its rough edges knocked off to be in danger of any drastic change, let alone an overthrow.

With some minor modification this a fair description of the situation that has existed in the "core" countries of the European Community for the past three decades—in other words a whole generation, with all of the implications of what that must have meant for the development of a political culture based on that reality. That is, it is a stalemate of class forces, which *could* lead to social stasis and/or chaos if either side should try to change the status quo radically. At the very least it would lead to much-sharpened class antagonisms and turbulence and a kind of confrontation in which all major players potentially stand to lose.[7] The European business and labor elites have, with a few exceptions, accepted that stalemate as a quite tolerable fact of life, one they are ready to live with and prosper under and that has to be integrated into their long-range plans and projections, whatever their real preferences. The result is that the broad reformist Left has postponed to an indefinite future any practical or even theoretical work on any realistic postcapitalist socialist project, even a frankly reformist one, while the business elites and their supporters have accepted as a fact of life a capitalism much modified by a social market economy and a welfare state. Perfection and purity are then left for transcendental experiences for those who need faith and to fringe parties, while politics are reduced to the art of the possible within the contemporary really existing capitalist societies of the European Community.

The Outmoded Capitalism of the Anglo-Saxon Powers

The United States had also been moving toward a neocorporatist type of political arrangement through the New Deal, the Fair Deal, and the

Great Society programs, although far less consciously than was the case in Europe. So was Great Britain, through postwar Labour governments and "Butskelism," that is, the increasing policy convergence between social Tories and right-wing Laborites. This was reversed by the Thatcher and Reagan administrations in what amounted to cold counterrevolutionary coups. However, these coups did not come out of the blue, for the leaders of both labor[8] and capital in the United States and Britain were historically much more confrontational than was the case on the Continent. They were also far less prone to think in terms of broad social goals. Decade-long assaults on the main trend of modern industrial capitalism, by proposing a more Darwinian environment where long-established gains and trends toward greater security were being reversed, have created great insecurity for the majority.

Presumably, in such a bracing environment only the fittest would survive, which perhaps accounts for the increase in the number of young males in large cities who live from the proceeds of crime and sales of drugs. The new conservatives also have sharply increased the income differences between the lower third and the upper tenth. Above all, they have labored hard to remove state-enforced and -policed restrictions on banking, stock manipulation, and export of capital and jobs.

The result was that much of the new wealth in the Anglo-Saxon countries was accompanied by the impoverishment of industrial capacity, the export of well-paying jobs, and a general decline in quality of life for the working and middle classes. The new wealth created in the 1980s was speculative, based on manipulation of paper and stocks, rather than producing things and services. Despite this parasitic nature of the new wealth, it was wrapped in the cloth of competitive capitalism and justified as the socially useful reward for success in the free market.

An Ideological World System No One Practices

One should keep remembering that a "pure" capitalist society or economy is a utopian fantasy, that has never existed outside of introductory and oversimplified economics textbooks. It has, of course, existed and still exists in the ritualistic speeches of conservative, probusiness politicians who have themselves never hesitated to lean on the state whenever it would improve the operating environment of their favorite industries. It also exists in the prescriptions being pressed on the credit-starved third world countries.

The virtues of a genuine free market economy and the rigor imposed by a harshly competitive environment were always for the others. This can be certified by the richly subsidized private farmers of the European Community, who more often than not vote for the parties of the Right, as well as by the highly protected industrialists of the European Community.

They vote against the Socialists and Social Democrats and continue to draw subsidies.

Nevertheless, all ideological posturing aside, neocorporatism of one or another variant is the shape of the *really* existing capitalism in most of the advanced industrial world. It will be the dominant form of capitalism in the future. Capitalism in its various forms is increasingly a hegemonic global system, as the abortive attempts at establishing an autarchic set of state "socialist" Communist regimes have both implicitly and explicitly admitted defeat by beginning to marketize, and even more by the moves to privatize, their economies and moving them into the single world capitalist market.

To be sure, there is no necessary relationship between the use of the market as an allocator, particularly of consumer goods, and as a determinant of costs and private ownership. Clearly, there have been a number of experiments with market socialism, more or less successful, and many public enterprises in the West often have to operate by market criteria. That is why the debate about privatization of the presently nationalized economies in Eastern Europe and the former Soviet Union indicates more than a desire to reform or modernize those societies.

The debate about privatization is today a more or less open debate about moving toward capitalism. The real question, which is not directly addressed, is, *what type of capitalism*? Ideology notwithstanding, the neocorporatist variant is far more likely to be found in formerly Communist-ruled countries than is any Manchester liberal, Thatcherite variant, despite ideological protestations based on the current fashionability of social Darwinism among the post-Communist elites. The addiction of the masses of people to the personal security that even a crude welfare state provides is well documented. Growing discontent and demonstrations in former East Germany provide a wonderful case study of what happens when an otherwise popular government tries to reduce entitlements, even in West Germany, which is also a welfare state if a less generous one. The problems accompanying the integration of former East Germany into a unified Germany should be carefully studied by would-be privatizers who propose to reduce social entitlements in Eastern Europe and the Soviet Union. This is especially so because they would be privatizing without the safety net the overall German economy provides. There are serious lessons to be learned from this experience, and they are not the ones that will come from the World Bank, the International Monetary Fund, and American economic experts.

The Post–Cold War World Will Be Increasingly Interdependent

The major developments since 1989 form the backdrop to any consideration of the future prospects and strategies of the social movements, trade unions, labor-based and social democratic parties and movements, and, for that matter, democracy itself anywhere in the world. They will have a lasting impact on the economic, social, and—ultimately, after a considerable delay produced by an ever-growing cultural and political lag—political realities in the United States as well. They are of most urgent theoretical interest and immediate strategic relevance to social and political activists and theorists in the advanced industrial societies of Western Europe.

In an ever more interdependent world, the success of the European Community affects the fate of the world in general and of the underdeveloped third world in particular. Understanding the probable priorities of the emerging European economic superpower is essential, if for no other reason than to understand the new framework within which political and economic decisions affecting much of the world will be working themselves out. Given the continued relative economic decline of the United States, the European Community becomes even more important as a source of potential aid. The trouble is that there are two clamoring claimants for that aid today, the old Soviet bloc, including even the fragments of the Soviet Union itself, and the third world. It is almost certain that there will be too little to go around, in which case the third world will probably go to the end of the queue for aid.

The development of the European Community after 1992 will be of crucial importance for third world nations. In a world where the United States plays a diminished, though significant, role and the Soviets have, for practical purposes, ceased to be a competing world superpower, sources of possible aid and support are becoming very scarce indeed—frighteningly so. Understanding the new European Community is therefore essential to developing any long-range relationship to a world in which aid will no longer come primarily as a result of superpower rivalry. New rationales and connections will have to be developed. And clearly, a Europe that feels secure is more likely to consider major aid for the South than one that faces major turmoil and instability on its eastern frontiers. Thus, it is wrong to counterpoise aid to the republics of the former Soviet Union and Eastern Europe to aid to the third world. Rather, aid for the transition to stable, functioning, democratic societies in Eastern Europe and the former Soviet Union is an essential step to creating a European Community that can send effective aid to the third world.

However, a Europe that *can* aid the third world is, unfortunately, not the same as a Europe that *will* do so. The latter would require political decisions and even some sacrifices, and such decisions are more likely in a Europe dominated by labor and social democratic parties and movements. That is why there is much more than a parochial interest in the political fate of European social democracy during the next decade. That fate will have a direct effect on how the North–South problems are addressed. It will have a major impact on the fates of post-Communist countries in Europe.

The third world nations are not only affected by the new developments in Europe directly, through the changing prospects for aid and loans, but even more so indirectly, by the success of new economic, social, and political models. It is already clear that the collapse of the single-party Communist systems is having a profound effect on the third world, especially Africa. Thus, paying close attention to the new developments in Europe is not a symptom of "Eurocentrism," a word that has too easily become a label of condemnation. To the contrary, to think seriously about the real prospects of the third world today, one must do so in a framework that includes the effect of European unification—arising after the end of the cold war and from the debris of communism—on the future North–South relations and about what new political options are available.

Increased economic and political integration of the European Community in 1992, combined with the greater penetration of national economies by the world market, will necessarily force new national and parochial strategies on the Western European labor movements and parties. This becomes a life-and-death question for the trade unions, wherever they have made major gains, if they expect to survive in the new economic and political environment. A shift to such transnational strategies for the trade unions and their allies is essential if they are to have any chance at all to deal with the transnationals[9] and the increased mobility of labor, as well as the constant danger of the flight of capital, all of which threaten the existing welfare states and social programs.

Immigration and a Unified Europe

Mobility of labor will be a major issue in Europe on at least three different levels. The first problem, relatively easy to solve, is caused by the mobility of workers (and their immediate families) in the countries of the European Economic Community (EEC) who will be able to move freely within the EEC countries, settle and work anywhere, and be entitled to equal treatment. That fact will increase the pressures for similar conditions and portable benefits packages throughout Europe.

The second problem will be the pressure by workers from other European countries, presently *outside* the EEC to enter, preferably as legal—but if that fails, illegal—long-range guest workers, or sojourners. There are millions of workers in the EEC today who are legally established guest workers from outside the EEC countries. The statistics are in dispute, and there is a growing number of illegal migrant workers, but some 8 million seems to be the most reasonable figure. Some have been there for years, even decades, and have not obtained or even applied for citizenship. They are often from countries such as Yugoslavia, Poland, and Turkey (which has applied for EEC membership), where this migrant labor relationship has lasted for decades and has become a crucially important part of the home country economies. These guest workers not only contribute much-needed hard currency in remittances to the local economy[10] but have represented an invaluable safety valve to deal with local unemployment or underemployment.

Another way they contribute to the countries in which they work is that in addition to working, mostly at jobs that natives increasingly refuse to do, they pay taxes and social insurance fees, although they often end up getting fewer benefits than they have paid for. For that matter, although they are increasingly eligible for child allowances, their families often remain in their home countries and thus do not use the resources of the Western European welfare states for which they pay taxes. Recession, slow growth, and new pressures in the largest economy to give a priority to taking care of the former East German and Eastern European German workers have made these workers much less welcome. Their presence has become a focus for ugly political agitation for chauvinistic parties on the far right. Economic and political uncertainty have provided a popular base for chauvinist feelings among young underemployed and economically marginal Germans. The large number of workers from the Moslem Maghreb (North Africa) and former French African colonies has created similar right-wing racist and chauvinist reaction in France.[11] Since unification, very ugly nationalism has already manifested itself among the young unemployed in Germany, and explicitly racist thuggery directed against nonwhite immigrants has existed in Britain for decades. Racism and xenophobia can be expected to grow in Europe unless a broad movement of the democratic Left mobilizes the resentments of the young unemployed in a more constructive direction. Such a movement will have to be far more imaginative about reaching the alienated young than classic labor movements have been. For one thing, the historically quite recent idea that a societal norm is one in which the majority of people are continuously employed in wage earning will at some point need to be called into question.[12]

Although explicit racism and chauvinism are still on the margins of European politics, they have had an indirect effect on mainline politics as well. At the very least, a smaller number of immigrant workers from outside the EEC will be permitted to enter in the immediate future. This is bad news for Yugoslavia, Poland, and Turkey, and even worse news for non-European and nonwhite would-be immigrant workers. Their status represents a challenge to the European unions and labor parties, because they now form a substantial part of the blue-collar working class in some of the countries.

The third problem of labor migration potentially facing the EEC is the creation of a "Mexicanized" pool of temporary illegal workers, forming a black subeconomy that threatens the jobs and living standards of European workers. This is already widespread in Italy, France, and Great Britain, with workers from Poland, Tunisia, the Middle East, and Asia coming in on tourist visas and working for brief periods. This "labor market" is often organized by shady entrepreneurs and is fueled by the growing gap between a prosperous Western Europe and its neighbors. In effect, Europe has its Rio Grande to the east and to the south and its own "wetbacks." The problem is exacerbated by the abolition of border controls within the EEC. Thus, entry of illegal workers is regulated by the immigration practices and border controls of the *least* restrictive country in the EEC. Given the dismal state of the world economy, the problem of immigrant labor will haunt the EEC to the end of the century. The danger is that the EEC will become ever more insular in response to a harsh international economic environment.

This necessarily means that it will become increasingly less relevant to think in terms of social policies, trade union goals, and the range of social and economic policy options within single nation-states. The ECC itself will be the major arena in which those issues, or at least the major parameters of those issues, will be fought out for the remainder of this century—Western Europe initially, possibly all of Europe by the end of the century.

The Slow Expansion of the European Community

Some directions of the European Community's expansion are reasonably clear already. Both the pace and the range of this expansion will depend on whether the Eastern European countries stabilize as functioning democratic polities in the near future and at least become societies less subject to the pervasive fears and insecurity that now generate massive desire for emigration, even from countries in which conditions are not particularly bad. That will determine whether, as is more probable, a relatively smaller Europe of eighteen states or, much less likely, a larger Europe of some twenty-six states emerges by the end of this century. In either case, much more continuous economic, cultural, and political relationships will develop between the ECC and Eastern European countries and whatever remains of the Soviet Union. These relations will be sometimes tense and stormy and will at times prove deeply disappointing to both sides, but they will be a constant feature of European politics.

The European Fair Trade Association (EFTA) or at least most of its member nations, will almost surely enter the Common Market. They have already created a joint "European space" and are moving to eliminate the existing economic and regulatory barriers between the two. By the end of this century there will probably exist a European Community of some eighteen member states, firmly integrated economically and politically. More will be found on the periphery in some type of intermediate relationship to the community, ranging from arrangements abolishing tariffs, visas, and passports to joint judicial, health, and educational authorities. Turkey and the new post-Communist democracies in Eastern Europe, which face a difficult future, are in that peripheral category. This will certainly be a future of ever-increasing *relations* with the expanded EEC, at least for those states that do not regress to repressive authoritarian national populism or clericalism.

However, treating entry into "Europe," if that is interpreted to mean the European Common Market, as an immediate option and solution for the present genuinely frightening economic and political problems of the new post-Communist regimes is doubly irresponsible today because that is clearly not in the cards. No substantial group in the EEC supports such a step. Harping on immediate entry as a program will only lead to disappointment and to a possible backlash against human rights and democracy because those ideals quite properly have been pointed out as conditions for a better relationship to new Europe. It is also politically irresponsible and demagogic because insisting on entry into EEC, which is not achievable, as the primary political goal deflects attention from what is feasible and will greatly increase the widespread feeling of economic and political insecurity in post-Communist countries. Becoming more like Europe is a more modest and realistic aim.

European Unification Will Include a Social Policy

What *is* possible for the post-Communist states in Eastern Europe is to continue increasing and deepening relationships with the newly emerging European Community; this is possible in many ways, both formal and informal, short of membership in the EEC. In *that* sense the new democracies clearly are going to be a part of Europe, provided they continue to strengthen democratic institutions, habits, and organizations. Thus, many institutions, like the new trade unions, legal protection of workers through insistence on the norms of industrial behavior proposed by the International Labor Organization (ILO), ecological legislation, safety measures, rights for women workers, and minimal social standards, should become truly Europe-wide, not limited to the EEC. Whatever social packages are inserted into the new rules of the game in the Common Market after 1992 must become the yardstick, adherence to which will govern favorable access to credits and markets in Western Europe for the new regimes.

Western European trade unions should make it their business to see to this, and they should pressure and bully the European Community Parliament into passing such legislation as soon as possible. Once decent codes are adopted by the EEC itself, it should not be too difficult to expand them gradually to become the norm throughout the "Common European Home" if for no other reason than that the employers in the EEC facing high social costs and wages, will not welcome "disloyal" competition within the market; that is, they will not welcome giving low-wage industries and services access to the European Common Market any more than the unions will.

We may even see unions being pressured by the *employers* in high-wage areas in the EEC to help organize workers in low-wage areas. It has happened before, even in the United States. There is precious little internationalist class solidarity among capitalists when markets and profits are threatened. Why *trade unions* will want to develop internationalist efforts to help unionize their brothers and sisters on the periphery of the EEC and in Eastern Europe and the former Soviet Union should be fairly clear. Here is a rare heuristic case in which solidarity and self-interest happily coincide. This in no way precludes many bitter local and national struggles from taking place over issues of social policy and economic equity, including struggles between regions and sectors of the economy and sovereign states for relative advantages. In all probability, most of the struggles will occur within these more familiar and comfortable frameworks. All that is being asserted is that the ultimate arena in which an increasing number of these issues will be determined in most cases will be the larger EEC. That community in turn will be constrained by the considerations of the world economy and market.

What this specifically means is that unions and social movements and democratic parties of the Left, hopefully in alliance and coordination, must develop more transnational ties and institutions. Clearly, to do this it is essential to maintain certain "European" social and economic standards and to develop Europe-wide codes of rights for unions and minimal and Community-wide social benefits. The EEC's *present* structure already provides for courts to defend human rights, and these have been used to some effect to protect political prisoners and the social and economic rights of women. They have repeatedly given lessons in human rights even to Great Britain, prohibiting such time-honored British practices as caning children in elite schools and paying women lower wages for the same work men do. The European courts also have banned death penalties. Thus, the European courts have been ahead of a number of the member states. Whatever "leveling" does occur in social legislation will tend to improve the conditions of women in most of Europe. It will also improve the conditions of the minorities and political prisoners. One reason is that when compromises take place in social legislation, the bureaucratic arena in which these compromises are negotiated, the "Eurocracy," tends to prefer universalist, high-minded norms, which are more modern than the practices of many of the individual member states. This is particularly the case with Mediterranean countries and Great Britain and Ireland, which have tended to lag behind most of continental Europe in legal and social norms as well as practices. Britain has been repeatedly shocked by adverse decisions by the European Court on human rights issues; they were told that children cannot be caned, even in elite schools; that women must receive equal wages for equal work; and that IRA prisoners are political prisoners! Next thing, horror of horrors, they may be told that their electoral system, first past the post (that is, the winner-take-all system in which the candidate with a plurality wins all), is undemocratic because it marginalizes smaller parties and permits parties that receive pluralities, rather than majorities, to rule. It is sometimes forgotten that Thatcher's landslides never received even bare majorities of voters. After all, proportional representation was used in the last election for the European Parliament, and the Tories lost. Proportional representation is more democratic than the archaic plurality system used in Britain and the United States. It will increasingly be the norm in democracies.

Ecology Is an Obvious Transnational Issue

Ecology is also clearly a subject for which national boundaries and legislation make little or no sense because so many of the issues go beyond each individual nation-state, the European Community, or Europe itself for that matter. National boundaries clearly are of little relevance here, as countries along the Rhine and Danube, not to mention the Mediterranean, already know all too well. In any case, the ecologists will have to organize on a supranational basis. As the bitter experience of the Chernobyl nuclear disaster showed, antinuclear activists are obliged to think beyond the nation-state as the arena for relevant activity.

For that matter, Chernobyl showed just how devilishly intertwined issues like ecology, industrial policy, and freedom of press and information all are; radioactive trout in northern Sweden illustrated how those issues cannot be treated as internal problems of a single nation-state. Most of the nuclear plants in Eastern Europe and the former Soviet Union are technologically so abysmally backward and dangerous that they will have to be dismantled as quickly as possible for general safety considerations. That cannot be done by national states alone, nor should it be left to them alone to decide how much risk to others in the region is acceptable. On the other hand, it is unrealistic to expect these wounded economies to bear the entire burden of phasing out an existing, already inadequate, and very dangerous energy system.

As the Germans discovered after unification, the plants in former East

Germany—which if anything were probably *superior* technologically and in the standard of maintenance to the ones in Eastern Europe and the Soviet Union—are death traps, which are not salvageable but will have to shut down and the sooner the better. They must, alas, also be replaced, and the readily available solutions are not particularly promising. They must be replaced with *some* reasonably priced source of energy and heat. Coal, which is plentifully and cheaply available in Eastern Europe, is devastating to health and ecology, and oil and natural gas are more expensive. Years of antinuclear agitation and education in Western Europe have borne some fruit, and new nuclear reactors are politically unlikely anywhere in Europe. This is underlined by the large and growing Green movement and concern with ecology in the former Communist-ruled states. The huge costs of conversion away from nuclear energy, however, cannot possibly be borne only by the already ravaged economies of the former Communist countries. Therefore, resources for dismantling the future potential Chernobyls throughout Eastern Europe will have to be mobilized on a European scale for what, after all, is a question of the general safety of all.

European Solidarity with the Third World

Policymakers and the general public must understand that European economic unification in 1992 and the necessarily consequent increasing autonomy of the European Community from its traditional Atlantic alliance will radically alter the game of social and international politics in Europe. It will change the parameters within which that policy is decided for one thing. It will also alter many other previously accepted solid realities in world politics and the economic balance of power.

Politically attractive as well as economically workable pan-European reflationary strategies become feasible, involving massive credits and aid to Eastern Europe and the former Soviet Union as well as the South. Such proposals are attractive because they represent the mix of altruism and direct benefits to the national economies of the advanced industrial counties in the European Community. This creates a basis for a sufficiently broad consensus to make these proposals politically feasible in the mid-1990s.

Probable Social Democratic political gains in Germany, as well as increased prospects of a Labour resurgence in Britain, improve the chances of a bold reflationary strategy. Without such a strategy it would be hard to generate enough support for the massive investment that is needed.

European Unification and the End of the Cold War

The Atlanticist cold war consensus, which has held together for four decades, is going through what may well be a terminal crisis today. The prognosis for a continuation of U.S. domination of Western Europe and for its ability to help shape or, for that matter, limit European social and economic policies at the end of this century are poorer than the prospects of a Europe, at least a Western Europe, in which labor and socialist parties play a major role. Belief in either the efficacy or the exportability of the Soviet and state "socialist" models of political and economic development has long vanished even, or perhaps especially, within the Soviet leadership. Its revival is one of the few things one can make predictions about with some certainty: it will not happen. It will not happen even if military and authoritarian regimes (unfortunately, not impossible) arise out of a failure to develop a stable and prosperous society in post-Communist states. It will be a different kind of authoritarianism.

The states of the European Community, with their strong unions and social movements and relatively advanced social policies, have more favorable prospects than *either* the class-confrontational, neoconservative "Anglo-Saxons" or the economically ruined former state socialist systems of Eastern Europe and the Soviet Union. This is particularly so if one thinks in terms of such important intangibles in assuring a quality of tolerable life as crime in the streets, the quality of public education, access to decent health care, and public spaces and transportation. For most people these "intangibles" are at least as important, if not more so, than abstract gross national product per capita statistics. In that sense the developing European Community, rather than the United States, represents the more likely and certainly more desirable future for advanced industrial democracy.

The cold war is over but it is not "free market" *capitalism* that has won, as many Western pundits and politicians claim. Rather it is authoritarian state "socialism" of the Communist politocracies that has *lost*. But it has lost to Western European *welfare state* capitalism, run, as often as not, by social democratic and labor parties. That was the really existing "capitalism" that was most familiar to Eastern Europeans and Soviets. In short, the cold war was lost to a form of neocorporatism, very much modified through broad social programs and industrial relations legislation mitigating the raw forces of the market and tilted in favor of organized labor and its allies.

Both the business elites and the Left in the European Community regard their own variant of capitalism as being more advanced, efficient, and therefore ultimately superior in performance to the more familiar U.S. model. I believe that they are right when it comes to the question of long-range performance and efficiency. The greater efficiency of this model becomes even more salient as a more educated and skilled work force begins to dominate the labor market. Such a work force is more responsive to systems that stress cooperation rather than hierarchical control from above. Neocorporatism, in other words, is more suited to the needs of a postindustrial society than the more confrontational American model, which requires many very costly layers of middle management to control ever more antagonistic and insecure employees.

This greater economic efficiency of neocorporatist models of capitalism is quite separate from the quality-of-life questions that are automatically posed by any observation of the social consequences of the sterner Anglo-Saxon versions of the system. Any familiarity with current U.S. health statistics, not to mention a simple evening walk through most parts of New York, Chicago, Washington, or Los Angeles, will serve to concentrate the minds of most Europeans to dwell on the differences between the two types of capitalism.

Transformation in Post-Communist States and the EEC

Responding to their own desperate economic and ideological crises, after 1987 the Soviet leadership under Gorbachev accepted previously unimaginable political and economic reforms as well as radical cutbacks in military expenditures and existing arsenals. The two are, of course, linked; a disproportionate share of the Soviet technological know-how and resources were historically tied up in the military sector. The military cutbacks were also an absolutely essential step in building sufficient confidence in a new Soviet nonaggressive posture to create a realistic expectation of substantial aid and credits to help the Soviet economy. Liquidating the adventures in Afghanistan and scaling down the Soviet role throughout the third world logically followed.

The Soviets also proved willing to accept and in some cases even encourage the transformation of the political and economic systems of Eastern Europe to ones in which the Communist parties are now firmly out of power. In a number of cases they have pushed reluctant local Communist party elites toward reforms and elections. Without such a push, the changes would have been much slower and probably very much bloodier. To the surprise of most observers, they even approved of a much quicker and less condition-bound unification of the two Germanies than any, including the most optimistic analysts and politicians, had expected. These dramatic changes strengthened the Western advocates of disarmament and the tendency of Western Europe toward greater autonomy within the traditional North Atlantic Alliance. This also, for all practical purposes, ended the cold war as it had existed since the late 1940s in Europe, well before the date of European unification in 1992. These developments have, in turn, speeded up the completely unpredicted and exciting moves toward the democratic transformation of Eastern Europe and the Soviet Union.

However, despite the irreversible demise of communism, the democratic transformation of the post-Communist states remains only a *possibility,* although it is one of the utmost importance to the future of Europe and its security. The failure of this transformation could result in a whole range of new authoritarian and militarist regimes. At least one of these potential new authoritarian military regimes, the Russian one, remains armed with the nuclear weapons of a world-class power. Therefore, effective support of the transformation of the economies and societies of former Communist states is in the most direct and obvious self-interest of the European Community and of democratic forces throughout the world. This is not a time to be stingy. Extensive long-range credits on favorable terms must be offered to East European and former Soviet leaders to help the process of modernization of their economy and society.

Tender shoots of new democratic institutions and experiments could well wither under conditions of desperate economic crisis. In turn, failure to solve the economic crisis creates an even sharper crisis of political institutions and legitimacy. A major consequence is the growing insecurity of the bulk of the population and the political elites. The old order is gone, but a new one has not yet taken hold. This leads to a breakdown of law and order and to increasing ungovernability of the successor states. That is why the European Community must offer truly massive support for this democratic transformation, in the most immediate future and for a prolonged period. Such a policy would also help the Western European economies, much as the Marshall Plan in the 1940s helped the U.S. economy. One clear effect of such a "Marshall Plan" would be to reflate the economies sufficiently to increase employment and growth. This, combined with the saving resulting from cutbacks in military spending, which are inevitable in an era of increasing detente, should generate additional resources for politically popular social expenditures and welfare state measures without requiring politically unpopular tax increases.

Such reflation has become even more necessary because the danger of a major and prolonged recession during the first half of the 1990s is very great. Both the United States and Japan are in economic trouble, and following their examples might wound the European Community at exactly the time when demands on it increase, in 1992. That is one more reason why a boldly imaginative "Marshall Plan" is needed, not just to aid Eastern Europe and the former Soviet Union but to protect the European economies from a major downturn. A deep recession could have tragic consequences for the future of post-Communist democracies *and* for the European Community.

Under such circumstances continued attacks on the welfare state become clearly a matter of hard ideological anti–welfare state bias rather than the supposed unfortunate side result of economic necessity. That is why Thatcherism had to go on the defensive in Britain, and its main symbol, Margaret Thatcher herself, had to withdraw as prime minister in 1990, well before the new elections. The electoral chances of the Labour party were sharply improving. Her style of confrontational "little Englander" politics were no longer acceptable even to the barons of the Conservative party. Opinion polls in Britain favor greater European integration, which will clearly improve the social services and living standards for most. More generally, this is also why demands for a "social Europe" meet with wide support and little organized hard-core hostility.

In periods of general prosperity, particularly those underpinned by state-supported pump priming of the economy through large-scale loans, neocorporatist strategies of class compromise are more likely than confrontational assaults on unions and social standards. This situation, of course, refers to "normal" modern capitalists but not necessarily to the right-wing ideologues who have dominated the politics and, above all, the political debates of Great Britain and the United States. That era will end with the end of the cold war. Class-confrontational politics of the Anglo-Saxon type never really took hold in Western Europe after World War II and are clearly out of place in an essentially bureaucratic and neocorporatist European Economic Community.

Not the least reason for this antipathy to class-confrontational politics in continental Europe is the memory of the consequences of the last time labor and capital and their parties clashed. The result was a paralyzing stalemate that helped the Fascists and Nazis achieve power. The relations of class and political forces are slightly more favorable to the Left today. But that Left is less organized and above all less ready to take political risks. The memories of fascism and Stalinism have not completely faded, and democracy is not taken for granted.

If there is one thing that the broad Left in Europe is certain about it is that democracy, preferably combined with an advanced welfare state, is the optimal political terrain. This is the case whether one believes that an ever-expanding egalitarian welfare state is the ultimate goal of modern European social democracy or that it is merely the optimal terrain from which to advance, at some point in the future, toward democratic socialism.

German Unification and European Autonomy

A general détente in Europe made the unification of the Germanies inevitable. The great disparity of economic strength, demographic power, and, above all, political legitimacy between the two German states made it equally inevitable that unification would take place on West German terms. That is, East Germany would, despite some ineffective last-ditch objections by the New Forum[13] in the East and the Greens in the West, come into the existing legal, economic, and political arrangements of West Germany. The Federal Republic, as West Germany was formally called, was the incomparably more successful of the two Germanies. Unified Germany is thus an expanded West Germany, albeit one with problems caused by the need and cost of bringing former East Germany to at least the level of the more backward parts of the former Federal Republic. In any case, the unification was amazingly smooth, and it ended what had clearly been a completely unnatural division. The result is a unified Germany that will be the most economically powerful member of the European Community that emerges after 1992.

The United States and the Western allies had been primarily responsible for the continued existence of a divided Germany, but they were also responsible for the phoenix-like rebirth and growth of their Germany. The Soviets, beginning almost immediately after the end of World War II, had repeatedly shown an almost indecent willingness to trade in their occupation zone and their East German party loyalists, initially for a maximum goal of achieving an Austrian-type settlement of a disarmed and neutral Germany. This deal for a unified but demilitarized and neutral Germany had been offered again and again and had always represented the nightmare of those who supported NATO. It was even more upsetting to those who believed that the cold war had to last forever. How could one even imagine a NATO without West Germany, which provided half of the ground forces and the physical ground on which the conflict would be fought?

A divided Germany could not survive when the danger of military conflict in Europe was reduced to a vanishing point. Why would the West and East German peoples agree to a continued and artificial separation in the name of now nonexistent security considerations? Why should generations born after Hitler's wars and crimes continue to be deprived of the most elementary right of self-determination? This would surely not be acceptable in the name of some quite abstract balance of power in the European Community. And then, the closer European integration became, the less potential danger there would be from a powerful Germany. Under the circumstances, the Soviets were willing to accept German unification and the political liquidation of their followers in East Germany for considerably *less* than the abstractly not unreasonable but politically unachievable goal of Austrianizing Germany. Unified Germany will thus stay in NATO. However, this will increasingly become a new NATO, de facto if not de jure The specific economic weight of a unified Germany and the European allies within NATO will prevent it from remaining primarily an instrument of U.S. policy; it will be a far more multipolar alliance. In any case, it is no longer clear that U.S. policies and interests necessarily coincide with those of an increasingly independent and powerful European Community freed of a threat of Soviet military expansionism.

One can expect various attempts at a reconceptualization of what

NATO is for during the 1990s. There will be increasing difficulty in finding a consensus. For example, if it is granted that its purpose is not to meet a real or imagined Soviet threat, it is now hinted in some U.S. circles, with not too much subtlety, might it not serve to restrain a unified Germany? The more polite formulation is to better "integrate" a unified Germany within the European Community. These formulations are hardly likely to warm the German policymakers' hearts. There are other ways, more congenial to German political public opinion, through which that aim could be achieved. One could be to dismantle NATO, since the Warsaw Pact is already dissolved, and replace both with a new security arrangement, evolving out of the Conference on Security and Cooperation in Europe[14] (CSCE). The German Social Democrats have steadily moved toward an increased skepticism about the present Atlantic alliance, pushed in good part by the relentless hostility of Washington for the whole past decade, on one side, and the pressure from the Greens and the new social movements on the other.

Germany thus had its unification in 1990, far ahead of all predicted schedules, and was able to stay in the European Community and NATO, the Soviets having raised no objections. To the contrary, most of the leaders of the viable fragments of the Soviet Union now *want* a powerful European Community that will make it possible for the successor states to enter a "Common European Home" at some date in the admittedly cloudy future. The absolutely indispensable economic motor power for that unified Europe, one that has to be powerful enough to help both the European Community and the Eastern Europeans and former Soviets as they stand at the doorstep of a common home, is obviously Germany. This encouraged a Soviet diplomatic offensive that was successful in projecting the image of a Soviet Union that urgently needed, for its own economic and technological reasons, truly massive cutbacks in military expenditures and a prolonged détente. That, in turn, dovetails admirably with the needs of a unified Germany and a European Community to generate an economic recovery led by an expansion of production and exports. The consequence is obviously a more assertive and active German foreign policy, which, as the disputes over the recognition of independent states emerging out of a disintegrating Yugoslavia illustrated, could pit Germany against the United States.

Within a neocorporatist status quo, a policy that has the firm support of manufacturing and business elites, as well as of full-employment-conscious trade unions *and* the banking community, which has to provide the credits, *and* even the normally conservative farm bloc, which thus is assured of placement of its surpluses for the foreseeable future, is almost the best of all possible worlds. If one adds the assurance that such policy is also needed for the long-range security of Europe, if not the world, and that it is genuinely noble because it makes possible the success of a massive spread of democratic institutions in formerly authoritarian societies, the German cup almost runneth over. It might well make them believe that they are favored by fate itself.

There is, to be sure, a dark side as well: unity costs a great deal. Despite election promises by Kohl and the Christian Democrats, taxes will go up. Social Democrats will reap somewhat delayed benefits from their caution about the costs and speed of unification. However, their increasingly likely victory in the future will probably represent no basic change in policy toward the former Soviet Union and Eastern Europe. If anything, they are likely to be more generous. After all, they started it all, with Willy Brandt's *Ostpolitik.* Why should not virtue also be rewarded in politics, at least sometimes? It would be a pleasant change.

There are many other benefits of the end of the cold war, for Europe in general and for Germany in particular. Military costs will ultimately go down, perhaps quite sharply. In the short run, the political beneficiary of this heuristic development, in which economic self-interest, national goals, and good European citizenship happily coincide, has been the party that was fortunate enough to be in power and to be the godfather of all of these unforeseen and unforeseeable developments. For reasons that I will argue further in a later chapter, the long-range beneficiaries are likely to be the Social Democrats. That might be a matter about which competent political analysts differ. Who the loser will be is really unarguable; it is that part of the American political and economic establishment that had a stake in the continuation of a hegemonic role for the United States. For at least two decades that role has been based primarily on military hardware and muscle rather than on superior technology and economic organization. At least in Europe, that role is not long for this world. It will soon become history.

European Unity, the Future of Military Alliances, and Security

The political developments in Western Europe are crucial for the fate and future of advanced welfare states and the democratic socialist parties. But Western Europe must first free itself from tutelage and domination by the United States. For that to happen it is essential that Western Europeans feel secure from military threat and potential political bullying from the Soviet Union and thus for the U.S. nuclear military protection to be no longer perceived as necessary. Just how necessary that protection has ever been, historically, will remain a fascinating question for modern historians. What is clear is that protection is not needed for any practical purposes when the Warsaw Pact is dismantled, Soviet troops are being massively withdrawn from Eastern Europe, and the Soviet Union itself is disintegrating.

This means that all issues affecting long-range European and world security are up for reassessment at this time. That debate should be well on its way by time of the unification of the European Community in 1992. The EEC's independence will be strengthened by the entry of former EFTA states like Sweden, Austria, and others, all of whom had shared at least a formal neutrality. The ideal time for such a development is a period of major military cutbacks and disarmament of the superpowers in Europe. The trend toward a growing autonomy of Western Europe was accelerated in the 1980s by the military and diplomatic recklessness of the Reagan and Bush administrations on the one hand and the very successful diplomatic peace offensive by the reformist Gorbachev administration in the Soviet Union on the other. The Bush administration has continued the unpopular U.S. role, which combines bullying with ineffectiveness in imposing preferred policies. This was evident in the blundering around the "war on drugs" in Latin America and the aggressive lead taken in demanding the use of direct military force in the Persian Gulf. The political debacle that followed an almost letter-perfect hi-tech war did not help U.S. long-range prestige in the Middle East or in Europe.

The United States has showed an absence of imagination and initiative in responding to the Soviet peace initiatives and the major democratic breakthroughs in Eastern Europe. While providing little useful political leadership to the alliance, the United States insisted on maintaining its military leadership. There was barely a fig leaf of UN resolutions and consultations with the Allies to disguise the fact that command decisions in the Gulf War were made by U.S. field commanders and the president of the United States. That merely postpones the recognition of a continued decline of useful political and economic influence on the part of the United States. It has long lost the role of the economic leader of the alliance through its own ineptness and refusal to pay for its own policies.

A sharp contrast is visible between the continual U.S. fumbling and lack of initiatives and the flexibility demonstrated by French president Mitterrand, in his role as the chair of the European Community in 1989, in changing the traditional French attitude toward the prospects of German unification and again in 1990 in his willingness to use diplomatic means to try to settle the crisis in the Persian Gulf. France resumed its independent policies in the Middle East as soon as the echoes of applause for the technically efficient, high-profile U.S. military performance in the Gulf died out. The Gulf War solved nothing; it merely postponed having to face a new reality, that military power is an excessively blunt instrument for foreign policy purposes and above all for assuring stable peace settlements.

The European Community, political parties, and unions have shown a far greater readiness to raise large sums immediately to help the chances of political and economic reforms in Eastern Europe. By 1992 over 50 percent of all economic aid to the former Soviet Union came from Germany. This again is in sharp contrast with the niggardly attitude of U.S. administrations, which have had to be forced by the Congress to increase their miserly offers of help to Poland and Hungary. Clearly, the United States cannot expect to play a dominant role in shaping future political options in Eastern Europe and the Soviet Union if it is unwilling or, more to the point, perceives itself to be unable to give substantial economic aid. This may in the long run be to the benefit of the post-Communist countries, since U.S. advice has been generally poor.

The United States certainly does not seem to be in much shape to give economic advice. It is nothing short of amazing that aid on the scale of just one of the obviously now useless weapon systems, like Star Wars or another nuclear submarine or the nonfunctioning troop carrier, is not even seriously considered. Clearly, the value of a like amount spent in aid to the former Soviet Union would have greater impact on security considerations. It would even help the U.S. economy. This is quite apart from the other benefits, including simple humanitarian ones.

Intermediate steps can be taken to redefine a European security approach that is independent of the traditional NATO alliance. A unified Germany could lead the necessary massive reflation of the Western European economy through a huge long-range program of exports of goods and technology to the former Soviet Union and Eastern Europe. In the most immediate future this should lead to massive exports of Western European farm surpluses to deal with the immediate food shortages in those areas during the first and most painful period of transition from centrally directed to more market-driven economies. Such exports can help buy the time necessary for the successful reforms and liberalization of those economies and societies. A higher profile at home of the military and political hard-liners in the Soviet Union, even a regime dominated by the military, does not necessarily mean a more aggressive stance abroad. This should be kept in mind even though in the immediate future this option is not too likely given the defeat of the coup against Gorbachev in the summer of 1991. The converse is also true: a liberal and popular regime can be very assertive in foreign policy. To be sure, many political observers, myself included, have long argued that for several decades no realistic prospect of a war, conventional or nuclear, has existed in Europe. Too much had always been at stake for both superpowers; neither could have risked losing a war in Europe, and therefore any supposedly limited European conflict would necessarily have escalated to a nuclear all-out world war.

Logic aside, however, evident self-interest has not prevented wars in the past. And the beginning of World War I illustrated that continued confrontations between military alliances, particularly ones armed to the teeth, can get out of control and assume a momentum of their own. That is an additional reason for moving forward with ever sharper military cutbacks and down-sizing of the huge arsenals in Europe. It is also a reason for developing ever thicker networks of economic, political, and cultural relationships that are Europe-wide, transcend the previous military alliances, and contribute to confidence building. The Soviet military cutbacks meant that this reality was firmly accepted by at least one superpower.

The United States is increasingly lagging behind the new opportunities to develop an entirely new framework for international security. This is, in good part, the responsibility of a bipartisan political establishment that persists in playing domestic politics with international questions and questions of military security. A massive reorientation of U.S. policymaking is needed. As good a starting place as any would be a sharp curb on the development over the past four decades of an institutionally unrestrained imperial presidency. A more reasonable U.S. administration could well lead to truly major cutbacks in military spending. A conscious effort to catch up with the new realities of a post–cold war world should make these cutbacks acceptable to the defense and military establishments. Clearly, at the very least a changed mission should be reflected in changes in military hardware. The major future tasks of U.S. armed forces is obviously no longer to prepare for a major ground war with a superpower in Europe or for an all-out nuclear conflict. A scaling down is obviously called for.

The end of the cold war as we have known it has become a reality. Lions will not lie with lambs in this new world, even if it were all that clear who is who. But a limited war in Europe with conventional or with conventional and "tactical" nuclear weapons will not take place in any now imaginable scenario. Even if it did, by some malign miracle, NATO as it now stands would win a smashing victory, with the enthusiastic support of the Eastern European and even the Soviet population, which will not fight against a Europe that represents its ideal and hope. A European Community that increasingly finds itself dealing with a major political and economic transformation on its continent, essentially with its own resources, will clearly develop greater autonomy and self-confidence vis-à-vis the traditional alliance leader, the United States. It may even perceive that leader to have entered into a phase of long-range decline. That all points to a Europe that is taking shape along lines not too different from those imagined by Charles de Gaulle. If anything, the European Community will be considerably *more* integrated culturally and politically than he would have preferred. He wanted a Europe of "the fatherlands"; it may develop into a far more cosmopolitan entity. He was also, let us remember, the nemesis of the "Anglo-Saxons" in their self-chosen role as the world hegemonies after World War II. There it may turn out that he was more successful.

2

The Decline of the United States

Costs of a Hollow Victory

A Widespread Malaise

There is a growing malaise abroad in the United States. It is most widespread among the pundits who write tomes about the decline of America as a society or, from their point of view, worse yet, about the decline of American power.[1] It is widespread today among the conservative intellectuals and even more among the formerly liberal neoconservatives, who deplore the erosion of standards, civility, and even the canon in education. It is widespread among political consultants, who make clear that the space for political maneuvering by their clients is continually diminished by a public that seems to lack the minimal doses of civic virtue necessary to either (a) vote for tax increases or, better yet, (b) accept slashing cuts in what is already arguably one of the least generous sets of social programs in any advanced industrial democracy. It is rife in the numerous journals of "responsible" moderate opinion, which deplore the continual erosion of a familiar good life, at least a good life for the white middle classes and unionized workers, without ever naming the culprit. Families are decaying; education is in shambles; politicians get the lowest popularity ratings in living memory; metropolitan cities are sliding into the third world; race relations are worse than they have been for decades.

Yet this general decline of the United States is commonly treated as if it were either the work of a malignant destiny or the result of a combined assault on America by greedy hordes of welfare recipients and ruthless Pacific Rim importers. Little or no responsibility is assigned to the American political and economic system. In a way, this is curious because the collapse of communism as a world system *is* linked to the general and systemic nature of communism as an economic and political system of organizing societies. On the other hand, it is widely understood today in intellectually respectable circles that anything as crude as naming a social or economic system—such as, just for argument's sake, capitalism[2]—as a possible culprit for the malaise that has stricken *our* society, not to say our world, is a sure sign of sterile old-fashioned dogmatism.

Reasonable undogmatic people are therefore now cast adrift without a compass in chartless sea, subject to unpredictable whims of fate. If human agency is not responsible for what ails us, then obviously human agency cannot change what is wrong either. That political change in this country is extraordinarily difficult is something on which all students of our political system agree—some deploring and others hailing this specific feature of democracy in the United States. Worse than difficult; it is futile. This view is deeply reassuring to all of those who do not do badly in a society that is in deep trouble. Thus, the natural inclination in the United States is for sensible people, who are properly socialized to the dominant value system, which is possessive individualism, to avoid having anything to do with politics. At most they vote, and that not too often.

But even if they wanted to engage in politics, it is difficult to do so except on the microlevel of single-issue groups or communitarian experiments in backyard democracy. I prefer to think of these microarenas as sandlots of adult politics, having about as much to do with genuine issues of the distribution of wealth and power as high school student governments have with politics. And like student governments they often involve nice, earnest people who are completely sincere and honest. Substantial systemic politics, however, is all but impossible in a country that has no recognizable political parties; that is, none with a structure accessible to programmatic changes to which elected politicians might feel some responsibility.

Declining Living Standards for the Majority

Decent unionized blue-collar jobs are increasingly unavailable, and those remaining are being wiped out as quickly as a tough confrontational management backed up with slick professional union busters, can get to it. For a decade these efforts have had the heartfelt support of the White House occupants and much of the federal administration. Jobs for the non-college-educated young that pay anything resembling a living wage are almost nonexistent, for whites as well as for blacks.

The rates of violent crime and the consumption of drugs are up. Although I do not agree with the current demonization of drugs (there are many other causes for crime and decay in the large cities), it is reasonably clear that the drug subculture and economy have at least the same relationship to urban crime as alcohol had to the growth of organized crime during Prohibition. Both involve the massive corruption of the law enforcement and judiciary systems and the cooperation of respectable financial institutions, at least to launder the ill-gotten money. Cities are less and less safe while the rich pay less and less in taxes. While violent crime is up among the lower classes, the middle class and yuppies do their best to increase the figures for white-collar crime, which has been reaching spectacular new heights. Banks and insurance companies are less secure, and that most secure of all gambles for the past two decades—real estate—has proved that values can go down as well as up.

To be sure, crime rates have always been relatively high in the United States, which may have much to do with social values that stress individual achievement, wealth, and fame without much regard to means or social cost. Still, the statistics should give pause to those who have not stopped celebrating the American Century. Our rates for homicide and violent crime are *four to ten* times higher than those of Western European countries and three times those of Canada![3] It is not even the case that this is an artifact of the explosive ethnic mix in our large cities. Murder rates in Minnesota, Iowa, and Nebraska remain higher than those of the ethnically mixed areas in Europe. A country that celebrates both the robber barons and the James brothers as national heroes cannot act surprised when others, more humbly placed, try other methods to achieve wealth and prominence. Nor does it help that there has been a continued erosion of whatever remained of a common, even if much mythologized, American civic culture.

We are not even two nations but a metastasizing decentered culture in which every subgroup and individual is on his or her own, feeling little linkage to any wider national community. None makes a claim on support of others on the basis of some jointly held overarching program or conception of common good. There is no commonly accepted way of compromising issues and demands; one simply tries to get the maximum possible for one's own group or cause. Urgent causes compete against each other for public support. Thus, advocates for giving absolute priority to dealing with AIDS compete with those who are appalled by the growth of tuberculosis, child malnutrition, and other diseases associated with poverty, instead of demanding national health insurance. All causes are born equal. There is no "master discourse," to use the god-awful current jargon of academe. Without that, everyone does his or her own thing. In this bastard version of Emersonianism, "one's own thing" can be "offing pigs," White Power, the Italian Anti-Defamation League, the Jewish Defense League, WITCH, antiabortion activism, or even deep ecology. No claim is based on commonly held values or politics, something that was claimed by the Left at its best. Egalitarianism and general democratic rights were universalist values. There is no logical reason why one should be against racism in a valueless moral universe unless one is a black or other victim. And it follows that no one but blacks or Jews or Italians or Koreans can be expected to support the grievances of those particular groups. I almost wrote *legitimate* grievances, but of course, in a decentered world without common values, there is no such thing—*every* grievance is as legitimate as the next.

It is only a question of the power that the aggrieved group can mobilize that will determine the ability to achieve its demand.

And alas, one of the larger aggrieved grass-roots groups in our country is the National Rifle Association membership, whose hobby, owning firearms, is under continual assault from wimpy liberals. So far the NRA generally has won, benefiting harmless hunters, rightwing gun nuts, Black Liberation Armies, and others, including the young in the cities. A regrettable side consequence may well be our homicide rates, but then imaginative killers are not limited to guns, we are told. Guns remain as American as apple pie, as a black revolutionary activist remarked in the 1960s. All of these and many other different drummers agree on explicitly denying that the general community or polity could have any claims that might override their own. Why then should we not expect that an ever larger proportion of the young population would turn to crime, as an alternative and more lucrative life choice than "square" work. The latter is, in fact, often not even practically accessible, given the decay of mass transit from the ghettoes. It is almost as if a divine agency has abandoned America for some terrible unstated sins, as if vast impersonal and therefore uncontrollable malignant forces actively work against us. No wonder conspiracy theories are so widely popular on the fringes of our media and politics; some are even based on fact.

Years after the passage of the Civil Rights Act of 1964 the situation of black[4] Americans is arguably worse than it was two decades ago. In the face of massive (nearly 50 percent) unemployment statistics, the rotting of inner cities, and the abject collapse of the school system, for some peculiar reason minority youth turn to antisocial behavior, even crime. The only response by federal and state governments, Republican and Democrat, to that increasing crime rate is an ever more costly penal system for which funds can somehow be found. With funds for correction—plainly stated, prisons—relatively abundant, the private sector is already eying this arena as a promising new frontier for free enterprise. Our rate of incarceration has *doubled* during the 1980s! It will double *again* by 1997. Our social system today produces the highest incarceration rates and the longest sentences of any advanced industrial society—at long last a statistic in which we are still number one. We also lead in another area: we are now the only advanced industrial society that still has the death penalty.[5] Additionally, our criminal system assures that, in New York City, the cultural center of the United States, at any one time roughly half of all black males between the ages of sixteen and twenty-five will be the object of some form of custodial care, a rate that compares with those in South Africa. The response by both Democratic and Republican candidates is to call for the death sentence, although there is not a single reputable study that shows that death sentences affect rates of capital crimes.

Life expectancy of young black males in our cities is less than that of males in Bangladesh! This is the result of a combination of factors: lack of decent available jobs and of access to medical care; massive increase in the use of alcohol and drugs, with diminishing funds for rehabilitation; and the sheer increase in violent crime. Perhaps underlying all of those are two major factors: the effective abandonment of the ghetto poor by the majority white population and institutions combined with their abandonment by the black middle and professional classes, who benefited from the abolition of formal racial barriers. The result is a truly frightening political nihilism that permeates the ghettoes.[6] Alas, this nihilism extends even to the admirable reform program of the Congressional Black Caucus, which is unfortunately almost completely unknown within the wider African-American community.

In the meantime our bridges and highways are slowly falling apart, the public transportation system is increasingly unpleasant, when it is not positively unsafe, and our health costs are going through the roof. Although the health insurance industry is enriched, we have appalling health statistics and life expectancy compared with those of Europe and somewhat worse infant mortality statistics than those of Cuba. New York City had infant mortality rates in 1991 resembling those of Shanghai. Tuberculosis has reappeared in the inner cities. A raging epidemic of AIDS has already killed more young males than the war in Vietnam did.

We seem to be light years away from a universal health insurance program for all despite the growing consensus of the public, the unions, and even some of the corporations and doctors that one is needed. It is clear that our present health system discriminates *against* those companies that have a decent—and therefore costly—health insurance system imposed by the unions. The effect is to increase the pressures favoring an antiunion stance by other employers. The political system is truly blocked on this issue on which a huge majority has been stymied for decades. The only initiative by Congress on the issue of health care so far has been the steady scaling down of the proposals of the liberal reformers. This is an excellent example of the growing tendency of the United States to fall behind other industrialized countries. This is despite fact that U.S. *spending* on health care continues to rise. In 1990 spending on health care had increased to 12.2 percent of the gross national product, an increase from 11.6 percent in 1989, more than a number of countries that have comprehensive universal national health insurance schemes spend.[7] Some of the explanation includes gross overcharging by the doctors and insurance companies, but a more serious reason can be found in the American fascination with expensive high technology. A huge proportion of our health expenses are spent in the last years of a patient's life, very little in relatively inexpensive and broadly accessible preventive medicine.

Our elderly and retirees are rightly terrified of the mounting costs of illness, and ever larger numbers of them are left to rot in scandalously overpriced and miserably run nursing facilities for the aged. There too the private sector makes its contribution to creating what is surely the meanest and most expensive system of care for the aged in any advanced capitalist democracy. Astonishingly, we are told that the greed of the old, the retirees on social security, is jeopardizing our nation. Congress is castigated for not being willing to do the courageous and responsible thing and cut back benefits for the greedy oldsters. Governors advise the elderly to face up to reality and do the right thing—die earlier without consuming an unfair share of scarce medical care. And yet the aged vote in relatively large numbers and are, at least compared to the rest of the population, relatively well organized. Who is the political system responding to then?

During the past decade the living standards of the middle class have stagnated while those of the working class have decayed. This is in a society that pays its chief executive officers incomparably higher salaries than those of the executives of Japan or Germany. During an era of wage cuts, layoffs, and budget restraints, a top CEO gets a 103 percent salary increase over his 1989 rate, to an unbelievable $11,400,000 a year.[8] Auto firms simultaneously give huge bonuses to their executives while demanding givebacks and layoffs from their workers. In a world where more and more material goods are being produced we are arguably materially poorer. The children of the present middle class will have worse and less secure lives than those of their parents. Workers, stripped of trade union protection, will have less secure and worse-paid employment. Insecurity about the economic future for the great majority is general and widespread in what is still the richest single country in the world. Opinion polls are clear that the majority believes their futures are bleak. This was the case even before the general recession of the 1990s, which set off a whole new cycle of cutbacks in social spending.

Self-Imposed Wounds: a Blocked Political System

We have freely elected those who have unleashed this massive destruction upon us—not only elected but repeatedly reelected, one might add. We have elected incompetent right-wing ideologues to the White House who did more or less what they had promised to do. This was a shock to our cynical press and politicians, who never expected that campaign promises would have any relationship to political and administrative actions. That is why so little attention is paid to the politically irresponsible, demagogic, and absolutely appalling content of political campaigns in the United States. We have quite lost the habit of treating politicians, particularly while campaigning, as adults who should be taken seriously and held responsible for what they say. Campaigning is now an apolitical art form—better yet, a craft—an exercise in placing the right spin on exquisitely balanced cameo appearances on monstrously expensive prime-time television spots. One should immediately add that it is an increasingly costly art form, accessible only to the rich and superrich. Serious campaigning for office costs millions nowadays. It is surely not meant to be *political,* nor to have anything to do with the exercise of public policy formation. It does not even pretend to have any relation to raising substantial debate about grave national and international matters of importance to the public. The demos is here to be entertained or, if more appropriate, terrified with subliminal symbols like the Willy Hortons, not, God help us, to be involved in formulating public policy. For that matter, in an increasing number of issues it is not only the demos, or the political public that is excluded. In an era of an imperial presidency, Congress itself is often excluded from the formulation of both foreign and domestic policy, as often as it is possible to get away with it. Now, as one contemplates the social, moral, and economic devastation wrought by a decade-long party celebrating greed, our public appears to be astonished only by the most spectacular of the consequences of the years of massive civic irresponsibility.

These things were not imposed on a nation defeated in a prolonged war but are the result of humanly created, consciously designed policies that were imposed on the most powerful and richest country in the world by its own ruling class and political establishment. Further, all of this was done to the United States not by a right-wing military coup but by the absolutely regular, normal workings of a pluralist democratic political system that has been the object of pride and admiration of a generation of pluralist theorists. It was greatly admired and often recommended for export. So much for notions of progress. So much for the "City on the Hill," the example to and leader of the free world. The task of leadership is a trifle easier since the major contender has given up the struggle, and the world, at least temporarily, has only one superpower, somewhat morally shabby and economically weakened.

Another result of a political system dominated by a shallow and greedy business establishment has been the decade of ideologically motivated reckless deregulation that has bankrupted airlines while reducing service and has created an absolutely unprecedented savings and loan scandal that has looted billions from the hapless public and will be bailed out by the same federal government that has been cutting every imaginable social service to the bone for a decade. It is only fair to note that both the looting and the bailout were a thoroughly bipartisan affair, involving exemplary and heart-warming cooperation between Republicans and Democrats, the Congress and the White House. My objection is not to bringing politics *into* such scandals but, to the contrary, leaving it out.

Our endlessly greedy and aggressively confrontational business elite has helped create as its political counterpart a remarkable, uniquely unrepresentative, unresponsive, and stagnant political system.[9] This blocked system bewilders democratic theorists. The power of incumbency and the cost of running for office are such that after celebrating the advent of multiparty free elections in former Communist-ruled states it might be appropriate to extend such novelties to the United States. It would do marvels for the U.S. political system if some of the prescriptions the State Department so freely issues to benighted Eastern European countries about how to run genuinely free elections (including fair access to the media for genuine opponents of the regime) were extended to this country. To paraphrase Gandhi's reply when asked what he thought about English civilization, political democracy in the United States would indeed be a good idea, long overdue. Even the development of a genuine multiparty system would be a very good idea; a real and therefore conflictual and politically defined two-party system would be a major step forward. It might begin to fill the notorious "hole in the American electorate" by getting as many U.S. voters to the polls as vote in other advanced industrial democracies. It would help to have programmatic political alternatives that are accepted as such. It would makes things more interesting, and it might even provide some choice.

The political system dominated by the business community has been reinforced by the gross commercialization of all mass media and an absence of any political dialogue. A systematic depoliticization of politics has been proceeding in the United States for decades. Politics has been treated either as an essentially corrupt business that is best left to professionals or has been reduced to numbingly simple slogans that can be contained in two- to three-minute sound bites. The idea that genuine political participation, civic responsibility, and debate are essential political virtues in a democracy has been exiled to basic civics classes, if that. It is something only for the export market. What has been under assault is any notion that there is a common good, that the community has any general obligations to its citizens and that they in turn have legitimate responsibilities to the society and the state. Instead, a political consensus has emerged in which resistance by elected politicians to any fair taxes is the highest civic virtue. Social obligations are treated as in traditional societies characterized by patriarchal familialism—that is, where there are no obligations to the general community but only to one's tribe, family, or guild. In the United States this translates to obligations to one's ethnic or racial group, gender (or even gender orientation), and profession or class. There is no general community; there are no common civic values; thus, there are no genuine citizens. On this there is a remarkable bipartisan consensus backed by the media, the responsible economic experts, and popular opinion.

More energy is generated in tax revolts than in trying to deal with increasingly miserable schools, massive homelessness, lack of public safety, and a stagnant or falling living standard for the large majority of citizens. Americans seem to accept, as if fated, that today's young will live worse than their parents did. The sole reaction to these social pathologies seems to be under no condition to pay any more taxes. This in the lowest-taxed industrial democracy in the world. Given the inefficiency and general inadequacy of an increasingly resented and grudgingly funded nonuniversalist set of specifically targeted benefits for some "others," which are characteristic of what there was of a welfare state in the United States, this is not hard to understand. However, this problem was still further grossly exacerbated by a political class and commercialized mass media that seems incapable of telling the electorate any unpleasant truths—truths like the one President Johnson could not utter in the 1960s, that a war in Vietnam would have to be paid for by the public with higher taxes; like the one Reagan could not bear to state during the 1980s, if he ever understood it, that Star Wars and a huge decade-long military buildup cost, and would have to be paid for. Instead, Reagan cut taxes on the well-off and the rich, for which they were duly grateful. The poor and the blacks either did not vote or did not vote for him. But the rich and the yuppies were truly grateful, and they did vote. They certainly *loved* Reagan. He made greed positively respectable and even patriotic.

The young professionals, who had rediscovered the joys of greed in the 1980s, as well as the former liberals, were grateful to the horde of neoconservative social analysts like Charles Murray, who assured them that social spending and welfare positively harmed the recipients. That led to the gratifying conclusions that social meanness was the highest form of social responsibility and, further, that cutting their entitlements was *good* for the poor, especially for the urban black poor. This scandalous self-serving ideology spread through the better-off classes in the United States like a wildfire throughout the 1980s. How nice it was to be told, with scientific-sounding social science jargon bolstered with obscure but scientific-sounding statistics, that greed was good, that wanting lower taxes was far from egoistical selfishness; to the contrary, it was an act of positive, though perhaps stern, social virtue. That new bipartisan paradigm helped turn our major cities into battle zones and social disaster areas.

A society that had easily found enough money for fantasies like Star Wars has ended up with Calcutta-like statistics for the homeless sleeping, living, and defecating on the streets. The stranger and more alien the big urban centers became, the weirder and more frighteningly different they were from middle-class (specifically, white middle-class) norms, the easier it was to justify denying the essential humanity of those living in them. It became more difficult to imagine them as *fellow citizens* with whom we had some civic ties and toward whom we had some moral obligations—

especially the poor, especially poor blacks and Hispanics. A widespread yahoo-like prejudice against the large cities and anything multicultural, tacitly played up to by most of the political establishment and media, threatens to devastate our metropolitan areas with new lows in social meanness accompanied by more open hostility toward the poor in general and toward blacks and Hispanics in particular. Decades of defeat and slash-and-burn cutbacks have devastated the urban black community especially and have not only created a fertile ground for endemic drug-based criminality but also have helped to bring forth an opportunistic black chauvinist social demagoguery that is the victims' imitation of the widespread racism of the dominant white community. It is here that one should paraphrase Marx's statement that the dominant ideology of a society is the ideology of its dominant class. Whatever else that class might be, that "class" is not black, Hispanic, feminist, or even comprised of the masses of increasingly insecure white blue-collar workers. However, all successful ruling classes manage to get wide support for their ideology, their definition of reality, and especially their definition of what are possible and therefore reasonable political and policy alternatives. Our situation today is not that different.

But then this not new. Although Marx is now unfashionable, he seemed to be describing our society when he wrote in midnineteenth century:

> Competition separates individuals from one another, not only the bourgeois but still more the workers, in spite of the fact that it brings them together. Hence it is a long time before these individuals can unite. . . . Hence every organized power standing over against these individuals, who live in conditions daily reproducing this isolation can only be overcome after long struggles. To demand the opposite would be tantamount to demanding that competition should not exist in this epoch of history, or that individuals should banish from their minds conditions over which in their isolation they have no control.[10]

The Decline of the United States as a World Power

These developments have occurred within a world economy in which a prolonged shift in relative weight and power has been taking place for two decades, essentially at the expense of the relative standing of the United States and its currency, the dollar. Japan's growing economic significance and the growing economic and political integration of the huge European Community will, sooner or later, begin translating into a shift in political power. This increasingly reduces the basis for the dominant role of the United States to its military power. That base of power will grow less and less relevant in a period in which the collapse of a rival Communist world system and the consequent end of the cold war make military power less utilizable for political goals.

This is not to say that there will not be conflicts, even military conflicts and confrontations, in the post–cold war world, as the 1990–1991 confrontation in the Persian Gulf showed. However, for these conflicts, the kind of massive projection of military nuclear power that had been the almost unique property of the United States is certainly worthless. Nuclear weapons are far less useful, if they are usable at all, in low-level counterinsurgency warfare, military adventures in Grenada or Panama, or military intervention against middle-range powers like Iraq. Above all, they cannot be used as an argument for the continued political and economic dominance of the United States in a worldwide alliance of advanced capitalist states. There is no generally perceived need for an American nuclear umbrella in Europe today. In any case, the European Community has at least two nuclear military powers, France and Great Britain, each of which has the capacity for adequate deterrence were it to become necessary.

It can be cogently argued that more can be done for European and world security by preventing a pathological breakdown of the former Soviet Union into a right-wing military regime than by reliance on a military alliance with the United States. That aim is conceivably achievable by generous economic and technological aid to the former Soviet Union and Eastern Europe, and the United States has been claiming the lack of means for much aid on any but a symbolic scale. This is a very odd claim for a country that has proved capable a monstrously costly military buildup, including Star Wars, for over a decade and that is spending many times more on the savings and loan bail-out than what a fair U.S. share of generous aid to former Communist countries and the third world would require.

What is absent is not the means but the political will and program. Politics is about setting priorities and making difficult choices, even sometimes about "that vision thing" President Bush has so much trouble with. His administration has been primarily concerned with media and polls management, not politics, not even genuine security. That is how hegemonic world powers decline and lose whatever claim they ever had to political leadership of the advanced industrialized world. The cold war was lost by the Soviet Union and the Communist alliance, but it was not won by the United States. The other bloc imploded and collapsed because of its own mistakes and internal stresses and conflicts, what Marxists used to call internal systemic contradictions.

The safety and security of the European Community and Japan no longer ultimately depend, if they ever genuinely did, on the military power of the United States. It is increasingly clear that Soviet economic and military power and potential was systematically exaggerated during the years of "high" cold war, that is, roughly between 1948 and 1978. The growing relative decline of U.S. economic power, underpinned by the sheer backwardness and unattractiveness of our particular variant of capitalist social order, spells the approaching end of the American Century which was so proudly celebrated by Henry Luce and others. It will probably barely survive this decade, having lasted at best (or worst) for five short decades.

What happens in Europe, Japan, and Asia will have more weight and significance in shaping the twenty-first-century world than what happens in the United States. It will certainly be of more significance than what happens in the third world. This is not a statement of *moral* choices or even what I believe should be the case; it is simply my best judgment on what the existing trends lead to. The United States and North America will be, at best, one of the centers in an increasingly polycentric world. The United States is no longer a model or example to other advanced capitalist states. Its primitively confrontational, union-bashing economic leadership has shown itself unable to think in longer-range terms and has thus permitted the degeneration and decline of essential social services and education infrastructures essential to any advanced industrial society. The focus on short-range profits, a necessary consequence of an industrial system run by accountants, makes the United States increasingly uncompetitive economically.

This long-range economic weakness of the United States is not caused, as current popular mythology would have it, by a grossly overpaid and overprotected work force. When social benefits are added to wages, U.S. workers are economically behind Canadians as well as most Northern Europeans. Minimum wages in France are well over the $5 mark, which is almost 20 percent higher than those of the United States. Rather, we are suffering economically because of an absence of long-range investment in research, education, and manpower training and of anything even resembling an industrial or energy policy. American workers are thus not only less well off than their counterparts in much of Europe, they are clearly also less healthy and less well trained and educated, and therefore they will fall even further behind. So will the U.S. economy and therefore society.

What U.S. business elites are still good at seems to be union-bashing and helping to elect and then utilizing a craven probusiness administration to loot American society in ways not seen since the days of the robber barons. The result is a crippled union movement barely organizing 14 percent of the work force, compared to 40 percent in Canada and 85 percent in Sweden. This figure is even worse than it looks because it is inflated by the relatively high degree of unionization in the public sector. It also includes far too many unionized workers in marginal industries, where the pay is miserable—in textiles, small garment factories, the toy industry, and the like—and where the union is tolerated because it is too weak to really matter. Unions that are forced to make any peace available with employers are, of course, only marginally better than no unions. However, their existence contributes to the image of a trade union institution that is bent on surviving at any cost and can make no general appeal for support from a wider public. Whatever else it is, it is not a movement making a general appeal on behalf of working people.

Why It Is Bad for Capitalists to Get What They Want

The United States has not lost a major war or been conquered by a cruel enemy, so the reasons for its decline have to be sought elsewhere. After all, this American Century did begin under the best of all possible conditions. Providence itself seems to have blessed this country and given it a unique opportunity to set the world right. When World War II ended, the United States was the sole major industrial power that had not been devastated. Its industrial and agricultural capacities not only remained undamaged, they had expanded during the war. The major prewar empires were in shambles, the world was in debt to the United States, the dollar ruled supreme, and its rule was underpinned with a series of international agreements assuring something like free trade and therefore American access to previously closed markets.

The United States was the one victor in the war that had not paid a crippling price for that victory, unlike Britain, which was financially dependent on the United States. Western Europe was in shambles, matched only by the devastation that the war had brought to the Soviet Union. The defeated powers, Japan and Germany, were even worse off. The United States also had the advantage of not being identified with colonialism, as were Britain, France, Holland, and Portugal, and of not having had a flirtation, no matter how brief, with right-wing authoritarianism. It was not only the paramount economic power, with an enormous military establishment and the effective monopoly of the nuclear bomb, it was also a *liberal democratic* power par excellence. Its racial problems were relatively unknown abroad until the 1960s. Therefore, there seemed to be no reason why decolonization should not have *increased* the influence and power of the United States. The United States prepared to replace Britain and the other colonial powers as the world policeman in less-developed countries of the world, but it preferred to do so by proxy. The United States therefore supported the first wave of decolonization, that of India, Indonesia, Burma, Ceylon, Nigeria, and Ghana. It was more ambivalent when it came to Algeria and Indochina, but it was still sufficiently pro-decolonization to earn the wrath of French and British conservatives.[11] Both the role and the image of the United States changed with the expansion of the cold war into the third world in the 1960s. American popularity plunged and never recovered throughout the third world during that decade. Perceptions, even if wrong in some details, are sometimes right in important matters.

Be that as it may, U.S. factories and farms could export everything they produced for the first two decades after the war. Loans provided by the

Marshall Plan were used to buy U.S. goods, as was the relatively modest aid to developing countries. This export boom, which seemed to assure *permanent* U.S. penetration into previously protected markets, was matched by a seemingly insatiable domestic market. Those were the "golden years." They lasted until Johnson tried to wage a war in Vietnam without raising taxes to pay for it. The U.S. economy was essentially fordist; high buying power assured an expanding domestic market for cars, consumer durables, and homes. These in turn required expenditures on infrastructure, above all, the huge network of highways. To be sure, public expenditures never seemed to match private ones, and much of the public investment went into highways at the expense of cities and mass transit, but that seemed to reflect consumer choice via the ballot box.

The problem was the old one. Capitalism needs to be regulated to be saved from its own built-in mistakes. The individual pursuit of selfish goals *may* produce public good in abstract capitalist theory. However, in practice the narrow interests of sectors of the economy or industry have to be regulated and restrained in the interest of the system as a whole. That is presumably the role of the state, the capitalist state in this case; that is, one that is run by parties committed to the maintenance of capitalism as an overall efficient system for all. That means regulating the banks, keeping up the infrastructure, and pushing technological innovation. All three of these will reduce the profits of some players at a given time; all three require an interventionist government. That is the clear lesson from the Pacific Rim economies as well as from Europe.

The trouble is that the official ideology of American capitalism, its master myth, is antistatist; that is where the Left, Right, and Center agree, despite the fact that American business has repeatedly used the state to maximize profits and protect itself from competition. Smart procapitalist governments therefore pay lip service to that ideology and then proceed to act as enforcers for the system as a whole against sections that need to be whipped into line. Thus, Roosevelt's New Deal saved American capitalism from far greater damage by bringing in bank regulations, Keynesian pump priming of the economy, huge public projects, and other such measures against the almost unanimous opinion of the capitalist class and its publicists. The Eisenhower, Johnson, and Nixon administrations all in turn had to discipline some sector of the capitalist economic jungle; that is, they had to assure that it would *not* be a jungle. Nixon, let us remember, cracked down harshly on the steel industry when it tried to play its usual confrontational role at the expense of the system as whole. He also devalued the dollar and went off the gold standard, sending traumatic shock through the system, but he most certainly *did* intervene. These "statist" interventions by Washington bureaucrats were profoundly ideologically objectionable to the American business and banking establishment; however, they were also essential for the smooth working of the economy. That was more or less grudgingly accepted by the so-called Eastern Establishment, the more sophisticated, flexible, and internationalist wing of the American economic and political elite. That internationalist elite has tended to vote for either liberal Republicans or Democrats.

The long decline of internationalism in the United States has paralleled the decline of the United States as a world power as well as the evolution of the United States from a liberal supporter of anticolonialism and moderate democratic reforms to a power that backs most of the remaining right-wing and militarist regimes and is primarily a military power. The Gulf War is an almost perfect illustration of this evolution of U.S. policy. It demanded no democratic reforms, not even the formality of free elections from the Kuwaiti regime it restored. We propose to continue selling arms to the region and will use the war as a celebration of U.S. military high technology in order to edge out the competing arms merchants, thus continuing to destabilize the area and creating new Frankenstein monsters. The war helped to turn Iraq's dictator, Saddam Hussein, into a regional power.

The problem for American capitalism, and therefore for the society that it runs as a whole, is that the Eastern Establishment lost. They lost in part because of overreach, in part because of the war in Vietnam, and in part because of their elitism. But lose they did, first more or less harmlessly with Carter, then to the real thing. The Reagan victory gave the conservative procapitalist ideologues the administration of their dreams. They got exactly what they wanted, and the result was unalloyed disaster both for the American people and for a modern American capitalism. Noncapitalist or even modest social democratic options, I hardly need add, were not in the running at any time since the 1930s.

The increasing internationalization of capital has encouraged the export of well-paid unionized jobs from the smokestack industries of the United States and their replacement by mostly "hollow" service jobs, most of which are both nonunionized and low-paying. In turn, this export of well-paid manufacturing jobs has helped to lock new, young, mostly black and Hispanic unskilled workers in the major cities into a vicious cycle of unemployment and marginal, insecure jobs. Thus, part of the price for the U.S. world role has been an erosion of living standards of blue-collar workers and the creation of massive black and Hispanic youth unemployment, with all of the resultant social pathologies, in our cities. It has been used as an argument to assault the already mean and marginal welfare state in the name of increasing the competitiveness of U.S. industries and society, and it is in no small part responsible for the present flood of drugs and crimes devastating our major metropolises.

The imperial role of the United States is increasingly being questioned and even attacked both at home and abroad. It is in question for many reasons, but the most obvious is the changing consensus of the estimate of both Soviet power and intentions. If the states of the former Soviet Union are, as most analysts, east and west, seem to agree, now facing such grim internal stresses and difficulties in moving toward essential economic and political reforms, then they are hardly in a position to play an adventurous and expansive role in the world. The specter of an ever and inevitably expanding Soviet empire, always dubious in the past, given the historically cautious and conservative nature of the ruling Soviet bureaucracies, is now impossible to maintain credibly. Official Washington no longer even uses that particular myth, stressing instead good relations with a properly chastened Russian Republic as the most significant heir of the Soviet Union. But the Soviets were always cautious.

A country can be both authoritarian and militarily nonaggressive, just as political democracies can be and have often been militarily adventurous and imperialist. It was Democrats, not conservatives, who tended historically to get the United States into its military adventures. Elites in the United States have only slowly absorbed lessons about the costs of imperial overexpansion and overcommitment in terms of security responsibilities. A whole wave of new books has carried the issue of U.S. overextension out of the Left and the margins of academe into public debate. None question that the United States will remain the major world power among the advanced capitalist democracies. It is the cost and hubris of empire that are in question. Books by Calleo and by Kennedy,[12] as well as those of numerous other authors in recent years, all raise the need to reassess what is possible and desirable for a major democratic power to attempt by the way of defending and defining its worldwide interests.

It is a terrible pity that the lesson of the cost in human terms of imperial hubris has been so expensive and that is has had to be paid not only by hundreds of thousands of American draftee soldiers but also by the millions of Vietnamese and other victims of the brief and bloody attempt to make this effectively an American Century. A not so minor casualty of that lesson has been the abortion of the brief flirtation in the United States with an advance toward the welfare state standards of Western Europe through either Johnson's Great Society programs or Nixon's abortive attempt at social Toryism.

We are now moving toward the reality of a multipolar world in which the centers of economic and technological action may well move to Europe and the Pacific Rim. The United States does remain a superpower, but, alas, this is mostly in the same way that the Russian Republic also, despite everything, still remains a superpower militarily. The United States is, of course, also a major, but note *a* major, economic power and will remain that for the foreseeable future. The trouble is that public opinion and the electorate seem to be carefully guarded from this new reality by both major parties. The closest that public debate has come to facing the new economic power relations has been in the protectionist themes raised by Rep. Richard A. Gephardt during the 1988 primary campaign. It is also present in the understandable but dangerously simpleminded and nativistic protectionist sentiment increasingly and urgently voiced by AFL-CIO leadership, some of whose unions have been badly battered by imports. It is not the cheap consumer goods imports that should be the focus of worry for labor and progressives so much as the export of capital and jobs.

Some of the capital exports are directed to "reservations," where underpaid and politically repressed labor is worked at sub-subsistence wages, but that is a moral and political rather than an economic problem. The export of capital to the third world and the newly industrialized countries (NICs) is not the major problem; it is the internationalization of capital and technology, placing both out of reach of any kind of social and political control. That and the vast amounts of purely speculative capital floating around argue that the primitive, currently popular notion of simply letting the rich keep more money is not only a utopian program for obtaining socially necessary investments for the United States but also produces an irresponsible and immoral economy. But then in this respect, as in so much else, a democratic socialist finds himself repeating much of what has been said by the Catholic bishops in that excellent social democratic statement, "Pastoral Letter on Catholic Social Teaching and the U.S. Economy."

A scaling down of the U.S. economic and military role throughout the world opens up the possibility of a major political and educational campaign to redefine that role in a way more appropriate to a political democracy than that of a world policeman or an empire. This may generate a debate around the proposals for a genuinely noninterventionist and democratic foreign policy that works to strengthen international agencies as a way of creating a more secure world environment. That in turn should further lower the temperature of confrontation between the superpowers.

American Exceptionalism: The American Left

It has been said by cynics that countries get the type of government they deserve. That may be a cruel truth, much modified by the working of international factors. However, it is also true that countries often seem to get the kind of Left they deserve. Whether as a government or as an opposition, a mass Left seems essential to the workings of advanced industrial democracies. The United States is the great exception to that generalization in not having a major organized Left.[13] This fact may also explain a great deal of what else is exceptional, backward, and simply wrong with American society. The major historical debate about the Left in the United

States has focused on the issue of American exceptionalism. American exceptionalism refers to a problem that has bedeviled the American socialist and Marxist Left from its very inception: why, in a country that had so many of the obvious heuristic conditions for the formation of a mass working-class party, was it so difficult to form one? Or why is the United States, alone among advanced industrial capitalist democracies, the exception to the rule that such states have a mass labor or socialist party as a part of the political system? [14]

There are many arguments advanced, with varying degrees of subtlety and vulgarity, but the basic ones seem to center on three notions. First, the working class in the United States did not have to battle for a democratic electoral franchise in counterposition to other class forces, and as a consequence, unlike Germany and the continental European countries, no mass workers' movement developed over the issue of franchise and the right to participate in the polity. This argument has been put forward both by serious non-Marxist observers, such as Daniel Bell and Seymour Martin Lipset, and by a number of Marxists, like Michael Harrington.

Second, modern America, the country in which the most successful and complete bourgeois democratic revolution has been carried out, was also the country of considerable economic opportunity. Thus, in the words of Sombart, a Social Democratic observer from Germany writing at the beginning of this century, "American Socialism was wrecked on the shoals of roast beef and apple pie." A more subtle version of this would focus on the fragmentation of the American working class along ethnic dimensions as successive waves of immigrant workers entered the American economy, usually filling the ecological niche vacated by the previous wave, that is, at the bottom of the socioeconomic ladder. Thus, the United States has developed an ethnically charged stratification system within the working class, making class solidarity far more difficult to mobilize than in Europe. Early unions were more often than not racist, sometimes even excluding white immigrants.

The third reason occasionally cited focuses on the peculiarities of the American electoral system, which make it exceedingly difficult, if not impossible, for minor parties to enter the political process. The liberal-inspired reforms of the political system make it less political. The tendency in America has rather been either for the displacement of an existing party or for struggles within an existing party, as the arena through which new claimants entered into the politics. That is, after all, how the Republican party was formed.

Whichever version of American exceptionalism one chooses to accept, serious problems were posed for socialists in attempting to deal with the consequences of this exceptionalism. Their responses were predictably abstractly theoretical and unconvincing in practice. The early Marxists and socialists, the Communist party (at least until the 1930s) and the Trotskyists have all tended to work with an implicit assumption of America's relative backwardness and political underdevelopment.[15] That was not the case with the utopian socialists and some of the Marxist socialist immigrants, who treated the United States as the promised land. Marx and Engels were ambivalent and not too well informed. Engels did write about the early American workingmen's parties in the 1830s and 1840s in New York and Philadelphia as examples of working-class parties to be followed in Europe. However, organized American Marxist socialists treated the absence of a mass class-based socialist movement in America as a question of a cultural lag that would automatically be solved in time. America then would catch up with the European experience. It would become "developed." They therefore basically, more or less mechanically, tried to adapt the tried-and-true policies of the European workers' movements to the inhospitable terrain of the United States.[16]

Thus, the early socialists placed an enormous emphasis on independent electoral political activity and a principled socialist program more or less copying the orthodox currents in German social democracy. The Communist party USA rushed to "Bolshevize" itself almost immediately after its founding and sought its salvation in a rigid adherence to the twenty-one points or conditions whose acceptance was required for any party wishing to affiliate with the Communist International. They were among the most loyal and orthodox parties in the Communist International. The American Trotskyists, who attracted or influenced a substantial number of more critical leftist intellectuals, at least during Trotsky's lifetime, followed fairly vigorously the general world strategy of the Fourth International, with roughly the same hopeless results as all other Trotskyist parties in the world: they remained marginalized. In the United States that meant that they remained on the margin of an already marginalized Left, ostracized by the Communists and mistrusted by the Socialists. They had only slightly better luck with the student New Left and antiwar movement in the 1960s.

The practical issues debated by the Left seem to have been relatively well defined and surprisingly few. The first major issue, placed on the table even before World War I, was whether one worked in the official trade union movement (then the AFL) or set up revolutionary industrial trade unions. The second issue was whether one stuck rigorously to running independent candidates on one's party's full program or whether it was appropriate to attempt to form some kind of a broader formation, usually defined as a labor party, as the electoral vehicle for socialist and working-class polities.

To this dichotomy, the national leader of the American Communists from 1930 to 1946, Earl Browder, as well as the so-called old guard Socialists based on garment and textile unions in New York in the 1930s, added a new strategic proposition: that it was possible to work electorally with a set of working-class and other alliances within the two-party system while maintaining an independent organized center outside. This positioned both Communists and right-wing Socialists to play a role of some significance in the liberal and labor wings of President Roosevelt's New Deal coalition. In turn this increased their influence in the unions, particularly in the union institutions involved in electoral and other political activities. The "purer" Socialists and other leftists who remained committed to independent political action were increasingly isolated and marginalized. With the progressive wing of labor passionately pro–New Deal it was hard to maintain a base in the unions and oppose Roosevelt. Again, schematically, the range of options: independent socialist candidates, an independent working-class labor party, or any combination of those with an attempt to intervene in the electoral politics of the two major parties.[17]

Most American radicals today hold the point of view, with some ambivalence, that it is impossible to completely avoid working within the two-party system. To put it differently, the political and class cleavage that is most relevant to American politics still mostly runs through the Democratic party electorate and supporters rather than outside it. On the other hand, there is a wide agreement that the Democratic party has increasingly abdicated the role of an opposition party and that in any case it is very difficult, if not impossible, to work inside that party in any meaningful way. The American party system, essentially apolitical and unstructured, has no analogue in Europe. Since the nearly universal introduction of primaries that determine the choice of candidates, control by the two major parties of the candidates who run under their labels has continually decreased. A Democrat can be a Ku Klux Klan member, an adamant hawk and right-winger, a laborite not too different from moderate European Social Democrats, an independent radical, or even a left-wing Socialist.[18] The crucial point, however, is that class-conscious and trade union–oriented voters, blacks, peace activists, and followers of popular social movements, insofar as they vote at all, vote for the Democrats. The effect has been that the most serious attempt to bring forward a radical reformist program within U.S. politics in decades, one that challenged the major suppositions of U.S. foreign policy and called for the introduction of a generous welfare state—that is, the 1988 massive presidential primary campaign of the Reverend Jesse Jackson—had to take place inside the Democratic party.

American Leftists and Labor

Throughout American labor history, significant groups of organized socialists were active both in the base and in the leadership of the official trade union movement. A question that kept coming up was the relationship of the organized labor movement to the workers who were unorganized. The issue reemerged in a more relevant form in the middle 1930s, when the industrial unions were organized in the bulk of American heavy industry. American Socialists and Communists participated in quite disproportionately large numbers as organizers and leaders of the organization of the Congress of Industrial Organizations (CIO). The new industrial unions emerged out of the more radical AFL unions and the mass of new, mostly mass-production workers who were swept in by a huge wave of working-class militancy, including massive sit-down strikes, that organized the auto, rubber, and steel industries. Large numbers of blacks and women were thereby first included in the unions. They have stayed and increased in numbers, although only recently in influence as well.

Many socialists and progressive trade unionists argue that a situation exists in the United States today analogous to that of the 1930s, one in which the official labor movement proves incapable or unwilling to reach out and organize the new layers of workers outside the traditional industries.[19] For labor even to survive as a viable force up to the end of the century, its leaders must not only understand the recomposition of the American working class that is currently taking place but also must develop strategies and tactics for organizing the vast new strata of women; white-collar workers; new, often illegal immigrants; technicians; and hi-tech experts in the new force.[20]

American leftists and progressives who focus on unions today do so in two very different ways. Either they work for unions as organizers, experts, publicists, economists, or other staff members or they attempt to relate to rank-and-file activities, usually oppositional, as grass-roots members. In the first case, as staff, leftists have to accept the discipline imposed by the union leadership, which for practical purposes means that they must work for the more progressive unions hospitable to leftists and generally social democratic politics and programs. In such unions leftists traditionally have been self-sacrificing organizers and highly motivated political staff. Practically, this means unions with a tradition of hospitality to socialist or Communist activists in the past or unions organizing new and unconventional workplaces. These are the unions known as the "progressive wing" of the official labor movement.[21] In the second case, where leftists work as union rank-and-filers, a long tradition also exists. Some are "native" to these unions; that is, they were already in them as workers when they became radicals. Others, more usually from organized socialist groups "entered"; that is, they went into unions in which they thought political work would be practically possible.[22] They have met with mixed success, but no Left is imaginable in America that does not have a relationship to organized labor, whether as elected officials, staff, or rank-and-file insurgents.

However, insurgence is not a program. Just as in the case of social movements and community organizations, there are both progressive and reactionary rank-and-file struggles inside the unions. The spectacular victory of the insurgents in the Teamsters Union's supervised election in 1991 may signal a wave of internal union struggles. The organized labor movement is in desperate trouble today; only an internal transformation may give it a change to survive as a significant political and social force. That transformation can come only through major internal upheavals analogous to those that formed the Congress of Industrial Organizations (CIO) in the 1930s.

There are union revolts motivated by nativism and racism, by the selfish, particularistic desires of strategically better-placed workers to improve their contracts at the expense of other workers, or even to demand that their children be able to inherit their jobs. In a capitalist society, particularly the kind in the United States, where individualist egoism and individual economic progress are made into fetishes by the media and by the entire system of political socialization from childhood on, it is unreasonable to expect class solidarity and the values of democratic collective effort to be widespread. The miracle is that they emerge so often out of union and social struggles, not that there are exceptions. Other serious problems are posed by the grim contemporary realities of labor and industrial relations in the United States. One is the prolonged economic downturn of the American and world economy. This downturn has been accompanied by a wholesale assault on organized labor and on the gains made by progressive social and political movements. The assault on the unions has been many-pronged, including well-financed antiunion think tanks, publications, and programs of the Right and the business community and, above all, the most antilabor administration the United States has had since before the Great Depression of the 1930s. The resulting atmosphere has been evident in repeated losses of votes by unions in organizing drives and in a campaign for open shops and a "union-free environment." Unions have had an almost universally bad press, and even liberal Democratic opinion has turned increasingly cold toward them, despite the obvious reality that the Democratic party cannot win elections without union support.

The narrow, shortsighted selfishness of many contemporary organized-labor leaders has created a situation in which unions can be treated as a special interest, by definition narrow and parochial. One consequence of this is that unions have maintained their strength primarily in the public sector, and there, unfortunately, their demands are often seen as counterposed to the other budgetary needs of fiscally strapped cities and state governments. That too has been a consequence of systematic cutbacks in social spending by Washington for a whole decade. Social meanness and zero-sum politics are maximized as scarce resources have to be divided among many particularistic publics uninformed by any generous program of social justice and coalition. Among the reformist proposals most often heard are those for a new social contract approach that would in effect freeze real wages and prices and force some kind of willy-nilly partnership between trade unions and American industries.

The second general issue is that of the recomposition of the work force or the rise of a new working class. Although this is a matter of great theoretical interest in attempting to understand late-capitalist economies, it also creates a major crisis within the present labor movement of the United States. The new jobs occupied by service sector employees tend to be nonunion, and the shift from production to services also represents a shift from relatively highly paid industrial jobs to routinized white-collar and service jobs that are, if anything, even more vulnerable to automation than the blue-collar jobs were. It is sufficient to think of the fact that the McDonald's hamburger chain now employs more persons than does U.S. Steel to realize what impact this has on the living standards of American workers and on the viability of the traditional trade unions.

Not only is a vast new field for union organizing opening up, requiring specific new approaches to a heavily female and black as well as younger work force, but the harsh consequences of these shifts have given rise to increasingly urgent calls for more planning under capitalism. As has been pointed out by a number of observers of the Left, Right, and Center, the unplanned, solely market-regulated nature of American capitalism has been one of its more whimsical myths. The question, as has been repeatedly pointed out by Michael Harrington[23] and Kenneth Galbraith among others, has not been planning or not planning but rather planning by whom, for whom, under what kind of democratic popular control, and for which social, economic, and moral goals.

One problem for American leftists has always been the frustratingly huge gap between their subjective desires for social transformation and the objective circumstances in the society they live in. This has made many American radicals and socialists impatient with the politics of the possible while at the same time left them unable to engage in the politics of transformation at home. They therefore identified passionately, if not always wisely, with transformational movements elsewhere, most often in the third world, that seemed to be carrying out their programs. Although there is something pathetic about this search for a successful "model" elsewhere, it has made American leftists sensitive to a range of theoretical debates about the third world and noncapitalist paths to development. American leftists also have been forced to confront the reality of racism in their own society in much more dramatic and intense form than have their European counterparts. That racism is also related to the role of the United

States as a superpower that maintains an unjust social order at the expense of the vast nonwhite majority of the world's population.

The American Left and the Struggle Against Racism

A major issue within the American Left that reemerges recurrently and has been particularly salient since the early 1960s has been the problem of black nationalism. The problem is how that nationalism fits with the general strategic relation of the struggles of blacks and of black workers in particular with broad class alliances the traditional Left has historically called for. The Socialist and Communist movements in the United States have always supported integration rather than black separatism. To be sure, the Communist party played with and even courted black nationalism during the "left" zigs of its line, to the point of supporting the establishment of a separate black nation, a state with the right to secede in the South. The Trotskyists, after some considerable prodding from Trotsky himself, also supported the concept that the African-Americans were a nation. However, the major thrust of the Communists' work throughout the Popular Front period in the 1930s when its influence was at a peak, was to work for integration. Communists were a major influence within the radical and more political part of the black community throughout the 1930s and 1940s. Communists had been active in antiracist campaigns, in opposition to lynching in the South, and in building integrated trade unions, particularly after the organization of the CIO. Communist historians played a major role in helping to develop a history of African-Americans, stressing their struggles for equality. As a consequence they were the most influential groups among radical black intellectuals and activists for decades, until the sharp decline in Communist party membership in the late 1950s and early 1960s. They had helped to form politically and educate a large part of the black trade union political cadre in the United States.

Most American Socialists were vigorously antiracist, although historically some of them had argued that black workers' basic problems were economic and would therefore best be solved in the framework of a general "color blind" movement. Early American Socialists firmly believed that socialism would solve the problems of racism. But then, they believed that socialism would solve every problem, including that of alienation. Nevertheless, many Socialists supported integration actively and helped to found the Niagara movement at the beginning of this century, which later evolved into the National Association for the Advancement of Colored People (NAACP). Socialists also formed other integrationist organizations, like the Congress for Racial Equality (CORE)[24] and the Southern Tenant Farmers Union.

The major Socialist black trade union figure, who began as an antiwar activist during World War I, was A. Philip Randolph, a pioneer in establishing the first black union in the AFL, the Brotherhood of Sleeping Car Porters. The union's journal, *The Black Worker,* played a major role in developing black trade unionist activists and leaders. That union had an unsung role as a network during the spread of the civil rights movement and sit-ins during the late 1950s and early 1960s throughout the South. Bayard Rustin, a lifelong Socialist, and other black and white Socialist intellectuals and activists played major roles as strategists and links between the northern labor movement and the civil rights movement in the South up to the assassination of Martin Luther King, Jr. By that time sections of the civil rights movement had begun to develop black separatist politics.

King's premature death represented the major break within the civil rights movement. He clearly stood *both* for black empowerment and for integration, and in his last years he increasingly linked the struggle for civil rights, as it obviously had to be, with opposition to the war in Vietnam and the campaign to organize poor people. Poor people very often meant poor black people, but King's campaign was always stated in terms of all poor people and the unionization of the poorly paid municipal workers. His death left a vacuum that has never been filled; the movement in good part fragmented and lost its universalist moral thrust, and the clarity and directness of the early civil rights movement was never duplicated. King's subsequent canonization should not let it be forgotten that this saintly figure was even more explicitly a socialist in his last years.

The demise of the activist and integrated civil rights movement of the mid-1960s left the political scene for radical blacks to nationalist, Moslem, and black Marxist-Leninist groups. Some of the fringes turned to "revolutionary suicide," that is, armed violence against crushing odds and under conditions of isolation in their own community, a hopeless romantic gesture that managed to get some fine young black militants killed or imprisoned.

This separation is only to a very limited extent bridged today in what remain the major leftist organizations, the Communists and Democratic Socialists, which have a number of important black activists and leaders. Most of the socialist and leftist groups in recent years have accepted a language and a view of black political struggle that is now more in tune with what the nationalist blacks had been proposing than with the traditionally integrationist view that dominated the Left until the mid-1960s. However, not all black nationalists are separatists. Many argue that they need strong, independent black political organizations to be able to make alliances as equals with the broader progressive community. Moderate black reform politicians have been able to win office in most large cities in the United States, including those in which the black voters are a distinct minority. Leftists in the United States generally have been and are more sensitized to issues of cultural and ethnic autonomy and politics than are their European comrades. They tend to view American society as racist and support the view that it should become explicitly multicultural—that is, that it should stress the non-European groups' cultural and historical contributions to U.S. history and help maintain their ethnic identity and pride.

An additional reborn issue has been the birth of an assertive new feminism, a substantial wing of which expressed itself in Marxist and quasi-Marxist terminology. It is fair to say that the debate has influenced both the practice and theory of all leftists, organized and unorganized, since the 1970s. Unsurprisingly, the influence was most clearly felt in the academy and the media. However, it is also felt in mainline electoral politics. Today it is inconceivable for any leftist or socialist intellectual journal or organization not to pay major attention to cultural, social, and economic issues associated with gender-based oppression. A whole new, essentially Marxist-inspired anthropology of the family has become part of the vocabulary and praxis of American intellectual radicals. This is even reflected in trade union work and in such women's organizations as the Committee of Labor Union Women (CLUW) and the drives to organize white-collar workers undertaken by Local 925 of the State Employees International Union (SEIU) and District 65 of the United Auto Workers of America (UAW), for example.

Mass democratic, egalitarian political mobilization will catch up with this richest of all capitalist societies. Its form and language will probably be quite specific, but my guess is that it will be neither the familiar language of European Socialist movements, even with the Canadian accent of the New Democratic party of Canada, nor yet the Left-Populist Rainbow Coalition rhetoric of the Jackson campaign. It will necessarily borrow from both as well as from the feminist and other social movements and will have to include the bulk of the forces now found in organized labor and the left wing of the Democratic party.

The peculiar specificities of the political system in what is the oldest of political democracies with a continuous constitution make the present two-party system the confusing multiclass and multi-issues arena that diffuses political issues. One consequence is the so-called hole in the American electorate that represents in part those voters who in the other industrial capitalist states vote for socialist and labor parties. Racism, which has been endemic in U.S. politics since its founding, combined with the steady and mass immigration of workers, has generated an ethnically charged class system that makes it more difficult to develop solidaristic class politics than is the case in more homogeneous societies. However, the Jackson campaign of 1988, as well as the past successes of militant industrial union drives, shows that economically egalitarian, democratic mobilization can help bridge ethnic and race barriers to the building of movements that push universalistic, egalitarian social and economic policies. The key is universalist demands versus so-called specially targeted social policies. This means pushing for national health insurance, free and universal preschool child care, massive housing, universal and taxable child allowance on the European model, and the rest of the policies appropriate to a humane, advanced, industrialized democracy, rather than the punitive and mean social welfare policies of the caricature of the welfare state that the United States has become.

To create a mass public for an advanced and egalitarian welfare state, the measures proposed and taken must not be earmarked only for the poor or the aged or women or minorities. They need to be universalist as an extension of citizenship in a modern industrial society. All of these measures, while emphasizing the need for greater leisure and variety in life, must be firmly based on an effective, gender-sensitive egalitarian policy of deliberate creation of labor scarcity, that is, decent, nonpunitive full employment. Thus, the social policies advocated by socialists and social movements should be seen not as an act of generosity or charity, welcome as those sentiments are, but as a civic right, or to use the terminology of U.S. social policy, an entitlement to decent work and social services in what is still the richest society in the world.

The end of the American Century should mark the end to the empire and the hubris that has forced onto an increasingly unwilling U.S. population the odious role of the world policeman, guarding an unjust international world economic order. This role must be given up, and the maintenance of world order should be turned over to genuine international bodies. Clearly, the present unjust international order needs to be drastically changed. Genuine security will require massive efforts to bridge or at least attenuate the North/South gap and to create a world in which want and famine are a thing of the past. It is worth noting, however, that since 1984 the United States has deserted the worldwide campaign for population control, having accepted crackpot theories that population growth is not a real problem. This was another case in which ideologically parochial national politics were played with a desperately urgent international problem. However, famine and hunger can be humanly prevented; food supplies have so far more than kept up with population growth. That is a national and international goal that genuine American patriots, who cherish and defend the real and legitimate interests of their country, will support. What is good for General Motors or the multinationals is not only *not* what is good for America, it is an economic, ecological, and often political disaster for the world. It is also morally untenable.

3

The Future of (Dys)topia

Eastern Europe and the Soviet Union

The unfolding revolutionary transformations of Eastern Europe and the Soviet Union during 1989 and 1990 represented both the general and the terminal crises of the state "socialist" systems ruled by Communist parties. They also represent a massive general retreat, turning into a rout—in many cases led by the ruling Communist parties themselves—from the old, officially long-held and brutally defended claim that some kind of utopia was being built in the Soviet Union and Eastern Europe. This is the end of the misnamed "actually existing socialism." That political system, the parties advocating it, the layers of institutions supporting it, and the masses of professional media people and intellectuals apologizing for it are in panic-stricken retreat, all of which occurred at astonishing speed. There are few cases in history of an old, established regime collapsing so utterly, so swiftly, and with so little resistance. The swift defeat of the abortive coup by Soviet hard-liners against the continual dismemberment of Soviet communism in August 1991 marked the degree to which the old system had died. It, or even a reformed version of communism, can no longer be revived. On the other hand, the fate of democracy, pluralism, and economic reforms is far less certain.

The political and ideological retreat, all but total in the original heartland of communism, includes a complete denial that there was any validity whatsoever to the Communist experiment, now being almost universally blamed for the obvious technological, economic, and political backwardness of these societies. Communism is also held responsible for the retrograde political cultures that now prove to be so vulnerable to authoritarian populism, militant clericalism, and intolerant xenophobic nationalism. It is blamed for the economic disaster that has devastated agriculture, given birth to a veritable herd of white elephants in industry, and created an ecological wasteland.

The long decades of suffering, repression, and sacrifice were not only in vain; they actually did lasting damage and set back the societies of Eastern

Europe and the Soviet Union. Some of these countries had not been industrially backward before the Communist takeover. Czechoslovakia, as the most striking example, had a living standard and a developed industrial economy that compared favorably with the more advanced countries of Western Europe. It had even benefited economically from the wartime German occupation. Nor had Bulgaria suffered any substantial war damage by the time of the Communist takeover in 1945. It was a food exporter, well known for the high quality of its agricultural exports. Eastern Europe and prerevolutionary Russia had been food exporters, for that matter. Czarist Russia had already begun a period of substantial industrial development before the catastrophe of World War I, without which there probably would not have been a Russian Revolution. East Central Europe and Czarist Russia had lively cosmopolitan artists, respected scientists, and an intelligentsia that was an established participant in a general European culture.

All that was devastated by long decades of Communist mismanagement and repression. What was achieved carried a monstrous political, ecological, and economic cost. Essentially, the achievements consisted of rapid, crude, and massive urbanization combined with industrial development that has often turned out to have been misdevelopment and ecologically catastrophic to boot. There also were some real advances: vastly expanded education, a crude universal welfare state, and massive social mobility. To these must be added real improvements in the legal, social, and economic condition of women, which may now be in grave jeopardy throughout the region. Even those few genuine achievements of Communist states were corrupted by crass privilege and favoritism on behalf of a greedy party elite, politocracy, or *nomenklatura*,[1] which consistently demanded and almost always obtained huge privileges for itself, its families, and its sycophants.

What now remains to be done is to dismantle as quickly and painlessly as possible the entire political, social, and economic edifices of these societies. On that there is wall-to-wall consensus among the former ruling parties and their new triumphant former opponents. The only relevant arguments on the political scene are how to go about the demolition job—how much pain in unemployment and lowering of social and living standards is unavoidable and how much is politically tolerable.

There are also questions of who if anyone is to be punished for the catastrophe and who is best suited to carry out the restructuring of these economies and societies. Unfortunately, many of the leading candidates for that job also propose to introduce religion in schools, outlaw abortion in societies where contraception is not easily available, deal with unemployment by pushing women out of the workplace, and reintroduce censorship. They also propose a massive purge of present and former Communists, as well as the dismantling of the party institutions and press; some even propose outlawing the party itself. Clearly, the struggle to build pluralist and tolerant democratic institutions and society only *begins* with the removal of the Communists from their power monopoly and the institution of free multiparty elections. But equally clearly, those are essential and minimal, necessary though not yet sufficient, preconditions for a civil society and a decent democratic polity.

The custodians and rulers of what had been called with unconscious bitter humor "really existing socialism" have helped to bury it. What they ended up burying were their very own authoritarian, state-directed economies or politocracies rather than burying capitalism, as they had promised with such breathtaking certainty. That was a very scientistic certainty based on the belief that official Marxist Leninism had mastered the laws of history and development. But then, a great deal about the state socialist politocracies has been based on broken promises, and there is no reason to have expected that an exception would be made in this case. History is by no means fair. Communist ideologues and their fellow travelers, as well as many critics of those systems, insisted that Communist regimes were indeed some of, if not the only, "really" possible variants of socialism. Conservative anti-Communists agreed, with enthusiasm, that communism in power was indeed the logical heir of socialism; some even would say that it was the logical heir of the great democratic revolutions. The very idea of socialism itself, which I insist must be democratic if it is to be at all, may also have been mortally injured. Or perhaps, to be more optimistic, that idea and project must now be reformulated in a new, crystal-clear language, making it plain that socialism is a part of the thoroughgoing extension of political democracy and individual freedom, both of which require substantial equality among citizens, and that it has nothing whatsoever in common with the statist authoritarian regimes that had claimed its name since the Bolshevik Revolution of 1917. Such a reformulation of a possible and viable democratic socialism is a long and painful project, of which this book is a modest part.

How the Communist Politocracies Developed

Any discussion of the former Eastern European, Soviet, and other variants of Communist party–ruled societies should begin with their similarities, political and economic, to each other—in other words, with their common character if there was one. I believe that the best way to describe these systems is as *politocracies*, that is, systems in which the political elites, ruling through the single Communist party, controlled the state and the economy and through those the society.[2]

This is not the place to develop an extensive rationale for my preference for the term "politocracy" to describe societies diversely described with terms such as "state socialist" or "currently existing socialism" or "authoritarian socialism." I borrow the term with considerable gratitude from the well-known Yugoslav political theorist Svetozar Stojanovic. I think it is superior in explanatory power to others, including independent Marxist, generally Trotskyist-influenced attempts to describe the society that emerged in the Soviet Union after the isolation of the Bolshevik Revolution and Stalin's counterrevolution in 1929–30 created an unprecedentedly brutal new social and political order.

Some kind of a new name, a descriptive term, needed to be found for these new systems.[3] My own early preference was for any label that would clearly indicate that these societies were new social formations, radically different from the previous authoritarian capitalist dictatorships and from any projected socialist or workers' states or so-called dictatorships of the proletariat, to use that unhappy phrase of Marx's. Today I prefer the term "politocracy." To put it as directly as possible, whoever ruled, whatever class was in power, it seemed clear to me that it was not the working class. The new political elites, which had emerged from a revolutionary socialist and Marxist tradition, did continue to use and manipulate, albeit ever more routinely and cynically, the language and symbols of a common socialist tradition.

That social and political system was exported, essentially by the Soviet armies after World War II and the defeat of Nazi Germany and its allies, throughout Eastern Europe. It was imposed on the Eastern European states with more or less force, from the top down, and survived essentially as long as Soviet military power was there to underpin it. Even the two exceptions to that generalization—Yugoslavia and Albania, where Communist party–led Partisan resistance movements won power through a bitter civil war combined with a war against the Nazi occupiers—initially benefited from the support of the Soviet Union through the postwar treaty settlements of Yalta and Potsdam that legitimated their victories.[4]

After the Chinese Communists won their civil war and revolution, the "generic" Communist model, modified and adapted for local use, developed considerable support throughout the third world. This was particularly the case with younger anticolonial and anti-imperialist intellectuals and leaders of national liberation wars. That model, in its modified third world form, legitimated the rule of small revolutionary minorities as the necessary shortcut for modernization and development of backward societies. The Soviet and Chinese models of economic development were widely admired and imitated. Even more attractive was their organization of state power, that is, the subordination of the state and the economy to the ruling revolutionary party and, more often than not, of the party itself to its maximum charismatic leader. To be sure, that charisma was often manufactured and maintained by chicanery and force, but the power was real.

Both the realities of and fantasies about these systems, which defined themselves and were accepted widely as variants of socialism, were something for which some kind of intellectual and, above all, moral responsibility was laid at the door of socialism itself, both as a project and a worldview. This is in no small part because a number of Western Marxists and socialists did continue to refer, and do to this very day, to these societies as socialist. By the 1960s this was usually accompanied with some modifier such as the euphemism "currently existing socialism" or simply "state socialism."

These societies, at least in their "authentic" forms—that is, those ruled by classic-type Communist parties[5]— have had an essentially similar class in power. I also now think that mature or *decaying* politocracies[6] evolved a wide range of possible political forms, with more or less autonomy for independent organizations and trade unions and more or less political rights and individual liberty. This entire range of development took place within an authoritarian political framework. Just as bourgeois societies provide a wide range of variants, from dictatorships and authoritarian states to pluralist welfare-state democracies, the politocratic regimes, during their prolonged decay, which lasted a good two decades, provided a wider range of variants than had been imaginable. The great exception is that bourgeois societies *also have* parliamentary pluralist variants; the politocracies never did and could not. In that sense they were sterile and could not develop, at least not into pluralist democracies.

A whole new type of social order emerged, neither capitalist nor socialist. It needed a name if for no other reason than to demystify the claims of the rulers of these states that they were the natural heirs of the great liberating democratic revolutions and the democratic mass workers' socialist movements. The states they ruled were clearly anything but democratic, unless language was to be turned to whole new and unprecedented usage. George Orwell, in his dystopic *1984*, stressed the need for his imagined totalitarian state to control language. Thus war became peace, and slavery was freedom. He even predicted a whole new profession, the rewriters and updaters of the past. A bitter Soviet joke of the 1970s described communism as the system in which the future—that is, the victory of communism—is certain; it is only the past that constantly changes.

The Collapse Is That of a World System

Official Communist ideology and the system of political power that underpinned it was defended by countless devoted, sometimes heroic, and often ruthless party cadres, activists and supporters of the Communist movement throughout the world. It was even accepted, albeit most often in a less chiliastic and more instrumental form, by millions throughout the third world. It was, lest it be now forgotten, a world movement that was perceived as either a terrifying or a liberating but irresistible wave of the future, whose victory seemed all but inevitable during the long years of high cold war in the 1950s, 1960s, and 1970s.

In the light of that genuinely frightening prospect, a whole generation of liberal and democratic leftist intellectuals turned into ever sourer and more politically and socially conservative cold warriors during the 1950s. They stayed that way for more than a generation. The non-Communist Left was turned into near irrelevance for decades, as junior allies of a West firmly led by the United States. There seemed to be no other alternative to the "irreversible and inevitable" spread of the Communist empire. That period seems gone, destroyed almost like magic. Future historians may well decide that it has turned out that the gray, dull Brezhnev era during the 1970s represented not a decline but the high watermark of communism as a world system and of the Soviet Union as a superpower. That era may retroactively even look like the good old time of stability and slowly growing prosperity in the face of the new post-Communist perils in what will have remained of a Soviet Union.

How far away in the past all of that seems today! And yet Jean François Revel's and other doomsday scenarios of the necessary collapse of democracies and inevitable victory of communism were written and celebrated only yesterday. The best known was probably Revel's 1983 best-seller *How Democracies Perish.* Statements and speeches today by both Communist reformers and Soviet leaders—above all, since the *anno mirabilis* 1989—confirm in detail some of the most relentlessly ferocious criticisms of these systems by both internal and external opponents. "The truths of yesterday have became the lies of today." It was the facts relentlessly piling up as more and more of the previously forbidden truths came to light about these politocratic dictatorships that were truly shocking to the sympathizers and supporters of these paths to an earthly paradise. They confirm what was hardly a secret to all who were willing to see, what had been there for all to see—that is, for those who were willing to see without ideological blinders. What there was to see, ever more clearly as the Communist states became less and less isolated and more visible, was relentlessly destructive of illusion and faith in "really existing socialism" as a system. It has proved fatal for the old Communist parties identified with that system outside the old Communist bloc, no matter how much they have insisted on their own fundamental transformation and reform.

It remains to be seen if those years of state "socialism" and Communist power have also been deadly to their chances of any left politics at all.[7] I do not believe that a broad democratic Left has lost a chance for a future even in post-Communist societies; the question is how long must it be in a purgatory of the sins of others, that is, ruling Communist parties. No current observer of the widespread visceral hatred for the old Communist system and all of its symbols and language in former Communist-ruled countries can fail to wonder whether any type of socialism at all, even a socialism very clearly identified with the social democracies of Western Europe, has not been deeply injured by the identification of Communist one-party tyranny as a variant, no matter how abhorrent, of socialism. One mildly optimistic sign is the large number of newly born parties, as well as the reborn and remnants of old pre-Communist socialist parties, claiming the name "social democratic" throughout Eastern Europe and the former Soviet Union. They are requesting some kind of recognition and fellowship from the Socialist International and the Western European social democratic parties. In this quest for some kind of social democratic legitimacy, the new and reborn parties are joined by more or less transformed, chastened, and reformed sections of the old Communist parties. There must have been *some* reason for this frantic scramble throughout 1990 and 1991 for some kind of social democratic credentials. Some local political actors must believe that such an identity is of practical political value today and a promising investment for the future.

The Delegitimation of a Political and Ideological System

It is questionable if even two or three decades of generous aid from Western Europe will be able to help clean up the economic and social mess the post-Communist regimes have inherited. It is even more questionable if aid on that scale will be available for years. Germany will have its resources tied down trying to integrate an economically and ecologically devastated former East Germany. After all, *these* specific former Eastern Europeans vote in a unified Germany and thus have to be paid urgent political attention. How much will be left over for helping other Eastern European states and the former Soviet Union is anyone's guess. One thing is clear, the first priority will be aid to the Russian Republic, and that will be for security reasons, as well as being a tribute to the massive natural resources that are potentially available. The attempted hard-liner coup against Gorbachev and the reformers in August 1991 underlines the urgency of massive aid. The failure of the United States to come up with real money will place the main pressure on the EEC and Germany.

That does not augur well for the immediate economic prospects of Poland, Czechoslovakia, Hungary, Bulgaria, Romania, and the states emerging from Yugoslavia. Albania's prospects are too dismal to be even worth discussing. The trouble is that the relatively better-off Eastern European countries cannot expect a fraction of the aid the wildly aroused expectations of their now much freer populations require. The fact that those societies are now far more open only means that the drastic contrast between their living standards and those of Western Europe are now all too clearly visible and stark. A demagogic yellow press keeps rubbing in the difference and encouraging impossible demands for immediate and sharp increases in living standards. But after all, one of the major reasons for getting rid of the Communist regimes was to become a part of "Europe"; for the masses that means to achieve a "European" living standard almost immediately, hopefully without having to develop capitalist working habits.

Wild, desperate, unrealistic hopes have been aroused, some quite irresponsibly, that some quick solutions are graspable by an act of political will. It should be reasonably clear that *none* of these countries will become a part of "Europe" if by that is meant entering the European Economic Community before the end of the century. At best, what is open is the hope for some process, some type of halfway house, where a gradual increase of contacts and ties with Europe will take place. Favored countries may get some or all of their debt forgiven and be treated with more consideration when new credits are requested. The citizens of more favored countries—in practice, Poland, Hungary, Czechoslovakia, and with some luck what remains of the Yugoslav federation after a settlement—will be able to travel in the European Community without visas. To be sure, this is likely to continue only if there is no mass exodus, like the Albanian one in the summer of 1991. The Community *will* almost surely try to help, but the probable amount of aid does not begin to approach what is needed for the expectations of the peoples of former Communist countries to be satisfied. What they expected was that their living standards would radically improve after the demise of communism. To date they have not; to the contrary they have dropped everywhere in Eastern Europe, in some cases drastically. What is worse, it is universally predicted that things will get worse before they get better. The only debate concerns how much worse and for how long a time.

An additional problem is that with the old Communist repressive regimes *and* the potential military threat of the Warsaw Pact both gone from the scene, there is considerably less interest on the part of Western Europe and the United States in the former Communist countries. Less interest, unfortunately, translates into less urgent pressure for aid. Potential immigrants—and there may well soon be a flood—are no longer courageous political refugees seeking well-deserved political asylum. Instead they are "mere" economic immigrants representing economic costs and social problems, and as such they have far less claim on hospitality. This is particularly true because the 1990s may well produce slow economic growth and a near recession *and* desperate would-be immigrants from the Maghreb, Middle East, and Francophone Africa, who will clamor to get into the island of relative prosperity that Europe will represent. It will do no good for Eastern Europeans to, quite properly, insist that they are and have always been a part of a general European culture. That claim is abstract, and tolerance for economic immigrants with strange languages and customs has never been high in Western Europe, particularly in time of economic stagnation and low growth. The prospects that growth will rise sufficiently to make a difference to the millions of Eastern Europeans who want to live better now, not in the indefinite future, are quite dim. The world economy is stagnant, and no dramatic change is expected soon.

The New Beginnings: Liberation and Reforms in Eastern Europe

All agree today, friends and foes alike, that the economies of the former Communist societies are in a horrendous mess that has to be addressed urgently, without delay. The trouble is that the overall political system *and* the social policies *and* such minor details as new constitutions, electoral systems, and new civil services *and* new political parties *and* independent trade unions, which in most cases have to be built from scratch, *and* habits of tolerance for political and ethnic minorities all have to be invented (or in the best cases, reinvented) at the same time. All of these things have to be done simultaneously. That is, both the economies and political systems have to be restructured radically while taking care of some of the most banal and urgent priorities in many countries, such as feeding the population and providing enough heat, fuel, and medical care simply to survive. Even well-functioning political systems with a high degree of popular legitimacy would have trouble coping with that much overload. In the case of the former Soviet Union, Bulgaria, and Romania, the situation threatens to get out of control and become catastrophic. In Yugoslavia, only a half decade ago the most promising case, economically, in Eastern Europe and the most likely candidate for a successful transition from authoritarianism and entrance into Europe, the situation *has* politically gone out of control. The political breakdown has gone so far that civil authorities lost control of the federal army (YPA) by 1991; and local nationalist elites that rule the republics have, at least in case of the three largest ones, lost legitimate civilian control of their own police and armed forces. The federal Yugoslav government is a shell, and the remaining republics should soon follow Croatia and Slovenia in obtaining recognition. Both the Soviet Union and Yugoslavia have faced the problem of disintegrative nationalism, which tore those multiethnic states apart. This is in addition to their already gruesome economic problems.

The situation is only slightly more tolerable in Poland, Czechoslovakia, and Hungary,[8] where economic hardships and drops in living standards are substantial but somewhat more manageable. Yugoslavia is a separate story; there the economy, otherwise probably the most salvageable in Eastern Europe, has fallen victim to the catastrophic rise of rival nationalisms and armed conflict resulting in the destruction of the Yugoslav state.

Czechoslovakia had always been relatively prosperous, and Hungary and Yugoslavia were both more familiar with the market than the other Eastern European states were. Poland is the beneficiary of considerable aid and has had a start on reforming the political system. But these are fragile advantages, subject to unpredictable changes. One reason for the rapid economic breakdown in the worst cases is that the old distributive system *and* the old law enforcement mechanisms have both broken down and have not been replaced with new ones. There is no generally accepted notion of the common good for which voluntary discipline and sacrifices will be made, and the old repressive structures capable of commanding compliance are thankfully gone. This is an intolerable and therefore obviously temporary situation. The question is, in which directions will these societies move? One thing is certain, far from catching up and surpassing the advanced capitalist nations, Eastern Europe and the former Soviet Union are in acute danger of at least temporarily plunging into the third world.

To understand the third world parallel with former Communist-ruled states one should remember that many third world countries, particularly the so-called NICs (newly industrialized countries) have *sectors* of the economy and achievements in the fields of culture and science that conform to world-class standards. It is the *overall* performance of the economy and society that is in dismal shape. Underlining the miserable economic performance has been an increasing technological lag, which has developed despite the vast expansion of higher education and a major emphasis on science and technology in the Soviet Union and most Eastern European countries for at least the past three decades.

The Crisis of Communism Is Worldwide

The reforms launched in the Soviet Union by Gorbachev in 1988–89 opened up the systemic crisis of the politocratic state socialist systems as a whole. These reforms were meant, at least by the reformers surrounding Gorbachev, to launch a second socialist revolution, that is, to create a more humane and open socialist system capable of adjusting to the needs of modern technology and economic efficiency.[9] The slogan was "Back to Marx." All familiar structures—the party at the center, the mass organizations, the structure of the government, the role of the political police, even the military—were being restructured beyond recognition. These were not reforms but an attempt at administered revolution from above. This explains, if any explanation is needed, why the hard-liners attempted a desperate last-minute coup in August 1991. The defeat of the coup accelerated the changes to a point of no return. That does not mean that the fate of democracy or economic reforms is at all certain. Disintegration and a Russian Peronism are very real alternative options, perhaps even the more likely ones. Poverty, insecurity, social chaos, and national mobilization combined with an ever more ferocious anticommunism are not a promising terrain for building a stable democratic polity.

Increasingly pluralistic and democratic elections spread through the Soviet Union, at differing paces and with mixed results. It is the case, however, that non- and even anti-Communist legislatures were elected in a number of republics. Several legislatures passed into the hands of nationalist majorities, which opted to secede from the Soviet Union. This was first the case with the three Baltic republics, Estonia, Latvia, and Lithuania, as well as with Georgia, Moldavia, and Ukraine, which have all voted to secede. By the end of 1991 the Soviet Union was something that could only be mentioned in the past tense. How far the process of disintegration will go is an open question. The fate of the new Independent Commonwealth is very uncertain. What is certain is that the odds for survival are bad.

The Baltic republics, with a better legal and historic case for international recognition than others, were recognized following the abortive anti-Gorbachev coup in 1991. However, for the other republics, with the possible exception of Moldavia, issues of this sort are not settled by legalities and diplomatic niceties but by relations of force. Separatist-nationalist majorities exist in the legislatures of the Ukrainian and Armenian republics, and it is an open question what results genuine free elections would produce in the Moslem Central Asian republics. The old guard managed to manipulate the elections in its favor; however, the chances of its staying power are very low. At the very least, this means that short of a reversion to more repression, the former Soviet Union, without the Baltic republics, will have to develop into a very much looser confederation, as proposed by the agreement for an independent commonwealth, if it is to survive at all. Such a development must take place early in the game, or it becomes an unacceptable option, as Yugoslavia demonstrated in 1990 and 1991.

The major cities in the Russian Republic have passed under the control of nonparty reformers. At least six or seven organized political groups or parties now compete openly for political leadership in the Russian Republic alone. However, if the reforms begun by Gorbachev in 1989 opened up the Soviet system to fundamental reforms, the stalemate of political and economic reforms by 1992 underlines the depth of the crisis of that system. The epicenter of the crisis is the economic system, a familiar but inefficient system that had all but collapsed without a new one taking its place.[10]

The Soviet political and economic systems are unreformable without gigantic upheavals that would wipe out the entire formal and informal *nomenklatura* that still rules. Since Gorbachev's own power base was the reformist section of that *nomenklatura,* he drew back, creating a prolonged stalemate. After the defeat of the August 1991 coup by the organized hard-liners in what remained of the party and their allies in the military and police, the struggle over the fate of the Soviet system passed from the circles around Gorbachev and the Parliament to the group around Yeltsin in the Russian Republic and to unorganized mass pressures from below. The gradualist liberals and reformers are sidelined, at least for the time being.

Whatever the ultimate fate of the republics emerging from the former Soviet Union as such, the economic and political bankruptcy of the "real-socialist" soviet model only emphasizes what was there for all to see under the thick layers of ideology and propaganda: the total loss of legitimacy of such systems throughout Eastern Europe and in the Soviet Union. The single nation-states will surely survive, and the multiethnic states will break up or be transformed to looser confederations acceptable to their various previously subject peoples, but the socioeconomic and political system of Communist politocracies is today either already dead or dying.

That crisis is worldwide. A whole political and economic model, defended and fostered by a world movement, has entered its terminal crisis. Politocratic socialism consisted of command economies that had managed scarcity following the soviet development model and had at their core the indispensable element of authoritarian one-party rule because it was indispensable for the control of the state. In turn, the state controlled the economy and dominated or tried to dominate the society. It was clearly a world model, with whatever nominal allowances were made for individual "national roads" to that Marxist-Leninist model of socialism; the goal and the methods were essentially the same. It was prescribed as the supreme and, above all, the *effective* solution for the problems of backwardness and underdevelopment in the third world.

The failure of this model in its heartland has only underlined its failure throughout the third world. It was not merely that these regimes massively violated human rights and deprived broad layers of the population of the most basic democratic rights; that is no small thing, but these regimes were failures even in what they claimed was their *special* virtue. They have miserably failed as effective economic and technological backwaters.

Just as the Soviet political and economic reforms have highlighted the general crisis of a worldwide model, the fate of the former Eastern European Communist state systems, their differences notwithstanding, can help us consider some of the possible futures. All post-Communist regimes are not cut from the same cloth, but they do share certain similar problems. The fate of the Eastern European states permits us to speculate about a more general question: Is there a general direction in which the former Communist-ruled societies will go? That is, what is the likely fate of the transformed politocracies? What are their prospects for emerging as stable, productive, and democratic societies?

Elite Contestation Led to System Transformation

Economic and political reforms, particularly administrative decentralization, and the increased autonomy of the individual enterprises (and thus the economy as a whole) have been on the agenda for a quarter of the century. Many of the reforms have been experimented with for decades on the much smaller scale that individual Eastern European countries afford. A whole generation of political and economic reforms have had their day in the sun throughout the region. Yugoslavian and Hungarian reforms have shown that a very considerable degree of marketization of economy is possible while maintaining social ownership. For that matter, the great *flexibility* of the market as an allocator and as an engine of economic growth is shown in Austria, undoubtedly an example of a capitalist and market economy but one in which a large sector of the economy is nationalized or under public ownership. Thus, private ownership and the market are not necessarily linked.

In any case, Hungary and Yugoslavia also illustrated that although marketization weakens the central authority of the state, it does not necessarily or automatically lead to pluralism and democracy. What it does is add other players with new social and political bases to those who contend for political power. Powerful and successful managers and technocrats joined the political cadres in the expanded ruling elite. This process is, however, much slower than most observers have thought. The "techno-managerial bureaucracy," as it was called by its critics in Yugoslavia in the 1960s and 1970s, still remained subordinate to the party's ideological and political cadres. However, although subordinate, the managerial elite was a distinct and self-conscious part of the ruling establishment, with definite interests. In short it was a player, although not the dominant player, in the power politics of the country.[11] This leads to at least a limited elite pluralism and competition, which, in turn, provides space for some politics. To be sure, it was oligarchic politics with limited players, but that makes it no different from the politics of most of Western Europe until the beginning of this century.

Conflicts about alternative ways to modernize the economy and the society within the ruling elite have produced cleavages in the previously monolithic systems, cracks in a previously solid wall through which new players could enter the game of oligarchic politics, initially as allies of leadership cliques and factions. This was, for example, the way that segments of the so-called humanist intelligentsia—writers, journalists, social scientists, and economists—were pulled into elite conflicts on one side or the other, usually on the side of the technocratic modernizers and reformers. Then parts of the elite turned to ever more dangerous power games and alliances by bringing in, very cautiously at the outset, workers and the popular urban masses, more often than not *against* technocratic reformers. The appeal there was to egalitarian populist rhetoric and, failing that, to nationalist grievances, real or imagined.

There was a *master* grievance, against the results of Yalta and Teheran, that made all but the Yugoslavian and Albanian governments essentially illegitimate. The Communist regimes were instruments through which Soviet domination was exerted over the region. In plain words they were puppets or were seen to be such by much of the population. To be sure, over the years the regimes became increasingly autonomous and even national, but this remained essentially within the boundaries of what the Soviet Union would tolerate. Nationalism was thus counterposed to the continued existence of these regimes. This was also the case with multinational regimes, whether or not they were subordinated to an external power. An existing political arrangement between various national groups within a single state could not remain based on the legitimacy of the Communist party and its state. At the very least it would have to be renegotiated. That is why the most massive parties that have emerged in post-Communist states have tended to be nationalist. Nationalism remained the residual identity of the large majority of the population that was counterposed to communism. It was often reinforced with religion. Both nationalism and religion lend themselves to organic politics of identity, unlike abstract political ideas, which need time to reach broad layers of population, if they ever do. Politics of identity rather than of program are more likely to survive and spring up as mass movements at the first chance they get after long years of Communist repression. That is why it was dangerous for sectors of the Communist political elite to play with nationalism. The future, if any, of the former Soviet Union and Yugoslavia will tell just how dangerous for the continued existence of a unitary, even federal, state.

Beyond Elite Reforms to Contested Elections

Since 1989 radical breaks with authoritarian Communist party rule have taken place throughout the whole region. The result has been the development of a range of transitional regimes with varying mixes of parliamentary democracy, administrative authoritarianism, chaotic disorganization and breakdown and transitional economies with equally bewildering mixes of state ownership and control, managerial autonomy within socially owned sectors, unevenly developing and unregulated private sectors and a massive gray economy.

All of these states now claim to be democratizing, more or less successfully, to genuinely contested elections. Whatever legitimacy is claimed for governments now rests on that claim. All of the new governments and in most cases their oppositions are at least formally committed to economic reforms that will introduce elements of the market into the economy, as well as some (in most cases unspecified) mixes of state, social, cooperative, and simply private ownership. All Eastern European governments are trying to develop the closest possible relations to the European Community at the most rapid pace possible. Poland, Hungary, Czechoslovakia, and Yugoslavia all belong to the European Parliamentary Union and to as many multilateral European bodies as they can get into.

All post-Communist Eastern European regimes now claim to be democratic. To be sure, that claim to democracy is flawed by the current confusion of the *ethnos* and *demos*—that is, the dominant or majority national group and the citizens of the state—throughout the region. It is as if all Eastern European and many former Soviet nationalisms had adopted a "Zionist" view of their respective states. The state is the national state of the dominant people; others are tolerated, at best. This makes democracy the instrument of national majorities against others.

There is little sensitivity about the need for religious tolerance or indeed for any separation of church and state among the post-Communist national populists who have won power in many of the countries. Thus, introduction of religious teaching in school and measures to "protect" the family and morality are spreading as well. It is also clear that women's hard-earned gains under the old Communist regimes are very much in jeopardy throughout the region. These problems, which have arisen even in the very early stages of democratization, must be firmly and quickly addressed by the European and American friends of human rights. Otherwise, a very real danger exists that post-Communist governments will end up as nationally intolerant, clerically obscurantist regimes in which democracy is reduced to formal regular elections. Although this *is* undoubtedly a step forward from one-party authoritarian rule, it is important to remember that in three of the Eastern European countries that rule was very much softened by the time of the free elections and modified by reforms. Hungary, Poland, and especially Yugoslavia were ruled by reform Communists who, in their last days of power, showed more sensitivity and tolerance in many ways than some of their successors do. What keeps the new regimes from being even more intolerant today is hope of eventual integration into Europe. That means that pro–human rights and democracy pressures can be very effective.

Western European and American political leaders worried publicly about the prospects for Yeltsin, after he replaced Gorbachev, and the various post-Communist administrations throughout Eastern Europe. The reform Communist prime minister of Yugoslavia, Ante Markovic, had been the West's—especially the banks'—openly favored politician in that country until he fell victim to the country's growing disintegration. He was favored even over explicitly anti-Communist but, alas, nationalist and therefore destabilizing Croatia and Slovenia and, of course, over the very thinly disguised nationalist Communists of Serbia and Montenegro. Russian visitors and delegations and observers are present everywhere talking about the Common European Home. In the United Nations all is sweetness and light since 1989, as the new states of the former Soviet Union and the old Warsaw Bloc nations hastened to prove their new good citizenship through denunciation of terrorism and support of the UN blockade of Iraq in the fall of 1990.

And yet, after the first obviously genuine joy at the toppling of the detested or in some cases merely despised Communist regimes, popular euphoria and mobilization began to dry up practically overnight. There is no new alternative vision of common good. After communism, what? A republic led by former dissident poets, playwrights, and historians? Good, and then what? What is it they are expected to do after pushing, with more or less kindness, the former Communist appointees and *nomenklatura* into political (we hope only political) oblivion. Once that particular catharsis is over, there remain some banal economic questions and decisions that have to be made. There the first problems begin.

The free market, which most of the former opposition and former Communists have fallen in love with as an idea, is very abstract indeed. *Everyone* today, including the old Communist cadres, is for all the good things associated with the market: a plentiful supply of world-quality goods at a decent, nongouging price, with a minimum of petty bureaucratic interference by the state. Almost everyone is also for rewarding hard work and initiative, even with higher incomes, provided that would not be rewarding those artful dodgers who have connections or relatives in right places, as too often seems to be the case.

Most ordinary people in former Communist-ruled states support a minimalist state today, given the nature of the state they have just begun to transform. However, even this minimalist state is far less minimal than the state considered appropriately minimal by the new intellectual enthusiasts for marketizing everything under the sun. Very few people in Eastern Europe are for the distribution of health and education based on the ability to pay. Almost no one is willing to accept massive, prolonged unemployment. No one, that is, except the new post-Communist and reform Communist governments; their economic advisors and techno-managers, domestic and foreign; and the journalists supporting the now increasingly admired "hard cure." The "hard cure" comes in many forms, from the dangerously utopian plan to privatize the Russian economy in five hundred days, to the so-called fire sales of previously nationalized enterprises in Poland and Hungary, where former Communist managers sometimes metamorphose overnight as the new owners and managers of the more lucrative chunks of the old economy. They include even the more reasonable, but still draconic, assaults against inflation in Poland and Yugoslavia. Even these monetarist solutions to the urgent problem of a superinflation passing the 1000 percent range caused considerable pain to whole sectors of the economy and hurt the population dependent on incomes that were either frozen or controlled. Although ending the superinflation was essential, if for no other than psychological reasons, making previously soft currencies convertible is essential to expanding economic relations with the European Community.

The effect of making the local currencies convertible was to open up the Polish and Yugoslav economy to imported consumer goods. By the fall of 1990 there was no black market in either goods or currency. On the other hand, income differences necessarily mean more when there are attractive things to buy in the increasingly well supplied shops, whose goods are ever less accessible to ordinary wage earners. An economic cure that essentially requires holding down or even lowering real wages, cutting down on the social entitlements, *and* at the same time consciously increasing the real and visible incomes and consumption of the upper strata is social dynamite. This is especially true in these societies, where the rich are *not* necessarily or even usually the powerful, nor those whose wealth seems to be the result of socially useful hard work. Thus, the new and visible wealth and privilege are rarely defended by the increasingly independent and sensationalist media.

Lacking a sufficient sense of national community to make sacrifice acceptable without the sneaking suspicion, usually justified, that the spivs and new rich of these societies are not sacrificing, it is clear that the lion's share of the sacrifice is expected from the workers. Worse, *after* the sacrifice what is generally offered is some kind of a Mexicanized economy that will be the backwater of Europe, with increasing class and income cleavages.

To be sure, just as in the case of Latin America, the Eastern European countries will now be, formally, completely independent of their own old superpower. Contested parliamentary elections will take place more or less regularly, unions will struggle on behalf of the workers with varying success, and there will be a market economy. That market economy will be modified by a fair dose of state intervention and by some welfare and social justice measures, at least for the strategically better placed workers. The universities and the intellectuals will be free to oppose and create and will have considerable access to those in power. That seems to be the one most probable future for the region and is what is meant by the increasingly popular metaphor of the Mexicanization of Eastern Europe and the former USSR. For some odd reason this does not inspire mass enthusiasm, particularly among the present or future unemployed.

A general, increasingly surly sense of political malaise pervades a landscape covered with broken promises, implicit or explicit. Most of the economies are in disastrous shape. The new, fragile multiparty parliaments have had no chance yet to develop new norms of behavior appropriate to the new political alignments. Everything seems to be both possible and permissible today in a political milieu where nationalist populist parties and movements compete for power and where the atmosphere is pregnant with potential political pogroms against the former Communists. That same nationalism and populism, Eastern European varieties of Peronism, can equally easily turn against national minorities, disliked neighbors, or even those who enrich themselves too quickly under the new regimes. These regimes are becoming increasingly nationally specific, and there is an almost frantic search for an accessible, politically usable past.

Some of the new Eastern European post-Communist regimes seem more stable than others. For example, the bets for a stable and democratic regime do seem to be considerably better for Czechoslovakia than for Poland, for Hungary than for Romania. Different parts of Yugoslavia may face radically different fates. East Germany's future fate is now as part of a united general German present and future. Bulgaria could well present a pleasant and unearned surprise, but that would be against outside odds, and the jury will be out for some time.

Some previous heroes of democratic dissent may show cloven hooves at a later date. A heroic, uncompromising, and stubborn trade union leader like Lech Walesa, for example, is less attractive as the democratically elected president of Poland than he was as the embattled leader of Polish Solidarity, the first mass workers' movement that challenged Communist rule. More than one previously close associate in the underground struggle against Communist authoritarianism now sees a potential new Pilsudski or even a Polish Perón. The reality is happily likely to be more banal; he will probably turn out to be merely a somewhat demagogic, democratic politician. That will represent an enormous relief to a Poland that is tired of heroes and needs some unheroic normalcy.

Hungarian populist historians were far more attractive as opposition figures than as a narrow nationalist and conservative government reflecting the prejudices of Hungarian Mitteleuropa intelligentsia. The economic advisors of the new democratic government in Czechoslovakia are for the moment in love with an idealized version of Thatcherism that exists only in their own heads. How congruent that will be with the democratic aspirations of a massive working class remains to be seen. One of the leading figures from the previously persecuted "Belgrade Eight," former *Praxis* philosopher Mihailo Markovic, is now the vice president of the ruling, only slightly altered, and even less democratized Communist party of Serbia.[12] Now he defends the party's continued domination of the political scene, political trials of opposition politicians, and the Caesarian "Presidential" Constitution, hand-tailored for the present Serbian leader, Slobodan Milosevic. Even more out of synchronization with his past democratic credentials, he continued to defend the lawless rule of the Serbian minority over an Albanian majority in the province of Kosovo for at least three years, as well as the murderous armed struggle of the Serbian minority, aided by the federal army, against the elected government of Croatia. Markovic is a Serb, and regrettably but not at all inevitably, the nationalist overcame the democrat and socialist. He is, alas, not at all alone.

Many of the valiant fighters against Communist authoritarian rule will turn out to be exclusive nationalists, demagogic and irresponsible populists, or intolerant religious authoritarians. More mundanely, they may turn out to be merely power-hungry, parochial political opportunists or quite mediocre, humdrum, self-promoting politicians. Democracy is, after all, a system in which quite ordinary people, not moral or intellectual giants, can play a role, sometimes even hold power. This commonplace fact is extraordinarily hard for some previously heroic underground leaders and the critical intelligentsia in general to accept.

It was always tempting for Western liberals or democratic leftists to assume that all enemies of tyrannous or oppressive domestic or colonial regimes were radical, even egalitarian, democrats. They were therefore necessarily doomed to repeated disappointments. Their assumption about the character of opponents of tyrannous or colonial regimes has turned out to be true all too rarely, whether in former colonial countries or in the emerging post-Communist states in Eastern Europe and the former Soviet Union. Nevertheless, previously politocratic Communist regimes are going through a historical transformation, in which many of the problems faced by the individual states share a common general background of political systems and economies, devastated by decades of political repression and grotesque economic mismanagement. How the process turns out will not only be important to the millions living in former Communist or modernizing authoritarian states; it will have a great deal to do with the prospects for stability in the emerging, unifying Europe and the rest of the world.

One should therefore look at a range of former Communist state systems to be able to speculate about the direction in which they may evolve in the twenty-first century. One certainty is that most, if not all, of these systems are evolving away from the politocratic, authoritarian one-party societies and centrally planned economies. How many will achieve stable democratic polities with relatively functioning modern economies is another question. So is the degree of pain and disruption that will accompany the transition from "real socialism" to a now uncertain and uncharted future. Populism, more or less authoritarian varieties of local neocorporatism and Peronism, religious and national intolerance, and vengeful anticommunism all have assured places on the post-Communist agendas, as do the development of reasonable, tolerant, and socially sensitive democracies.

The Consolidation of a Post-Communist Consensus

Generations of leftist and Marxist intellectual dissidents have argued that these societies had never been genuine socialist societies and had thus represented no test of the possibility of socialism, let alone a democratic socialism. However, those societies did unfortunately bear on the validity of at least some assumptions that had been shared by socialists in general. At the very least they cast a negative light on the performance of highly centralized command economies.

For many on both the left and the right, the proposition that some organic relationship existed between Communists, democratic socialists, and radical reformers, that they were a part of a continuum, was so obvious as to hardly require argument. It was not only *the enemies* of democratic socialists who assumed such a link to exist. Five minutes spent with some of the leftist Labour party members in Britain or with "progressives" in peace-movement think tanks in the United States or Western Europe—not to mention most of the third world or liberation theology activists—would make that clear. In its most benign form it was expressed in perennial wistful calls for the "unity of the Left," clearly meaning the Communists and their allies, including the democratic socialists.

Cold war ideologues in the United States often worked with the same assumption and thus looked with suspicion at any Socialist or Social Democratic government because it was automatically presumed to be "soft" on Communist repression. The West German Social Democrats had long maintained ties with ruling Communist parties in Eastern Europe. To be sure, those ties consisted of exchanges of visits and conversations, through which considerable useful leverage was exerted on behalf of democratic dissidents. However, the ties also led sometimes to a soft-pedaling of public pressure and criticism of those repressive regimes, in the concern that such criticism would negatively affect quiet, behind-the-scenes negotiations and diplomacy. This was a trap, although one that honest democrats can fall into. It sufficiently compromised the German Social Democrats so that they did poorly in the first free elections in a unified Germany. It is true that regular contacts, helpful though they were in aiding dissidents and pushing for reforms, did involve treating the Communist parties as legitimate political institutions and partners in dialogue. Many victims of communism believed that went too far.

For social democratic ideas (i.e., ideas combining democracy and egalitarianism) to have a chance in Eastern Europe they must be shown to have no continuity with that Communist past that is now being so massively rejected. A legion of right-wing theorists and publicists, throughout the world and most particularly in both Eastern and Western Europe, have been claiming that the mildest of reforms lead straight to the gulag.[13] The current political and economic reforms of post-Communist states *are taking place under conditions of a general and visible moral and ideological crisis of both* Communist politocracy *and* the general socialist project. A wide but very shallow consensus exists in the region that the new post-Communist systems should be politically democratic and that the economies should be market-driven, with a multiplicity of forms of ownership, among which social ownership would play a minor, if any, role. In practice there is far less agreement. Worse, there is no real agreement about how the disagreements are to be resolved.

This can be seen in the uncritical acceptance of ideological insistence on the market as the sole master instrument of economic reform. I am not questioning here the desirability of introducing market principles into the economy as one of the needed measures to leverage the remnants of the *nomenklatura* out of economic control. What I am questioning is the present love affair of many Eastern European reformers with the "market" as a synonym for the economic dogmas of Milton Friedman and the social policies of Margaret Thatcher. To make things worse, under the cover of a nominal agreement about economic reforms lie vast differences. Paying identical lip service to economic "reforms" are technocrats who want to retain a powerful input of the state into the economy, fanatic followers of Milton Friedman's utopia of the untrammeled free market (which exists nowhere in the whole world), moderate social democrats who believe in a social market economy (i.e., an advanced welfare state), and all other possible variants in between.

Another problem is that for too many in the new post-Communist democracies, "democracy" means untrammeled majority rule (of *the* people, or the largest national group) unleavened by tolerance of differences, national minorities, or disagreement. That should not be surprising; large parts of the political public think the same in Western Europe and the United States. This is a poor recipe for a democratic polity under the best of circumstances. In contemporary Eastern Europe and the successors to the Soviet Union, with the problems posed by national rights, multiethnicity, religious exclusivism and intolerance, and anti-Semitism, such an approach can be deadly for human rights and democratic pluralism.

Nationally charged populism is now widespread in Poland, Hungary, Romania, and at least the two largest republics of Yugoslavia. Similar explicitly right-authoritarian politics are found in many of the former Soviet republics, from the Baltic to the Caucasus. Such politics have a history in the region that is hardly reassuring. What is at stake today in former Communist countries is not an intellectually stimulating seminar on transitions from authoritarian to democratic societies. What is being decided is the fate of real-life economies and, more to the point, societies increasingly sick of austerity and shortages. *No* proposals have surfaced that do not admittedly involve considerable doses of pain. Most of that pain will be borne by the workers, who are those least responsible for the present economic mess.

The most acute form that pain will take is the universally predicted loss of job security and consequent more or less massive unemployment. Given the political predilection of much of the region to populism charged with nationalism, it can almost certainly be predicted that the political actors will not resist the temptation to engage in social demagoguery to deal with that pain since readily available economic solutions are not available. That demagoguery will most easily be directed against the real or imagined enemies of the nation (the people) who are the usual suspects—other national groups, minorities, Freemasons, Jews, the Vatican, former Communists, present leftists, liberals, foreigners, and the other predictable groups.

The alternatives to that demagoguery are difficult and will require the building of a civil society and democratically rooted mass social movements, trade unions, and political parties. Those, in turn, require rebuilding a political public and the acceptance of a *general* political community or a modern-day equivalent of a polis, with sufficient assumption of community that sacrifices can be accepted. That means to turn away from the notion of politics as a place where there is no common good or interest, where instead hard-edged homogeneous groups, most probably based on nationality, struggle against each other. To move the emerging post-Communist political culture to such a conception of politics is a hard task; it requires a democratic and egalitarian movement—in other words, a modern democratic socialist movement.

After years of grinding drabness and shortages, much of the population is mesmerized by an attraction to Western consumer goods and a consequent exaggerated attraction for "Western," that is to say, consumerist, materialist, and petty-capitalist values; in a word, that same possessive individualism that is all too familiar in the United States. After all, why should citizens of former Communist-ruled states have a more attractive civic culture than the United States and much of Western Europe have? Consumerism is especially widespread among the educated middle classes, including sections of the political elite, as can be seen by the mythification of the market as the solution for all economic problems. It can also be seen in the increasing differences in life-styles and access to goods between the more privileged strata and the working class. Forty years of politocratic "socialism" has all but destroyed any fabric of social solidarity in these societies. That is an important historical criticism of the effect of Communist party rule.

The Blue Collar Workers: Indispensable and Difficult

Economic reforms, all agree, will require massive sacrifices by the working class, at least temporarily. Calls for temporary economic sacrifice are difficult to make, however, because it is clear that work you are paid to perform is not the way to advance in these societies. This is made evident by seeing who has done well and who continues to do well economically: political hacks and those who work the legal or the not so legal boundaries of the gray or alternative economy. This is still the case in the countries that have had free elections and have replaced the ruling Communists with democratic reformers. The possibility of effective political and social change that is progressive and egalitarian is generally treated with cynicism. That cynicism is reinforced by the increasing tolerance of corruption, economic wheeling and dealing, and individual advancement that exists within all of these societies.

To make things even worse, features of the economic reforms that people rightly *do* believe would be delivered in the imaginable future are greater economic inequality and unemployment. There is no insurance at all that greater rewards will go to the economically more efficient and productive. Greater economic inequality will hardly encourage workers to accept the unemployment and speedup that are necessary features of the proposed economic reforms. If the speedup is to pay back the debts these societies have to the Western financial institutions, it must be accompanied not by pay increases but by pay decreases. Pay decreases must further be accompanied by cutbacks in the inadequate welfare state *and* massive dismissals of surplus workers. This will be exacerbated by the closing down of numerous inefficient plants that are not worth modernizing. Things will be made still worse by massive dismissals of the hordes of unneeded white-collar workers. The lower ranks of these are often wives, who provided the essential second income. It is likely that they will be the first to become unemployed.

The decades of Communist rule have created a large and homogeneous working class. The process that took place in Western Europe in generations was compressed into three short decades in Eastern Europe. Several consequences follow. The first is that the regimes have favored the industrial working class and the cities against the rural sector and the peasantry. It was in the cities that the almost universal crude welfare state first developed, education became massively accessible to the working class, and the rapid upward social mobility of workers and peasants into the new layers of state, party, economic, and organizational bureaucratic hierarchy took place. Much of this mobility was more the result of the structural changes in the economy than of consciously planned policies. As a consequence, the "rewards" were distributed, as often as not, as a result of mere chance and the good luck to have been in the right place when the party cadres desperately searched for any promotable bodies. An entire old prewar bourgeoisie and its industrial and state bureaucracies needed to be replaced.

The new regimes emphasized central administration and control and therefore needed many more bureaucrats than had the old ruling class. The party cadres within the working class, few as they were, experienced truly meteoric careers. Until the newly expanded universities began to produce new experts and technicians, most of those in the managerial cadres were workers who had been promoted through the party. Although not necessarily competent, they were loyal. One unanticipated effect of this rapid social mobility was to increase the distance between the remaining manual workers and the Communist party, which was based increasingly on white-collar employees, technicians, and managers. With a whole second generation of workers entering the mines and factories in the 1960s, the chasm between the party and the working class increased. New informal lines of solidarity and mutual support against the bosses, the managers, the state, and all things external to the working class began to form normally. Not only were the workers now increasingly abandoned by the party in the workplace but throughout the massive new quasi-slums and housing projects, almost homogeneously working class in content, as well. Thus, if you were a blue-collar worker, you did not work next to a party cadre member and were unlikely to live next to one. After all, if party membership was good for anything, it was good for obtaining a better job and housing.

The blue-collar workers of Eastern Europe and the former Soviet Union today resemble the industrial proletariat in the smokestack industries of an earlier period of great industrial militancy and class consciousness in Western Europe. Continued labor turbulence is therefore the future forecast. To make things worse for the new post-Communist governments, the workers now can vote, and any excessive repression of their new unions would be met with protests from the European Community. That now matters a great deal because the goodwill of that Europe is needed to obtain the essential credits and continued political legitimacy. Also, from the point of view of the regime, the police are of dubious reliability when it comes to beating up coal miners or steel workers. All of this adds to a formula promising continued checkmate between the class forces. It also suggests a continued consolidation of class consciousness and development of independent new unions by the workers, on the one hand, and self-consciousness and a sense of separateness by the post-Communist ruling strata on the other. These are obviously class societies, as they were under the Communists; the new regimes are simply franker about this reality.

An Ambivalent Standoff with the Intelligentsia

The explosive potential of industrial turbulence represents the major problem of post-Communist regimes in the long run, but the short run is not rosy either. The gap between promise and performance in the economy and the lag in technological innovation and progress are evident. There is a growing and, what is even worse, increasingly visible income gap between the top leadership and the managers and the bulk of the population. Advancement must go through newly established hierarchies in which the requisite pieces of paper—diplomas and certification of new, non-Communist political reliability (or at least harmlessness)—are needed.

There is clearly no need for continued additions to white-collar officialdom; on the contrary, cutbacks in the cost of the state apparatus are expected. What then is to happen to the masses of university-educated philosophy, economics, political science, and law graduates? Many of them are deserving supporters of the post-Communist political establishment, even victims of the past Communist regimes, and need to be rewarded. Can one possibly purge enough Communist timeservers to provide sufficient new jobs without major disruption? How will that look in a *Rechtstaat*, a law-abiding state, which supposedly respects its own universalist laws?

For years the Communist regimes have permitted the continued expansion of the universities. Their democratic successors, often dominated by university-trained intelligentsia, have now inherited the problem. Cutting back seems an obvious solution. But that in turn creates underemployment of university-educated graduates, who create a surly, unproductive, and above all ungrateful stratum of lower officials and administrators—they obviously are not going to become manual workers without as yet unimaginable economic pressures. However, the currently unimaginable often becomes tomorrow's reality in Eastern Europe.

The options of what to do about further overproduction of university-trained "generalists" are quite limited. One can drastically cut down on admissions to the universities, at which point the critical question is, just who is to be admitted? If competitive examinations are used, universities would clearly discriminate in favor of the children of the middle class and intelligentsia, and the gap between the professional middle classes and the workers would increase. In the very unlikely case that class quotas are used, a number of the children of the middle class would be doomed to downward mobility. The entire intelligentsia would regard itself as victimized, having always regarded access to the university as its normal class privilege.

One major characteristic of the Eastern European and Soviet intelligentsia is that a good part of it still believes that it is the carrier of a special historical mission for its nation. This mission they expect to be recognized and, they hope, properly rewarded. It is hard to square such a mission with popular democracy because, essentially, the intelligentsia is still viewed collectively as the "philosopher kings" of their nations. It is also hard to accept that the historical role of the intelligentsia has been a cover for demanding a special and privileged place—for the intelligentsia in general and for writers, historians, and poets in particular—not only in politics, as mentors of morality and democracy, but also where massive allocations of scarce resources were demanded from the society. The intelligentsia dominates the new post-Communist parties.

The old Communist regimes did meet these economic demands, for the most part, on a scale the previous bourgeois regimes could not have dreamed of. They funded huge increases in size of the universities and other cultural institutions and massive subsidies for theaters, films, fine arts, museums, academies, publishing, and writers. In exchange for relatively minor conformity, the intelligentsia was subsidized quite generously. No favor or good deed remains unpunished in politics, and the intelligentsia massively supported the anti-Communist opposition. Unfortunately, if the new post-Communist regimes are at all serious about economic reforms, they will have to cut back drastically on the subsidies for culture, jobs for intellectuals, and universities. All of these are already bloated beyond all reason, considering the real economic resources of these societies and the sacrifices the working people will be expected to bear. Resources will therefore become scarcer.

The price will be an increasing cynicism and apathy on the part of the younger intellectuals and the educated young in general. Why these in particular? Because they are the latecomers to the party. They have arrived too late to receive the perks their predecessors had under the old regime, sometimes even when they were in genteel opposition to the Communists: the apartments, the summer homes, trips abroad, and for some, even the reassuring certainty that they were on the winning side in the march of history. That has been lost, and austere times are coming. The virtues of the intelligentsia are not particularly marketable. And yet ideologically, for the time being, the market reigns among the intelligentsia above all. The price of that contradiction between interest and ideology will probably be the development of an ideological vacuum.

The cost of this increasingly widespread vacuum is cynicism and apathy about politics and even about oppositional politics, above all among the young. This has also spread across the class barriers so that there is a genuine youth subculture, which today is mostly apolitical, hedonistic, and materialist. Certain "fashionable" topics—currently ecology and human rights (as distinct from democracy)—serve as a focus for single-issue activities, particularly if the issue is fashionable among the young in the

West, who are being copied relentlessly. The young do not join left-wing or socialist groups. The rejection of the *language* of socialism, however, does not necessarily extend to the basic *values* of socialism—democracy, equality, community, and participation.

In state "socialist" politocracies the demand for democracy was, quite properly, the primary socialist demand. That is, everything began with that, with freeing society from the total domination of the party and the state. That created the space for autonomous social, cultural, political, and popular institutions and thus a civil society. These in turn are minimal prerequisites for a democratic socialist society. That minimal necessary but not sufficient step has been taken throughout Eastern Europe.

The prospects for a stable, peaceful European Community living alongside a politically chaotic and economically devastated Eastern Europe and states of the former Soviet Union are quite dismal. It is a more immediate potential threat than the long-range time bomb of the third world. On the other hand, a *successful* transformation of the region from authoritarian Communist regimes to stable and decent democracies would automatically mean that the European Community's greater integration in 1992 would be only a way station to a Common European Home, which would one day include all of Europe from the Atlantic to the Urals. Such a Europe would have an immense impact on the future of the world community.

A Historical Pattern: The Fragility of Authoritarianism?

Other authoritarian societies have made the transition to democracy in Europe, and they represent an invaluable reservoir of historical experience. Unfortunately, most advisors who are now popular in Eastern Europe and the former Soviet Union seem to lack any practical knowledge of comparative politics. They concentrate, like Professor Jeffrey Sachs of Harvard, on economic issues or on issues of political economy, such as ownership. Other advisors are even narrower and know about techniques of electoral politics, learned in that bastion of contested pluralist politics, the United States of America.

Far more useful for understanding the problems of transition from authoritarian to democratic polities are the experiences of Greece, Portugal, and above all Spain. Comparisons have to be made with caution because, with few exceptions, the Eastern European Communist regimes had been imposed from the outside by force and with the aid of the Soviet armies. The obvious exceptions are Yugoslavia and Albania, where the Communists came to power mostly through their own efforts. Nevertheless, the presence of the Red Army in the battles to liberate Belgrade and the *general* domination of the Soviet Union in the region made the victory of Yugoslavian and Albanian Communists all the more certain. By the same token, the case could be made that the Czechoslovakian Communists took power in Prague in 1948 through the successful pressure tactics of their mass organization, but that was immensely aided by the prestige of the victorious Red Army and its presence. It is now clear that the real penetration by the Communist parties into the political cultures of these societies was far more limited than in the Soviet Union. Amazingly little transformation of popularly held values have taken place after two generations of intense attempts to politically resocialize the population.

Much of the transformation that did take place can be better explained by the impact of modernization, urbanization, and industrialization and the consequent spread of literacy and social and geographic mobility. In a way that is very good news because it argues that those who feared that totalitarian dictatorship would be able to transform the belief systems and behavior of the bulk of the populations were wrong. Whatever the future may offer, it is unlikely to be any recognizable variant of Orwell's negative utopia in *1984*. A whole generation of political scientists and analysts believed firmly that totalitarianism was irreversible. It was irreversible, the world was told, because it would *successfully* brainwash or resocialize the subject populations.

If Communist totalitarianism was irreversible, it was also the wave of the future, albeit a negative future. That was the viewpoint of a great many intellectuals and analysts, east and west, a view held by those who celebrated the wave of the future and those who cringed from it in horror. The Communist system, negative enough in reality, was thus demonized in a way that made the cold war a crusade against an "evil empire" rather than a conflict between competing fallible social and economic political systems and states. That assumption of the irreversibility of Communist rule grossly exaggerated the pliability of human beings. There had been innumerable warnings that this represented an inaccurate picture of a far more complex reality.

Repeated revolts and resistance in East Berlin in 1950, in Hungary in 1956, in Poland throughout the period, in Prague in 1968, culminating with the development of the most massive workers' resistance movement in Europe—the first Solidarity in Poland in 1980—all made clear to those who were willing to see that the regimes had not won over the populace. That record should also give pause to those who would locate the cause of the changes in Eastern Europe primarily in the reforms from above launched by Gorbachev. The presence of an energetic and powerful reformer at the helm of the Soviet Union no doubt helped immensely to make the transformation relatively peaceful and so far almost bloodless. However, both the speed of the collapse—once the process began, regimes toppled like ninepins—as well as the nearly universal nature of the shift away from the Communist regime and from its professed values throughout the region, show that the roots of the rejection of those systems and of the malaise were very deep.

Traditional values and beliefs retained a great deal of resilience. Indeed, one could even make the argument that the general rejection of Communist values, enshrined as they had been in the all-intrusive authoritarian party rule, preserved the traditional values and even traditional religion precisely as a symbol of resistance to communism. That certainly helped explain the popularity of rather traditional religion and nationalism among young urban intellectuals, a group that massively rejected the same values in the rest of the industrial world. Those values, representing traditionalism, sexual repressiveness, sexism, authoritarianism, nationalism, xenophobia, and chauvinism, were certainly preserved far better in Eastern Europe and the Soviet Union than in the rest of Europe. They had almost nothing in common with religion other than the use of it as a source of identity, or rather a counteridentity to the officially promulgated one.

Culturally, communism proved more repressive and retrograde than capitalism modified by the welfare state. In practice, as Wilhelm Reich had very insightfully noted in an earlier era, authoritarian politics and general repressiveness, particularly in matters sexual, went hand in hand. The popularity of Wilhelm Reich was never great in Eastern Europe, even with the anti-Communist opposition, although his *Mass Psychology of Fascism* was a bit of an underground classic in Yugoslavia, Hungary, and Poland. An extreme and analytically powerful statement of an antiauthoritarian Reichian blend of sexual and political liberation is found in Dusan Makavejev's great movie *WR, or the Mysteries of the Organism*. A document ahead of its time, it was made in 1969, still basking in the glow of the wonderful late 1960s, when demanding the impossible was not limited to Parisian students. In practice, the ruling Communist parties did their best to reinforce sexually and culturally repressive values.

I would add that this was also more generally true in attitudes toward popular and youth culture. The Communists in power were crushingly dull, boring, and culturally conservative, whatever else they were. That fact went a long way to explain the general rejection of the Communists among the young and educated urban strata, which had in many ways been the beneficiaries of the new Communist system and which the Communists expected to be their allies in the task of modernizing those societies. The acceptance of the Communist parties as the legitimate political authorities was far lower than had been anticipated by either the friends or the enemies of those regimes.

The ability to rule by administrative fiat from above, enforced by sheer repression, began to unravel extraordinarily quickly when it became clear that fraternal "aid" in the form of brotherly tanks and troops was no longer available. To make matters even worse, throughout 1989 the Soviets made it clear to their former client states in Eastern Europe that they favored reforms and would not support massive repression of popular demands for change. That was probably the final nail in the coffin of the old hard-liners. The ultimate safety net was gone and would never be replaced. What remained was to beat as orderly a retreat as possible and hope that the dismantling of the Communist state system would not be accompanied by excessive demands for retribution against those who had built them, brutally defended them, and so generously benefited from them. Given the gross brutality that had been necessary to build and maintain these systems, it is nothing short of amazing how little violence and vengeance has accompanied their abject collapse. Despite all of the ambiguities accompanying the early halting steps toward democracy, that should be kept in mind. It is a sign that the struggle to build new democratic polities in Eastern Europe and the former Soviet Union, even under the horrendous economic burdens these societies have to bear, is far from hopeless.

There are nationalists and populists and clerical rightists in the region, but that is not something unique to Eastern Europe. There are also millions of ordinary, decent people who have been given a rotten break by history *and,* let this not be forgotten, by the superpowers, *including* the United States, when they divided the world after World War II. Eastern European democrats have produced generations of heroic fighters for democracy and built the largest workers' movement in Europe, under impossibly repressive conditions. Nevertheless, the peoples of Eastern Europe and the Soviet Union did manage to amaze both the world and themselves by their valiant struggle against and overthrow of Communist dictatorial regimes that had been assumed to be, for all practical purposes, eternal. They did all of this with precious little help or support from the West. They deserve to be supported and aided, not written off merely because there is no longer a cold war in which their suffering can be put to use.

Just as the end of the cold war has removed apocalyptic fears of nuclear annihilation without removing the fear of wars, the Eastern European and Soviet transformation should have removed the fear of absolute totalitarian regimes as the wave of the future without, alas, guaranteeing the victory of democracy or that there will not be rollbacks of some of the present achievements. But even were this to happen, the resulting authoritarian regimes will never have the same terrorizing effect on or power over the imagination that the totalitarian regime of Stalin had. That would be an aberration, not a wave of the future. The future is uncertain, but it seems that Orwell's nightmare, in his dystopia, *1984* (as stated by the negative hero, O'Brien) that the future is a boot smashing into a human face forever is now an unlikely outcome. That, at least, is a relief. Once that is said, it must be added that the road of transformation of authoritarian societies into stable democracies is likely to be long and troubled in Eastern Europe, the former Soviet Union, and yes, the third world.

Those trying to travel that road deserve the generous help, sympathy, and solidarity of democrats everywhere. What should accompany that solidarity is honest critical analysis. Euphoria about the collapse of Communist regimes must not blind democratic friends of Eastern European and Soviet reformers to the great perils to which the transformations to democracy are exposed in societies in which there are still great scarcities. Unfortunately, that kind of situation can always provide political space for a regime that is capable of asserting a centralized and authoritarian command over needs.

4

North/South

The Third World in the New International Environment

The upheavals that began toppling the Communist regimes in Eastern Europe in the fall of 1989 stripped the political reality of the Communist systems to their bare essentials for all to see. What was seen confirmed the truth that had been stubbornly denied for decades, especially throughout the third world, despite massive evidence and testimonies of hundreds of disillusioned witnesses. Hatred for a known colonialism and imperialism, the exploitation and greed of capitalism, had all too often combined with a contempt for the widespread hypocrisy and manipulation in the "really existing" liberal parliamentary democracies. This made too many good people all too willing to believe that the often not too well known enemy of those known evils and injustices must have some virtues.

The major colonial powers were, for the most part, pluralist parliamentary democracies at home during the period of their repression of colonial peoples. The *democratic* French republic waged the brutal wars in Africa, Vietnam, and Algeria both before and after World War II. *Democratic* British governments smashed Zulu and Ashanti resistance and colonized much of Africa and the Middle East. *Democratic* parliamentary Belgium and the Netherlands were both brutal and racist in their colonies. That paragon of democracy, the United States of America, had robbed Mexico of half of its territory, conquered the Philippines and Puerto Rico, and reduced much of Central America to a colony in all but name. It was not a right-wing cynic but an immensely popular liberal president who said of Somoza, his pet right-wing dictator in Nicaragua, "He is a son of a bitch, but he is *our* son of a bitch."

These imperialist states were, as their subject anticolonialist intellectuals and activists noted, also capitalist. When support for their anticolonialist activities developed in the metropolitan countries, it was among groups and individuals on the left. For decades much of the Left in advanced industrialized countries accepted at least some of the myths about the Soviet Union and other Communist-ruled countries. Those myths were also very attractive to young modernizing anti-imperialist intellectuals in the colonial world. Later, particularly after the death of Stalin, military aid and support against the United States and the former colonial powers made the Soviet Union even more attractive. That aid was quite limited, but other sources, particularly for military hardware sold on generous terms, were scarce or nonexistent.

A power like the Soviet Union, as an enemy of the old colonial powers, could *not* be all bad to the third world radicals and their supporters. For decades it was at least a source of political support and arms against the West and the United States. In short, the enemy of my enemy had to be a friend. That naive Machiavellianism proved to be inadequate for a complicated and nasty world in which *two* superpowers threatened peace and in which the *reality* about the enemy of our own superpower was devastating. The fact that the U.S. media and the U.S. government have often lied about the U.S. role in the world and about the alleged military threat from the Soviet military alliance did not mean that they were always wrong in describing their rival.

Communist-ruled countries did create crude and almost universal welfare states with considerable, sometimes even spectacular, achievements in education and public health. However, Communist politocracies also had been subjected to decades of crushing and stultifying one-party tyranny, and the bottom-line cynical justification for that dictatorship, that it provided a shortcut to rapid economic growth and modernization, also proved wrong. Their relative performance has been quite poor when examined over a protracted period.

The Communist regimes, presented as models of development for revolutionary third world regimes, had been lagging behind other comparable industrializing societies for decades. Much of the development was misdirected, creating industrial white elephants seemingly impervious to technological modernization. In addition to the economic, moral, and political price future generations will have to pay, much of Eastern Europe and the former Soviet Union have been turned into an ecological horror show. Despite the fact that nominal Communist dictatorships survive in China, Vietnam, Cambodia, Laos, and Cuba, these cases are now, sui generis, the exceptions that prove the case for the crisis of communism as a world system—that is, a world system that was once seen as a rival, even the gravedigger, of world capitalism. None of these countries, with the exception of Cuba, present themselves as models for export. To the contrary, these countries today represent beleaguered fortresses of unique national paths to "socialism." Most of them are desperately dismantling their centralized command economies and rushing into privatization and economic reforms, like the introduction of the market and invitations to foreign investors. To be sure, they hope that these "capitalistic" reforms will not jeopardize the rule of their party.

Past economic and industrial growth are no longer respectable arguments in favor of the Soviet-type regimes in the third world. A number of societies, in their own ways just as unlovely, have provided much more impressive levels of industrialization and overall development, including, in some cases, spectacular agricultural development, through which previous food-importing countries became food exporters despite substantially greater domestic consumption. South Korea, Taiwan, Hong Kong, Thailand and Singapore, although also authoritarian, have produced sustained rapid growth for decades on end at a much smaller end cost to their populations. They also have been far more productive and efficient at introducing new technologies and scientific breakthroughs than have either the Soviets or the Eastern Europeans, let alone their third world allies and would-be imitators. Perhaps more to the point, economic development over time, at least in South Korea, Hong Kong, and Taiwan, has produced lively and democratic trade unions and massive popular oppositional movements that are very promising. These developments have taken place against the will and efforts of their ruling elites. What they promise is that, through massive and sometimes bloody struggle, these societies have a very good chance to develop into pluralist democracies with institutions of a civil society.

All of these Pacific Rim countries have invested massively in education and infrastructure. They have relied heavily on government intervention in the economy, lip service to the ideology of the market and private ownership notwithstanding.[1] That the transition to democratic development will be hard and will face many setbacks is reasonably clear, but that is still a more realistic hope for democracy and development than any we have seen in the third world to this date.

Third World: The Politics and Career of a Concept

The 1990s promise to be a grim decade for substantial parts, perhaps most, of the third world, a grim decade leading to a grim century. Most of the reasons are economic and are linked to the huge indebtedness of the poorer countries to international financial institutions as well as to private, mostly U.S.-based banks. A major reason for the miserable economic condition of most of the South is the continued disadvantage built into the imbalance between the prices of commodities and semifinished products of the third world and the costs of energy, high technology imports, consumer goods, and military hardware that they import from the North. In part their relative economic and political weakness has been aggravated by the fact that what used to be known as the nonaligned movement[2] has disintegrated. The term "third world" was always chameleon-like, meaning too many things. In that way it resembled the nonaligned movement to which it was closely allied and whose fate it shares. A political invention, it was meant to be used in whatever way was most convenient. It included both conservative and radical, aligned and nonaligned countries. It also included states that were historically long established, as well as those that had been created so recently they were not included in even the most up-to-date atlases. It has included nations established through popular struggles against colonial oppressors *and* nations that were spending an inordinate proportion of their income in repressing peoples who did not want to be incorporated into a unified nation.

The term "third world" has at times included nations that were in most respects more like European countries than newly freed former colonies. Thus, for example, why was Argentina under Perón in the third world? It is a nation vastly rich in natural resources but also one that has all but wiped out its native population to replace them with European settlers. How about South Africa? Or for that matter today's Taiwan or South Korea? Is the third world just a synonym for the nonaligned countries?[3] If so, then Yugoslavia was properly a part, even a leading part, of the third world. What does nonalignment mean after the end of the cold war—nonaligned with what? There is also a problem with the term "third world peoples." My own somewhat shamefaced use of that term in this work is limited to the former colonial countries and to the underdeveloped (yes, that too is a tricky term) countries.[4] Its application to Americans of partially African descent is, to say the least, problematical. When applied to U.S. military personnel of African-American or Hispano-American descent, it is truly grotesque, particularly in real-life situations like Panama or the Persian Gulf. There are other absurdities. For example, is an upper-class blond Argentinean or Mexican a member of the oppressed third world, whereas an impoverished Andalusian peasant or immigrant into the United States remains a member of the oppressors?[5]

How did a problematic concept like "third world" become so popular? In the three decades after World War II, years of great stability and economic growth in Western Europe, realistic prospects for radical social transformation beyond the existing welfare states became increasingly remote. However, during that same period, dramatic, massive transformations were taking place in the former colonial countries and the less developed parts of the globe—in what was to be known as the third world by the 1960s. As the more orthodox Communist and Marxist movements began to run into ever-increasing ideological and organizational trouble in Western Europe, many of their theorists, intellectuals, and fellow travelers turned to the emerging third world for hope.[6] In part, this paralleled the increasing influence of both Maoism and the nonaligned movement. These developments were both implicitly a critique of the orthodox Communist parties and of the alliance led by Moscow; they were anti-imperialist but not pro-Moscow, therefore the *third* world.

In the 1980s the third world disintegrated into competing political and economic entities, breaking up what was in any case an artificial category. Some states, particularly those on the Pacific Rim, emerged from third world classification as newly industrialized economies (NIEs) or newly industrialized countries (NICs), as did, somewhat more uncertainly, Brazil and Argentina. Other states clearly regressed through a combination of external pressures and internal mistakes. Many fell back economically, primarily because of fluctuations in the price of the one commodity on which their economies depended. Periodic price drops in commodities like copper, cocoa, or sugar might cost a country, or even a region, as much as all of the aid received from the West or the United States. Furthermore, by the end of the 1980s there was also a wholesale retreat from the paradigms and visions of an era when consciously directed, centrally planned, rapid development seemed to be feasible and, above all, efficient.

For at least two decades blueprints for centrally planned economic models were exported to the third world wholesale. To be fair, the predilection toward centralized and bureaucratic planning came from at least two sources: the more familiar Marxist-Leninist model *and* the bureaucratic Fabian model. A wide range of liberal consensus among Western academics, focusing on what was known as "modernization" in the 1950s and 1960s, favored at least some central planning as a tool. Both the Fabian and the Marxist-Leninist variants were eagerly accepted by third world elites, often educated in universities in Moscow or China or in the London School of Economics or other progressive university centers in the West, where they had learned about and accepted the virtues of centrally planned growth.

The most influential work on growth and underdevelopment for Marxist-oriented students after World War II was probably Paul Baran's *The Political Economy of Growth*,[7] reinforced by excellent and well-written books by Paul Sweezy and Harry Magdoff. Its central thesis was that in the underdeveloped countries the state had to be greatly centralized and that it had to nationalize whatever financial and productive resources were available in order to break down the inevitable resistance of the internal bourgeoisie, landlords, and their allies to rapid economic development. Centralization and repression were indispensable to achieve the initial breakthrough and to crush the resistance of the privileged classes and elites. Somewhat more restrainedly, most authorities on the subject believed, some with regret, that softer approaches were not likely to work. Democracy, trade unions, and pluralism would have to wait.

State control was also essential if a policy of import substitution was to be adhered to. Import substitution was the general orthodoxy of the UN developmental agencies and of most developmental economists, left or right. That general consensus did not begin to shift substantially until the early 1980s and the conservative swing in the West that produced Thatcher and Reagan and their ideological counterrevolution against state intervention into the economy. As late as the mid-1970s there was a fairly wide agreement that *some* kind of state intervention and planning was necessary to achieve effective growth, not to speak of growth with any kind of even relative equity. By December 1990 one of the last of the hard-boiled Afro-Communist[8] regimes, Congo Brazzaville, bit the bullet and publicly announced that a whole era had ended. The ruling Workers' party declared at its 1990 Congress that it had joined in the political and ideological retreat of the world Communist movement. With that act it formally joined with the other African regimes that had previously defined themselves diversely as Marxist, Marxist-Leninist, revolutionary, and the like. An experiment that lasted as much as a quarter-century in some of the countries had come to an end. Congo, its ruling party declared, would no longer legally be a one-party state. Its ruling party declared itself to be no longer Marxist, whatever that had meant. It also declared itself to be a Social Democratic party and it would adopt a social democratic program as soon as one was written.

Would that it were that easy to create social democratic parties and programs anywhere, let alone in the third world! But then the choice of a one-party state and of a stern Marxist program more than two decades ago had not taken place with very much more preparation. If anything, there had been less popular comment and debate, not to mention participation. I vaguely recollect that decision being hailed at the time in various fashionably leftist salons and journals in New York, Paris, and London as still further evidence that the tide of history was pressing ever leftward. I admit that my uneasiness at the time was not based on any particularly well-informed insights into the specifics of the class and political scene in Congo Brazzaville. But then neither was the joy of those who were celebrating the emergence of yet one more revolutionary party and regime in the third world. By the spring of 1991 the murderous civil war in Ethiopia was concluded, and the victorious, previously orthodox Marxist-Leninist opponents of the Marxist-Leninist regime in Addis Ababa proclaimed their newfound devotion to pluralist elections, an end to collectivization of land, and a market economy.

By 1991 the previously much despised, even more ignored, and more or less free elections began to sweep Africa. Thus, sub-Saharan Africa joined the trend already unfolding in Eastern Europe and Latin America toward, at least nominally, pluralistic and democratic regimes. This was good news indeed from a region where such news has become increasingly sparse. To be sure, this wave of elections in Africa temporarily disguised the same ambivalence toward democracy that had already surfaced in the other cases of transition from openly authoritarian one-party regimes to regimes based on contested elections. This ambivalence is based on a fundamental difference, whether this process is taking place primarily in response to pressures from below or is mostly a case of liberalizing reforms from above; in real life there are few "pure" examples of either. To the contrary, the changes are a result of a mixture of many factors, including the changing international political and economic scene. Another important factor is the presence or absence of substantial opposition.

It is the case, however, that although elections sometimes have toppled long-established regimes and leaders, at other times they have merely provided a fig leaf to disguise continued rule of familiar leaders and cliques. This should surprise no one and is by no means unique to Africa. It is a phenomenon rampant throughout Latin America and in much of Eastern Europe, where the continued monopoly over mass media has sometimes helped the old *nomenklaturas* and elites stay in power despite the thinnest of disguises.[9] Genuinely contested elections that substantively challenge the established order of things are not all that common in many long-established and highly developed parliamentary democracies.[10] The United States comes to mind almost immediately as an example of a situation in which formally free elections clearly do not necessarily mean genuinely contested elections.

Third Worldist Ideologies: Academic Elitism

Third worldist doctrines were originally developed mostly by radical or Marxist academics who had little or no active connection with any Socialist, Communist, or labor movement or with any organizations in their own countries. They were pessimistic about the prospects for socialism or even significant egalitarian reforms in their own or any other advanced industrial country. The workers of the advanced capitalist countries, whether organized or not, were considered to be totally co-opted by their economic and social systems; they were not as radical as these revolutionaries of the chair but were interested in mere material gains.[11]

On the other hand, according to many academic third worldists, the workers and peasants in the third world did not have a rosy outlook either, because their countries were doomed to underdevelopment by the immutable fact that the world market would always impose terms of trade on them that are unequal and therefore exploitative. What they must do, therefore, is break from the world market and try a path of independent development, which most charitably can be described as autarchic; they would have to go it alone.

Since going it alone would necessarily impose great privations on most of the people in those societies, it is unlikely that such a path would be maintained if any vestiges of democracy, bourgeois or proletarian, remained. What is needed, therefore, is the stern tutorship of an enlightened elite, somewhat like the third world graduate students of these professors. Unlikely to get the power they would need to carry out these tasks, the real-life role of these students was to be the ideologues of the various repressive third world radical, modernizing elites. As often as not, such elites would base their rule on the armed forces, which, led by radical modernizers, would be the surrogates for the all but nonexistent proletariat. There is more than a family resemblance between third worldist academic views and the views of Mao and Trotsky. The originals were both more stylistically powerful and conceptually and theoretically clearer.

One reason these theories were so appealing in the universities and among intellectuals was that they addressed the not too deeply buried elitism of the Western-educated intellectuals from the third world. The world market or world system theories happily relieve the participants in these societies of any responsibilities for their economic and political choices and actions. If decent civil societies and democratic paths to development were never possible in the first place, how can one be blamed for not taking them? It is gratifying to be assured by these respectable academic theorists and radical professors that the Western world since the industrial revolution, and the United States since World War II, were *alone* responsible for the disastrous socialist experiments in the underdeveloped world.

Not coincidentally, it is this same world economic system that has done untold damage to the unionized sectors of the American manufacturing economy and degraded the living standards of unionized blue-collar workers (among others) in our country. This is important because part of an academic Marxist critique of the official U.S. labor movement's complicity and collaboration with American foreign policy in the third world was to argue that American workers benefit from the unequal exchange the world market imposes on goods from the South in trading with the North. From that not completely inaccurate insight one can go two steps further: to argue (1) that American workers "exploit" the South by simply participating in the U.S. economy and through that in the world market[12] and (2) that American workers *consciously* help exploit the third world. Struggles by socialist or labor movements in advanced industrial societies are therefore either useless or positively harmful, because the working class of the advanced capitalist countries participates, consciously or not as the case may be, in the exploitation of the third world.

It is therefore "objectively" reactionary to fight for higher wages and living standards for unionized workers in the United States unless they happen to be living in absolute economic misery. In effect this would mean only farm workers or textile workers in the miserable sweatshops of the

South and Appalachia or the new sweatshops in large cities with their own third world workers—still a minority of the workers in this country. Happily, therefore, one is not only exempt from having to support the economic struggles of most workers in the United States, but that is an act of solidarity with the third world. It also neatly fits in with what is good academic careerism—at least what was good careerism in those parts of academe where sensitivity toward the third world was much admired, whereas an interest in workers in the United States was both old-fashioned and suspect.

Human Rights: A Defense of Universalism

For the third worldists, solidarity also has usually meant regarding third world nationalisms as progressive. Why is there such unwillingness to face the fact that many of these states very rapidly become dictatorial or military regimes that oppress subject national groups more ferociously than did the former colonial nations? For that matter, they often harshly exploit their own majority peoples. Some have engaged in well-documented near-genocidal attacks against their own majority populations and subordinate national groups. Cambodia, former Spanish Equatorial Africa, Uganda, Ethiopia in Eritrea, Somalia, Sudan in the Nilotic South, Indonesia in Timor, Burma against the Kachin and Shan peoples, and Iraq against the Kurds are among the better-known horror stories.

Little or nothing is done about them, and the United Nations, as well as much of the progressive world opinion, when faced with these horrors, keeps prattling about sovereignty and noninterference in internal affairs of sovereign states. The depressing fact is that many of these states were set up in the first place without any trace of consent of the future subjects who were to be ruled, within boundaries imposed by former colonial powers.

There are several reasons for this continued tolerance of national oppression. The most popular theory is based on the proposition that these were "underdeveloped" nations, that had gotten that way primarily, if not exclusively, because of European and U.S. colonialism. They could therefore not be judged by standards that Europe and the United States adopted only in the very recent past and in any case often violated—particularly when non-Europeans were concerned. This view assumed that third world countries would all develop political democracy and individual freedom of the "Western" type, and this would more or less parallel economic development. In any case the evident injustices in Western societies gave them no right to criticize the newcomers on the road of nation building, given the huge costs that Europeans imposed on their peoples and the world during their own road to development.

What is essentially wrong with this view is that it ignores the fact that *knowledge* of the existing and potential political, economic, and institutional alternatives is not limited to individuals and groups by the level of economic development of their society.[13] That is, the political alternatives before the revolutionary movements, and by inference the modernizing political elites in underdeveloped countries, were not limited by their "stage" of economic development. Countries were not going through stages because there is a single world market of which they are a part, and information and knowledge can reach any part of the world system. Many leaders of national independence movements and the intelligentsias of the newly independent third world countries had access to the same knowledge of possible alternatives that their opposite numbers in the metropolitan countries did. They had often gone to the same universities and military academies as the leaders of the metropolitan countries. These were not noble savages, who had to learn for themselves by trial and error. They were men and, more rarely, women, with access to the most advanced theories about politics and economics. Benazir Bhutto went to Oxford and was president of the Oxford Union; the generals who toppled her government went to Sandhurst. Leaders of many third world countries are as well educated as, if not better educated than, their opposite numbers in the advanced North. They should therefore be treated as responsible adult political actors and not patronized by high-minded northerners.

Further, no economy is only "underdeveloped." Most economies and social structures are far more complex. Underdevelopment usually refers to the overall averages about a country. It is also a part of the global economy, participating in the international division of labor. A country that is "underdeveloped" in terms of its overall gross national product or average income may be very developed indeed when it comes to those sectors of the economy, usually extractive, that are linked to the world market. Underdeveloped countries may have parasitic cosmopolitan cities with large educated middle classes. They may have rich sectors of the legal or illegal economy that do not appear in official statistics. They may have, and more often than not do have, classes and strata that live in ways unrelated to the overall averages of the living standard of the country. They also may have sectors of the society that are technologically right up there with the most developed parts of the world. Unfortunately, this is usually the case with military and police technology and the most modern instruments of surveillance, torture, and repression.

In any case, the term "underdeveloped" tells us too little about the potentials of a society. Some countries are potentially very rich but "underdeveloped"; others have hardly any option of a reasonable strategy of development because of size, lack of natural resources, or other factors. Still other countries have been underdeveloped either by systematic external exploitation or by gross mismanagement and misrule by their own national rulers.

A second view is more relativistic, based on the idea that oppression and democracy are culture-bound concepts. To object to violations of human rights in third world countries is to attempt to impose alien values on different societies and cultures, based on presumptions of Western superiority—in more contemporary jargon, on "Eurocentric" concepts of right and wrong. These, in turn, are based on the assumption that certain universal norms exist, but that too is a Eurocentric, culture-bound notion. Burning widows, caste discrimination, chattel slavery, female circumcision, death penalties for blasphemers, child marriage, and torture of political opponents are thus all merely customs that belong to other cultures, as valid as our own. It is then argued by cultural relativists that it is the height of arrogance to demand that societies abide by some abstract "European" norms. In any case, Europe and the United States violate their own norms; only the United States has used a nuclear bomb against civilians, for example.

This line of reasoning assumes a far more autarchic world than the one that exists. The horrors that a Bokhassa or an Amin imposed on their populations were not products of a reversal to a "real" existing historical past. The invented past and traditions they laid claim to were imposed with modern weapons and enforced with modern methods of torture and surveillance. Islamic fundamentalism now uses modern cassette tapes to spread its messages and, when it can, modern armies. Kurds are repressed in Iraq with the use of the most modern poisonous gases.

I for one have no trouble accepting the charge that the values I defend are universalist in origin. Those values include human rights, rights for women, political democracy, egalitarianism, and individual freedom. That is why it was morally and politically *right* for French democrats and intellectuals to oppose torture in Algeria and to defend the Algerian and Vietnamese right to independence in the first place. These universalist values are products of the long evolution of European democratic thought, which owes a major debt to non-European civilizations, philosophies, and religions. It owes a special debt to Islamic civilization, which preserved and often enriched Greek, Persian, Judaic, and Hellenistic ideas during the six centuries when Europe was an intellectually stagnant backwater. Great Arab medieval social theorists like the Tunisian Ibn Khaldoun had no problem acknowledging their debt to Greek and Hellenistic scholars; to the contrary, they gloried in it. It is the less scholarly supporters of "third worldism" in the U.S. academies today, who themselves know almost nothing of Islamic, Indian, and Chinese contributions to what is an increasingly universalist world culture, who rail against Eurocentrism.

Solidarity with the democrats and socialists in the third world must begin with the assumption that concepts like democracy, the right of organization, individual rights and liberties, and equality for women are not culture-specific "Western" ideas to be doled out in the South in small doses when the elites decide that it is appropriate. These are goals in a universal struggle for democracy and socialism desirable in themselves *and*— this is crucially important to understand—are also indispensable tools for developing decent stable societies capable of balanced growth. Democratic leftists must reject the racist and neo-Darwinian notion that democracy is something reserved for the developed societies. The rights of peasants and workers must not be sacrificed to some abstract notion of progress as defined by self-selected vanguards. The emancipation of women cannot not be postponed into the vague future. I have always found it strange that educated radicals in the third world, including women, who enjoy the individual liberties of Western democratic societies, including sexual emancipation, often argue that equality for women is a culture-specific form of Western cultural imperialism, as is the defense of the most elementary democratic rights.

The third reason for supporting third world nationalism and failing to object to human rights violations in those states is based on the proposition that they are on the right side of a world conflict against imperialism. That is an idea whose origins lie in the past. Its most benign recent ancestor was the Italian independence movement of the nineteenth century, the Risorgimento of Giuseppe Mazzini, with its assumption that democratic nationalism was the foundation of a larger cosmopolitan democratic community. That nationalism was based on popular will and sovereignty and the repressed national identity of peoples and was supported as an elementary human right. Thus, throughout the nineteenth century, high-minded European democrats supported the national liberation and unification of the Irish, Poles, and Italians and far less often that of the South Slavs, Greeks, Armenians, or even the Algerians and Indians. Since Marx and Engels's time some leftists have always supposed that there are more and less "progressive" nationalisms. The same progressives who might enthusiastically back black nationalism in the United States or South Africa, or Cuban nationalism, often refuse to support Kurdish, Israeli, or Berber nationalism. There was the broadest imaginable coalition against the Biafran war of independence, uniting the Right and the Left—the Soviet Union, the United States, Britain, Israel, and Egypt—in supporting the unity of Nigeria. There is an almost worldwide coalition agreeing that Kurdish nationalism is, well, inconvenient. Fulfilling its demands would disturb at least four existing nations. Therefore, Kurds, a people numbering between twenty and twenty-four million—that is, *larger* than most nations that hold membership in the United Nations, larger even than two of the "nations" that rule some five million of them—are doomed to continued suffering and repression. To add insult to injury, they are subjected to the continued administration of Iran, Iraq, Turkey, and Syria, *none* of which are particularly good about granting even *individual* rights to their unwilling Kurdish subjects, not to speak of genuine cultural autonomy or even linguistic rights

Clearly, not having an independent national state of one's own is more tolerable in a reasonably pluralistic democratic state that permits wide linguistic and cultural autonomy. It is particularly intolerable under assertive nationalist rulers, left or right, who insist on "building national loyalty" among unwilling subjects. That was illustrated by the bitter armed resistance of the Mosquito Indians to what were probably well-intentioned attempts by Sandinistas to make them Spanish-speaking Nicaraguans,[14] the armed struggle of the Nilotic southerners against Sudanese attempts to make them a part of an Islamic state, and of course the resistance of the Kurds to make them "Mountain Turks." In all of these cases the former, less modern regimes had left well enough alone and were satisfied with a merely formal acknowledgment of central authority. "Modern" integralist nationalism endangers old, established coexistence in multiethnic states and communities.

Support for national independence movements in the third world assumed (a) that the nation in question did exist in the consciousness of sufficient majorities so that it could win a plebiscite and (b) that the new unified and freed nation would practice democracy and tolerance toward its minorities. A romantic Rousseauistic faith in the essential goodness of human nature was extended to nations. They were naturally good and democratic, almost in the state of nature, close to the "noble savages" of a romantic era. It was difficult to extend support of plebiscitary nationalism to artificially created former colonies where mutually antagonistic peoples were unwillingly packaged together. However, there was a great deal of dangerous innocence and ignorance abroad

The Devil You Know: The Role of the United States

The major obstacle to popular economic and political change in the third world since the massive decolonization following World War II has been the United States in its role as the world policeman, apparently doomed to maintain right-wing but presumably solidly anti-Communist regimes in the face of ever more desperate opposition and revolt. That is the visible and increasingly unpopular role. The less obvious role, which has been the foundation of the post–World War bipartisan foreign policy, without the primitivism of a Reagan administration in Washington, has been the maintenance of the present capitalist world economic system as such. It is, as has already been pointed out, the system that exploits the third world, not conscious policies pursued by this or that administration.

For decades the United States had propped up reactionary regimes with only the tiniest of fig leaves of democratic forms. Conservative regimes were repeatedly "certified" to be democratic and respectful of human rights in counterposition to more democratic and less repressive radical regimes that the United States happened to oppose. U.S. treatment of Guatemala, which has waged a murderous war against its Indian majority, comes to mind. Military aid went to Islamic fundamentalist "freedom fighters" in Afghanistan, rather than to SWAPO or the ANC. The polite pressures for free elections in Paraguay and Chile contrasted markedly with the repeated, insistent, and highly detailed demand for free elections in Nicaragua and with illegal acts of war such as the mining of harbors and arming of "contra" insurgents against a government with which the United States was legally at peace. These acts of the United States reflect the policies of the past decade, not a vague past. As the major power maintaining the present unequal world economic arrangement, the United States almost automatically, and often to the surprise of its own political publics, ends up supporting conservative stand-pat or, at best, moderate reformist regimes.

That status quo is, as even the pope repeatedly states, fundamentally unjust. On the other hand, in the recent past a near symbiotic relationship of the two superpowers in much of the world has repeatedly bent various third world struggles to fit within their cold war competitive relationship, thus greatly exacerbating already bloody realities. Hatred for the United States and its local allies builds support for local revolutionary movements and parties, and it is a justified hatred. On the other hand, fear of proto-Stalinist repression and revolution creates allies for the West and the United States in the third world. Most of the allies of the United States, however, are motivated by the fear that, whatever else a radical change of their societies would achieve, the property and privileges of the small pro-Western elites would be destroyed. This is why the proposals for U.S.-sponsored democratic social or economic transformation of third world societies, which reemerge under liberal Democratic administrations, were and are illusory even when well meant. U.S. allies in the third world may be—very rarely—for more democratic and law-abiding governments, but they are never in favor of fundamental economic redistribution and social equality.

Under President Carter the United States was helpful in fighting human rights abuses in many countries friendly to the United States. On the other hand, a large number of the regimes engaging in those human rights abuses had been set up with the active help of U.S. agencies, and their police forces had often been trained and financed by the United States. This should help explain why the United States is not taken all that seriously when it raises issues of human rights. Death squads and massacres by the military and landowner cliques in Guatemala, El Salvador, Indonesia, or the Philippines do not seem to rate the ire of the United States, whereas, for example, the Sandinistas, who, warts and all, were immeasurably less repressive than any of their neighbors except Costa Rica, have been repeatedly denounced as major human rights violators. This opportunistic use of the human rights issues, as well as the issue of government-sponsored terrorism, is nicely illustrated by the shifting official position of the United States toward Iraq. It was denounced as a major violator and supporter of international terrorism in the 1970s; then, during the Iran–Iraq war, it was taken off the list of governments that violate human rights and support terrorism when U.S. policy "tilted" in favor of Iraq. When the military confrontation over the Iraqi incursion into Kuwait approached in the spring of 1991, Iraq was practically demonized and its leader, Saddam Hussein, likened to Hitler. After the U.S. victory, when it was decided that it would be inconvenient to deal with the consequences of a political breakdown of Iraq, Saddam's Hitlerite qualities were forgotten; and his internal Shiite, democratic, and Kurdish opposition, previously encouraged by the United States to revolt against Saddam, were abandoned to his regime's not so tender mercies. And American commentators wonder why U.S. protestations about human rights and government-sponsored terrorism are not taken all that seriously.

Another example of the devastation caused by long-range policy inconsistencies of the United States within third world societies is its role in the international drug trade. Although administration after administration declares verbal wars against the drug traffic, the United States has an obvious, clear, and well-documented major responsibility for the development of this twentieth-century plague. It is the uncontrolled demand of the American domestic market for drugs that fuels the entire industry in its present malignant form. Present-day drug trade has close parallels to the other noble experiment of the United States, Prohibition. Much of the trade and refining of drugs originate with U.S. clients in the Latin American military, Thailand, the Afghan "freedom fighters," Turkey, and other governments and groups friendly to the United States. The vast sums of money generated in the international drug traffic are now creating large-scale corruption in third world countries, acting as yet another barrier to social change and democratization. It goes without saying that these same huge amounts of drug money have purchased entire small island governments as well as local governments and respectable banking houses in the United States proper.

All of the other sins and errors of commission and omission of the various U.S. administrations, however, are less important than the central role of the United States in maintaining the present world economic system. It is that world capitalist system that remains the major problem of would-be reformers and democratizers, not the particular policies of given administrations in Washington. There the United States remains bipartisan, as it does in its self-selected role as the policeman in the Panamas and Persian Gulfs of this world. As long as that remains the case, the greatest source of instability in the third world is not Communist or radical subversion but the pressure of the world banking system on those economies. U.S. policy toward the debts owed to domestic and international banks has effectively imposed a moratorium on any policies dealing with poverty, inequality, and injustice. It does so by insisting on austerity in already miserably poor countries. A dogmatic insistence on fiscal austerity and market-type economies demonstrates the same rigidity that primitive Marxists had toward collectivization of land and central planning.

The Enemy of My Enemy Is Not Necessarily a Good Friend

Organized support for anti-imperialist nationalism emerged after the Russian Revolution of 1917. The Soviet Revolution, isolated by a hostile world, found allies not in a revolutionary working class in advanced industrial countries, as its leaders expected, but in nationalist liberation movements directed against imperialism. In the 1920s practical alliances were forged between the Soviet Union and the radical nationalist governments of Kemal Ataturk's Turkey and Sun Yat-sen's China. The Communist International developed ties throughout Latin America, Asia, and, with less success, Africa. Two dynamics were set up: the training of third world revolutionary leaders in the European Communist parties or Moscow and the development of networks of support for colonial revolutionary struggle in Europe and North America.

Despite all of their inexperience, often uninformed heroic adventurousness, and catastrophic misjudgments and mistakes, the Communist International managed to develop more cadres and supporters outside Europe in twenty-odd years than the larger parties of the Socialist International did during their entire existence. The Communists were the first to break with the historic focus on Europe in the international workers' movement. This made international communism a potential ally or even mentor for a generation of future revolutionaries in Asia, Africa, the Caribbean, Latin America, and the Middle East.

Such alliances became much more common after World War II, when the language and symbols of radical nationalism and anticolonialism became pseudo-Marxist-Leninist, just as they had been pseudo-liberal democratic in the nineteenth century and sometimes pseudo-fascist or at least corporate-statist between the two world wars without ever changing their essential character.

That character remains essentially national-populist: the nation, the oppressed nation, sometimes defined in religiocultural terms, becomes the substitute for class in the socialist and Marxist movements. Islamic populism, Arab "Baath socialism," or for that matter most left branches of Zionism are examples. Both Mussolini and Perón stressed the concept of the have-not exploited nation, whose interests were more urgent than those of contending classes, in ways very reminiscent of contemporary Arab or African "socialism." All conflate *ethnos* and *demos*, the nation and the citizens. This makes democracy very problematic for the subjects of a national state who are not members of the dominant nation.

In the post–World War II period the Soviets aided a number of anticolonial revolutions. That aid increased substantially after the death of Stalin, under Khrushchev and especially under Brezhnev, who expanded military and economic ties throughout the third world. The Soviet Union did not have to be attractive: Growing hatred for the United States as the prop of neocolonialism and increasing contempt for its hypocrisy as a liberal capitalist democracy backing most of the reactionary regimes around the world made the Soviets appear at least as a lesser evil.

Where arms were concerned, the Soviets were friends of most radical and revolutionary regimes and groups in the third world. They were also many other things, but that was less relevant during the past twenty-five years in the poverty-stricken third world, where change was desperately needed and the United States was consistently the aggressive enemy of radical social and economic change. In the early 1980s the Soviets helped the Angolans, Ethiopians, and Nicaraguans, as well as some other radical third world regimes and movements. There have been grotesque examples of what regimes were considered "progressive" by the Soviet policymakers. Good evidence of the progressiveness of a regime was often its desire for Soviet, rather than U.S., arms.[15] Two of the worst examples were Uganda under Amin and former Spanish Equatorial Africa, which was ruled by a mad despot who managed to kill or drive out more than a quarter of the population. One of the welcome results of Gorbachev's glasnost is that past misjudgments about African despotic regimes are now acknowledged by the Soviet African experts. More somberly, *all* Soviet support—military and economic, even moral and political—will be reduced in the years to come. Decline in Soviet aid was capped by 1990 with an implicit partnership with the United States in creating a "new world order." This order is one in which elephants and pygmies retain their respective roles. That is bad news for the third world because it increases the tendency of the United States and Europe to neglect the needs of the South.

Both the United States and the Soviet Union had consistently subordinated the needs of the developing countries to their imperial rivalry for decades. I write *imperial* not *imperialist* rivalry. The traditional definition of imperialism, as a primarily economic category, has been difficult to apply to the Soviet Union or, for that matter, even to the United States today.

Military strategic considerations (even mistaken ones), maintaining allies, or simply complicating life for the rival power often explained much more.

The bulk of the support, critical or otherwise, for the Soviet and Eastern European state "socialist" countries within the third world had been historically based on two claims made on their behalf: that they were progressive and anti-capitalist, having abolished private property in the means of production and distribution, and that they were anti-imperialist because they were the most powerful rival of the existing imperialist world system dominated by the United States.

"Politocracies" rather than "socialist" would be the term best describing the Soviet-type authoritarian countries before their disintegration; this is a shorthand term emphasizing that these societies were not any kind of worker-run states. Rather, they were run by the political elites for aims determined by them. However, this description of the Soviet-type states made them *more* attractive to the modernizing political elites in the third world. Despite all of their egalitarian and populist rhetoric, these regimes were themselves essentially ruled by small coteries of political activists or young army officers. Therefore, the authoritarian and nondemocratic character of Soviet-type regimes was one of their major *attractions*. The masses were expected to participate, they were going to be educated and politically developed, but they most certainly were not supposed to interfere with the wielding of political power and the determination of economic and social goals. Above all, they were not to develop or maintain independent institutions and organizations. Participation in mass organizations under the control of the ruling party was highly encouraged under radical third world regimes and was pointed to as evidence of regime support. It was also counterpoised to the inferior "bourgeois" democracy of competing parties, organizations, independent unions, and press. That was the point of convergence between the Communist and third world "socialist" realities.

There were also a great many differences, not the least of which were (1) the immense poverty of the third world "socialist" countries and (2) their lesser efficiency even at repression. The absence of competitive democratic political tradition, as well as past caricatures of Western European parliamentarianism, which all too often proved to be shell games with parties representing the old elites alternating in power to the exclusion of representatives of unprivileged and poor rural groups, have helped give parliamentary democracy a bad name.[16]

A Third World Universal: Nationalism and "Nationalism"

Revolutionary regimes in Congo Brazzaville, Ethiopia, North Korea, and Benin all had the great good fortune, like many other third world revolutionary regimes, to come to power without any revolutionary or mass struggle. They also emerged in fortunate lands where a ferocious nationalism and a passionate Marxist internationalism were presumably not in contradiction, unlike the case of the more benighted European countries. But then I do distinctly remember that whereas *Western European nationalism* was presumed to have been born with the original sin of imperialism, that, apparently was happily not the case with the Communist-sponsored nationalisms of Eastern European countries and the Soviet Union. There, in the lands of really existing socialism, apparently no contradictions at all existed between socialist patriotism, a progressive social and economic program, and internationalism.

Why then should the revolutionary third world regimes have been expected to be different? And indeed the major identifiable component of third world ideology was nationalism or rather an attempt to create a nationalism, sometimes out of whole cloth. This feature of the revolutionary "Marxist" African regimes of Angola, Benin, Mozambique, Congo-Brazzaville, and Ethiopia was shared with more moderate "Socialist" regimes like those of Zambia, Tanzania, Senegal, and Algeria, as well as the conservative regimes of Zaire and Nigeria. Nationalism was what most of the nonaligned nations had in common on all continents. Nationalism cut across ideologies, alliances with superpowers, or even, surprisingly, religious ties. It sometimes appeared that it was all that the third world states had in common. Nationalism focuses on the people—many times an abstractly imagined people, to be sure—rather than on classes. It is the oppressed *nation* that is the focus of loyalty and pride and the instrument of opposition to imperialism. This neatly obfuscates the role of the parasitic intelligentsia and state bureaucracy and makes third worldism very acceptable indeed among new leftists in the industrial North. They too reject the relevance of class and defend the interests of "the people"—poor people, minority people, and the like.

Another feature of that "nationalism" was that it is, in practice as distinct from ideology, a *state-identified* rather than a *nation- or people-identified* nationalism. That is, in the overwhelming majority of cases it was a nationalism identified with the frontiers of the state, despite all of the talk about the people. Therefore, even more than usual, that "nationalism" was an invented category that had to be enforced, sometimes with great violence, over peoples who had a national identification that was in conflict with the frontiers of the nation-state that claimed them as often unwilling subjects. One need only refer to the decades-long wars trying to enforce national unity on unwilling Eritreans, Kurds, West Saharans, Kachins and other peoples in Burma and the near genocide in Timor. The long repression and national struggles of the Palestinians, Tibetans, and Kashmiris is the result of attempting to impose internationally recognized frontiers on unwilling subject peoples. Some of the more brutal civil wars in newly independent Africa, despite the exasperating presence of ideology and superpower meddling, were essentially national disputes, such as the war for Biafran independence, the civil/national war in Angola, and the like.

This persistence of conflict over national rights is not particularly a third world specialty. Defining *new* state frontiers, however, is more likely to produce disagreements about who are and are not the subjects of the new state than old, established frontiers are. To be sure, Basque and Irish nationalism have also involved at least minorities of those nations in armed conflict with old, established European states to which they had been assigned or by which they had been conquered centuries ago. Less violent struggles for Breton and Occident national identity in France, those of the Welsh and Scots in Great Britain and of the Walloons and Flamands in Belgium will probably be attenuated within a European Community that increasingly assumes a political and social character. However, nationalism will be far more difficult to handle within Eastern Europe, not to speak of multinational states such as Yugoslavia and Czechoslovakia and whatever remains of the Soviet Union. This at least hints at one solution, which in many parts of the world is unfortunately a long-range solution for what is a current problem. The development of larger supra-nation-state entities like the European Common Market will probably both lessen intrastate national tensions *and* encourage greater regional identity and autonomy. Why, for example, should the Scots continue to go to London for their regional economic or social grievances when the relevant decisions will increasingly be made in Brussels?

Almost without exception, democratic anticolonial leaders had, at the outset of their struggles, projected much larger heterogeneous regional entities than the national states that emerged from the processes of decolonization. In the 1950s when the victory of national independence movements was already in sight, the vision was one of a Caribbean federation or at least an English-speaking Caribbean federation, not a number of microstates, each trying to develop independently. In Africa the hope was, if not for a Pan-African federation, at least for large regional entities like the East African Federation (consisting of Kenya, Uganda, Tanzania, and Zambia) and a West African federation or a federation that would group countries from the Atlantic to the Sudan. Because such larger entities could not pretend to be nation-states, their multinational as well as multiconfessional and multicultural character would have to be explicitly recognized from the outset. They would therefore have to permit more diversity and abstain from trying to develop a monolithic "nationalism" attached to the new states. Clearly, such a project would run into massive opposition from the state bureaucracies, the urban intelligentsias, and the military, all of whom have a direct stake in continuing the existence of states that at least assure them of living better.

The sheer cost of the huge governmental bureaucratic structures and military has been a major obstacle to the development of many third world countries. This is not even because many of the bureaucracies have developed over a few short years into a genuine new class formation, full-blown kleptocracies or class formation that are clearly parasitic, living on loot and theft. They do so through their "ownership" of the state. It is not even only because these, most often urban-based rulers have historically mismanaged and made horrible mistakes in dealing with the problems of rural societies. And those have been heavy burdens indeed.

As has been pointed out by Paolo Freire and Rene Dumont,[17] the size and cost of *government*, the institutions of repression and administration, consume the lion's share of whatever resources could be mobilized to aid these societies and economies. *All* bureaucracies, national, international, and local, are many, many times larger than they had been under the exploitative colonial regimes. *All* armies and police forces are exponentially larger *and* more expensive than the forces of repression that had been necessary to maintain the colonial regime. These horrible costs, imposed on wounded economies, cultures, and societies, were justified by the urban intelligentsia whether the government was pro- or anti-Communist, formally democratic or openly one-party. The costs are justified in the name of national pride, sometimes in "nations" that exist only in the imagination of their urban rulers, if that, the products of totally arbitrary straight lines drawn on maps by colonial powers. They continue being justified in the name of defending the sovereignty of these pseudo-national pseudo-states when it is clear that the role of the armed forces is overwhelmingly that of internal repression and the maintenance of the given political and social order.

Decolonization and the Abandonment of Subalterns

The problems posed by nationalism have been exacerbated by the utter abdication of minimal moral, financial, and political responsibility by former colonial powers for the consequences of their past and present action. This is not just a question of the nature of the world economy and the exploitative relations historically set up between metropolitan countries and most colonies. The more difficult issue to discuss in anti-imperialist circles concerns those artificially created former microcolonies that never had a national or economic basis for existence.

This is the case with a number of smaller island colonies in the Caribbean, the Indian Ocean, and the Pacific, where the original inhabitants were wiped out or displaced by new settlers, who were often semifree or slaves. Independence was a convenient way of extricating the colonial power from any political, social, or financial responsibility or from the obligation to accept immigration to the metropolitan country. Previous colonial populations have been left to the not so tender mercies of whichever ethnic group emerged as politically and militarily dominant (often one and the same thing) in the former colony. This dominant group frequently imposed discriminatory measures against other national groups. The victims, sometimes more numerous than the ruling ethnic group, would be stripped of all redress in the name of respect for the national sovereignty of the new internationally recognized "state."

Former Dutch and British Guiana and the Fiji Islands are examples of an old colonial power simply abandoning subaltern peoples to their fate, as is the tragedy of the Asians in East Africa. (The Asians were economically and socially more adaptable to the limited opportunities in heterogeneous colonial societies.) In the three Guianas, a most cursory comparison of the political liberties and social and economic conditions between the three ends up with some startling conclusions. The conditions in French Guiana, which has formally become a part of France and therefore of the European Community, are light-years ahead of the other two. Decolonized former British and Dutch Guianas are miserable, oppressive dictatorships in which the descendants of Africans oppress descendants of immigrants from India, and both ignore the few remaining Native Americans. In both independent Guianas the living and educational standards have gone down for decades. Continued rule is maintained by a combination of aid from the CIA and toleration from the United Nations and the rest of the world for any oppression, including racial oppression, as long as it is garnished with proper nationalist rhetoric and is within a sovereign third world state. But these were never states; both the Asians and Africans were settled by Europeans to work plantations. There never was a demographic, economic, or historical basis for creating separate Guianese states out of the leavings of colonial empires.

Third World Military: A Clear and Present Danger

The single most radical, democratic demand in most third world states would be the abolition or severe reduction of the armed forces. It is the essential first step toward creating genuine civil societies, without which democracy and the free participation of citizens in governance remain a shallow sham. It is the presence of large armed forces acting as occupying armies in their own societies that makes a mockery of free elections and of any civilian government, not to speak of the judiciary systems, of much of Central and Latin America, Asia, and Africa.

Most of these praetorian forces were created on a large scale in the past quarter-century. They are armed and trained by the industrial North or by one of the superpowers. The United States has played the most significant role in creating these muscle-bound and costly obstacles to democracy throughout the world. Sometimes these praetorian institutions or their leaders decide to assert their independence from the United States and go into business for themselves. Panama, Pakistan, Surinam, Bangladesh, Argentina during military rule, the Philippines, and, potentially, Guatemala are all examples. Even when they assert their anti-imperialist and even "leftist" credentials, they remain a menace to democracy and reform because their very existence corrupts political processes and makes democratic and civilian rule impossible.

Thus, the demand to abolish or at the very least to weaken the military, subordinating them to civil society, is an essential first demand in the third world. If such a demand were extended to *all* nations, including the established states of Western Europe and North America, the world would surely be a safer place. The interesting question is how many of the present states, North and South, would survive; how many of the present governments and socioeconomic arrangements would survive?

Although the demand to abolish armies seems utopian today, it is good to stretch one's imagination when thinking about nation-states and the world order. Unimaginable changes have taken place since World War II. Unimaginable changes have taken place within the past two years in Eastern Europe and the Soviet Union. Why not, therefore, attempt to imagine desirable changes in the third world and the post–cold war world order. Some kind of international action will have to be taken during the 1990s. There is an urgent danger that the third world military will be strengthened rather than weakened.

The end of the cold war threatens to make third world nations the dumping ground for military exports. As the production of military weapons for the superpowers and their direct allies goes down, the pressure to sell military products elsewhere, at bargain rates if necessary, will increase. It is a multibillion-dollar industry for the West and a major source of hard currency for the successor states of the Soviet Union. To make things worse, considerable military productive capacity exists in NICs, which also need export markets. It is not only the superpowers that are culprits in pushing arms sales. Even Sweden, Yugoslavia, Brazil, and the Netherlands have sold arms to decent and not so decent regimes in the Middle East, Africa, and, throughout the third world. The pope reminds us that arms sales to third world nations are a scandal and a standing reproach to the prospects of decency and development in that impoverished part of our world.

Social Change, Free Will, and Necessity

Of course, some radical third world regimes have achieved a measure of success. In the best cases they have produced superior statistics for literacy, child mortality, and life expectancy—better than those of other regimes with comparable or even superior overall economic indicators. In the mid-1970s *Time* magazine did a cover story on socialism that surveyed the world and concluded that radical third world regimes were considerably *better* than others at their level of development in producing and delivering decent health and educational services for most of the population. Those statistics tell us a great deal about how gross national income is *distributed*, a question of great importance in poor countries, where huge income differences exist and therefore income averages mean next to nothing. They also tell a great deal about the social and economic priorities of a government. Third world countries are not uniformly underdeveloped; sectors of their economies and even their technologies may be world-class. After all, at least three third world countries, India, Pakistan, and Iraq, have the capacity to build nuclear weapons. Therefore, how resources are distributed is a key question, particularly in societies whose resources are inadequate to begin with in proportion to their population. Maldistribution can make things even worse.

There is something to this argument that is very appealing, but it applies as much to mild reformist regimes like those of Costa Rica and Sri Lanka as to full-blown one-party regimes with charismatic rulers. Thus, the question of *relative* cost of development and progress remains. On the other hand, it is also true that it is sometimes necessary to have a bloody revolution or civil war to remove a parasitic landlord class or foreign occupiers *even* to produce results as modest as a mildly reformist popular regime. In far too many parts of the underdeveloped world one could say that violence may, tragically, be necessary at times, to break the stranglehold that the traditional elites have over these societies. They have mostly proved impervious to parliamentary change, particularly in countries with powerful semiautonomous military and police forces, as in much of Latin America.

Often, therefore, the possible political and economic alternatives in the third world are not those found in a civics classroom in the rich North. These countries are inhabited by flesh-and-blood men and women who react to the demeaning backwardness, oppression, and exploitation of their countries. Such societies desperately need change, and many third world activists and leaders are educated, cosmopolitan men and women aware of the fact that life can be better, that it *is* better in other countries. Therefore, they also understand that life in their own countries is miserable for the vast majority, not because of fate or the will of a God or gods but because of systems and decisions constructed by living human beings. It is natural for them to assume that what was constructed by human agency can also be altered by human activity.

Thus, one of the central issues in the third world is the role of free will, or rather the degree to which possible political alternatives can be affected by conscious human agency. That is a profound challenge, which will be repeatedly taken up by new generations, who find continued injustices in their societies to be an intolerable provocation. Sometimes a sheer act of defiance against a corrupt and incompetent system, an unjust economic environment, and a distant superpower is necessary to remind oneself of one's essential humanity. It is that element of existential despair, the choice of personal risk and commitment, that links revolutionaries from a general Marxist background to Catholic activists who embrace a theology of liberation. The pity of it is that personal commitment and anger are not substitutes for rational choices and good judgment. Both are needed to improve society for the vast majority.

There Is a Role for a Democratic Left in the Third World

It is clear by now that authoritarian and autarchic shortcuts to development do more harm than good. Many countries are also of a size that precludes an independent developmental strategy. It is grotesque that the Left in general and third world countries in particular accept the boundaries inherited from the old colonial empires as the framework within which to attempt modern nation building and economic development. We were thus offered the separate and independent roads to socialism of a Grenada, a São Tomé, Benin, and for that matter a Nicaragua.

In his time, Leon Trotsky dared raise the question of whether socialism could be built in one country, even one as large and resource-rich as the Soviet Union. Today leftist and socialist intellectuals are petrified even to whisper a hint that the "socialism" being built in one of these microstates might not have any chance of success, even if the CIA did not engage in its malevolent and depressingly predictable work. They are terrified lest they be attacked for arrogant Eurocentrism and a lack of respect and sympathy for the victims of colonialism and the present unjust world economy. Devastating damage is done to the concept of socialism when it is handled like a medal issued for good intentions. Third world socialists have a right to expect from their allies and friends in the North the truth as they see it, not endless manipulation of that truth from a debilitating burden of guilt. If socialism as a concept and a workable program is in a crisis in Western Europe and the Soviet-type societies, then surely the same applies to the third world.

Since the end of the cold war in the late 1980s, the Soviet Union has been deemphasizing the utility of force in achieving change in the third world and urging the few remaining third world radical regimes to adjust to the existing, necessarily capitalist world market. It is among these regimes that the strongest reservations are heard today about Soviet glasnost and perestroika (i.e., political liberalization and economic reforms) and above all about the new Soviet international line of avoiding confrontation with the United States and the capitalist world. In this respect, Cuba's Castro speaks for a dwindling range of Soviet allies and friends when he criticizes current Soviet policies. The effect of the reforms in the Soviet Union and Eastern Europe has *drastically lowered* the amount of help and political support available to revolutionary movements in the third world. That help was mostly military in any case, except for the subsidies of wheat and oil to Cuba and massive purchases of sugar at above world market prices. The Soviets repeatedly demonstrated in the past that they were ready to abandon the national liberation movements, even when led by Communist parties, when reasons of state dictated. The change in the Soviet line should have been less of a shock than it was for friends and supporters in the third world, but then few of them had ever been interested in historical truths about the one source of potential aid against the United States and its allies.

Truths and realities, historical or current, and genuine options in the third world were depressing enough even before the dismal decade of the 1980s. Hope for external help is sometimes all that remains, and it is therefore doubly hard to give up. Traditional Soviet advice on economic and political development has been generally bad, if sincerely given; other external sources of advice or experience have not been all that helpful either. The current fetishization of the market by most Western economists, with repeated references to the Pacific Rim countries, is not helpful for societies that are far poorer and less centralized. Reasonable strategies would stress the need for flexibility and a variety of economic approaches through a mix of ownership and management forms. Although quite right, these would seem too slow to the more desperate of the third world leaderships facing immediate economic and social catastrophes.

There is a real role for third world socialists beyond hoping for an external salvation. It is a difficult and often heroic role. One is to lead relentless struggles for the expansion of democracy and empowerment and the mobilization of the broadest layers of the population. That means fighting to build democratic and participatory unions and popular organizations of peasants, workers, women, minorities, and the young. Typically, they engage in efforts to spread literacy and establish educational and cultural institutions independent of the state. That is what radical Catholicism has emphasized in building base communities and self-help networks among the poor in the countryside and the slums of Latin America. Much can be learned from the liberation theology movements in Latin America and for that matter from the women's and other community organizations of the African liberation movements before they took power.

The vitality of organizations developed during the struggle for national liberation against colonialism had made me optimistic about the prospects of the postrevolutionary regimes in countries like Guinea-Bissau, Angola, Mozambique, and Algeria.[18] This is in contrast to the countries that gained their independence without a prolonged struggle that required mass mobilization over protracted periods of time. That optimism turned out to have been premature if not mistaken. The huge emancipatory potential of mass organization from below has been repeatedly illustrated in the third world. So, unfortunately, has the capacity for revolutionary elites to take over these societies.

The forgotten lesson that the Spanish anarchists tried to teach the revolutionary movements of the poor and rural masses in authoritarian societies is to be suspicious of bureaucrats, officials, and the state—above all, your own national bureaucrats and state. The anarchists and rural socialists in the poorest regions of Spain before the 1934 civil war, when Spain had many of the problems of a third world country, provide interesting lessons. These iconoclastic grass-roots activists, without a centralized vanguard party, spread a genuine sense of empowerment and self-confidence, pushing the previously passive rural groups into the front lines of political and social struggles. This included women, who are all too often ignored by the third world liberation movements and represent a major resource for democratic change from below.[19] The rural anarchist traditions in Spain and Italy and in Latin American countries are more in tune with the realities of underdeveloped societies than the centralized models imported from Fabians or Soviets. For that matter, decentralized, market-oriented agriculture and both individually owned and cooperative small trade and appropriate technologies are more appropriate to deal with scarcity than with state ownership and control. This does not preclude some planning and fiscal controls. The mix will necessarily vary from country to country. In countries with weak civil societies one should support a weak state; where civil societies are strong, a strong legal state can expand egalitarian social services to the entire population, and in such societies the state can be kept under democratic control. Popular control is absolutely essential; although that might take unfamiliar forms in some third world countries, the rights of self-organization, free expression, and the election and control of those who govern are basic and uncomplicated.

The Need for Genuine and Massive Solidarity

The issue of aid to underdeveloped countries is complex because many of the forms that aid has taken have done more harm than good. Much of the aid had been linked to the cold war, and the political price has been to drag the recipient countries into the superpower confrontation. This has speeded up the tendency for the newly independent countries to spend increasing shares of their resources on arms and to divert precious resources. It has also strengthened the military in these fragile societies, which have only rudimentary civic institutions.

Socialists and democrats in the advanced industrial societies should propose an equivalent of the Marshall Plan, which so successfully helped rebuild the economies of Western Europe and Japan. The analogy must not be pushed too far; the aid would be funneled through international agencies, which would include the Russian Republic, occupying the old Security Council seat of the Soviet Union. What is essential is a massive systematic effort over time as distinct from ad hoc aid. To be effective, that aid must produce egalitarian growth leading to self-sustained, balanced, and *ecologically sound* development. That in turn would be a major shot in the arm for the stagnant industries of the North, and it is one reason such aid is in the self-interest of the North. The second reason is that it is illusory to think that any genuine peace is possible for any prolonged period if the vast majority of humanity is doomed to hunger and need. The third reason for the North, particularly the European Community, to give such aid is of utmost importance: the European social democratic movements and parties need a project to mobilize the idealism and imagination of the younger and better-educated publics they must now address if they are to survive. I cannot imagine a project more likely to achieve that aim than a war on hunger, exploitation, political oppression, and needs, an attempt to create the first genuine human world community.

5

Democracy for the Twenty-first Century

The Question of Socialism

The relative stability of their electoral base throughout most of their traditional strongholds has not prevented a crisis of morale and a programmatic disorientation today in most of the democratic socialist and social democratic parties in the world. This is despite the fairly steady growth of the electoral prospects of the socialist parties during the past decade, in countries as different as Germany, Japan, and the United Kingdom. To be sure, that growth has been neither stable nor unilinear; there is a relative stasis between the traditional parties of the Left and Right. As a consequence, a jaded electorate turns to nontraditional parties that do not neatly fit within the familiar political spectrum. Examples are the unexpected successes of parties like localist "leagues" in Northern Italy and libertarian right-wing groups like New Democracy in Sweden and the German People's Union in the 1991 election in Bremen. The more pathological versions of this turn away from democratic politics can be found among the neo-Nazi skinheads in Germany and the growing anti-immigrant agitation in the European Community.

In Eastern Europe and the various republics of the former Soviet Union, basically antipolitical nationalist movements have massively emerged in Georgia, the Ukraine, Russia, Armenia, and Azerbaijan, as well as Hungary, Croatia, Serbia, Romania, Poland, and Slovakia. Similar movements now exist throughout the area, and although they are antipolitical on the whole, the majority tend to be attracted to the symbols and language of the Right rather than the Left. When it is not the explicit political Right, it is the revival of traditional, nationally specific religious identities, coupled with a call for respect for traditional family and patriarchal authority.

It is ironic that this rise of a populist Right should be taking place at just this particular juncture in history, since the great schism between the two historical branches of the international workers' movement, communism and social democracy, has been unequivocally decided in favor of the latter. However, the massive collapse of communism as a world system has also raised substantive questions about the possibility, and for that matter even the desirability, of basic social change and even modernity as such.

The collapse of the Communist authoritarian systems that have usurped the name of socialism for over half a century has raised questions about democratic socialism, with which they had nothing in common but the name. But then, historical outcomes are rarely fair. Thus, the ability of democratic political systems to consciously control their economies and social development toward broadly acceptable and desired goals, without this turning into an utter disaster, is in question. To be sure, it has been in question for traditional conservatives and other defenders of the status quo for a long time.

The end of ideology[1] and therefore of ideological politics was predicted many times before, with just as much certainty and considerably more sophistication than today. The last time this view was in fashion was in the late 1950s. That particular epoch of the end of ideology was followed by a completely unpredicted massive explosion of political commitment by the young in the United States and much of the world, by major electoral victories of the parties of the Left in Western Europe, and by the Prague Spring, which was the precursor of the end of communism. So much for prophecies of the end of ideology. Incidentally, they are always stated as if they are good for the indefinite future, as if a final conflict has been resolved for all time. Clearly, at least judging from precedents, a great deal of caution is appropriate with such predictions.[2]

Socialism is now almost universally blamed for the crimes and mistakes committed in its name. A similar and equally unfair fate has overtaken democracy.[3] Monstrous crimes and misfeasances have been committed in its name throughout the world. There is hardly a dictatorship that has existed anywhere since World War II that did not claim to be democratic, whether the dictatorship was purported to be radical or conservative, legalistic, traditional, or populist. Every single Communist and post-Communist regime has professed to be democratic—*genuinely* democratic, unlike its rivals. It is almost refreshing today to run into the very few governing elites or leaders so out of tune with modernity and fashion as to be frankly opposed to any form of democracy, even to the very word.[4] To be sure, the United States led a massive coalition into a war in 1990 to defend and preserve just such regimes in Kuwait and Saudi Arabia.

Socialism Was Born as Part of the Democratic Revolutions

In many ways the present crisis of socialism is part of the more general crisis of democracy. This is the case in mass-industrial societies, as well as in the third world and the large number of societies that fall between the two, the so-called newly industrialized countries (NICs). Democracy and social equality, as well as the expansion of citizenship rights, have been intimately associated since the French Revolution. The slogan of that democratic revolution was *liberty*, *equality*, and *fraternity*. It is worth remembering that the rate of literacy and the experience with participation in self-government of the broad masses in France and the United States at the time of *their own* democratic revolutions were then on what we would consider today to be third world levels. So, for that matter, were their levels of urbanization and proportions of population involved in agriculture. Germany, on the other hand, was among the most industrially developed and literate societies in the world in the 1930s, when it succumbed to Hitler's dictatorship and launched its genocidal horrors. Its much better educated and developed working class, with the most massive and most thoroughly organized parties, unions, and institutions in the world was defeated by the National Socialist barbarians. The superior organization and development of Germany merely assured that no massive resistance to Hitler could organize and survive. That is to say, the superior degree of organization of the German state and society extended to the organization of repression. So much for the necessary association of democracy with literacy and development.[5]

From the very beginning there were those for whom "equality" was not mere equality before the law, the famous equal legal right of both the millionaire and pauper to starve under a bridge. That is not what the French Revolution was about to the Jacobin activists, to Gracchus Babeuf, the first modern socialist, and to the *sans-culottes*. The demand for *social justice* was raised in the first Commune, during the French Revolution. It was also there as a central demand during the democratic revolutions of 1830 and 1848, by which time numerous full-blown socialist programs were around. "La sociale," the rallying cry for social justice, is the root of the word *socialist.* Karl Marx and Friedrich Engels certainly did not have to invent it; they were relative latecomers to the concept. The Communist Manifesto is, after all, a polemic against the numerous already existing and popular varieties of socialist programs and proposals.

Contemporary social democracy is only the most legitimate and obvious heir of the nineteenth-century democratic revolutions. This is widely recognized by neoconservatives and their allies in academe today and is one of the reasons there is such widespread historical revisionism about the great French Revolution. It represents a logical part of an attack on the democratic traditions and ideological roots of the broad democratic Left. History is supposed to come to a stop. Change as such, we are told, is evil and dangerous; democracy itself is a dangerous utopia unless it is completely defanged of its potential for popularly initiated social change and reduced to mere process.

Two sharply counterposed traditions of democracy are conflated and confused: democracy as the rule of the demos, or the people, in its historical continental European usage and the paler, "cooler" Anglo-Saxon variant, in which democracy is treated as the gradual extension of suffrage and citizenship rights descended from the seventeenth-century liberal Whig tradition. In the United States and Great Britain, democracy is thus changed to this tamer and more respectable Whig notion, through which the demos will, at best, be allowed to have its "objective" interests indirectly expressed through legislatures composed of elites—that is to say, their betters. Thus, the U.S. Congress is mostly a house of millionaires in the case of the Senate and of lawyers in the case of the House of Representatives.[6]

One effect of the reduction of democracy to the rule of self-perpetuating elites is a systematic distortion of political and economic priorities. Crudely stated, what interests the elites is not necessarily what interests the majority of the citizens. Nor do they feel the same priorities and pains. This was put very well by Leslie Gelb in *The New York Times*,[7] which is not exactly the stronghold of radical criticism of the American political system: "Ever since World War II, foreign affairs—war and peace—have been the glamour field. . . . To growing public problems, elites sought private answers. Bad public schools: send the kids to private schools. Traffic congestion: put a phone in the car. The city a hellhole: buy a home in the country." Then, in words not too different from those any European social democrat would use:

> Issues like health and education become "hopeless" and "wasteful" to them. Governments do not perform many tasks well. But they do more than a satisfactory job of building. They can build housing for the homeless, roads and airports to speed transportation and new schools to replace the dungeons of inner-city education. These are capital investments that generate new tax revenues—pride and dignity. . . . *All this requires money, the kind of money unflinchingly committed to the fight against Iraq* [my italics]. . . . And it requires the sustained interest and participation of America's movers and shakers, who can choose to merely live in their country or to make their country livable.

Just so. I would add only that it would all be simpler if the "movers and shakers" did represent the demos; that is, if democracy in America worked, or at least worked more equitably and fairly.

The Crisis of Social Democracy Is Much Overstated

The ideological crisis of social democracy in Western Europe seems to have been, at least temporarily, alleviated in the electoral field by a shift in the definition of strategy and goals. The present social democratic programs make it quite explicit that these parties are broad defenders of progressive social policies and the welfare state, rather than movements committed to a basic transformation of the social order to some kind of as yet undefined socialism. This shift has succeeded in broadening the support of social democracy beyond its traditional trade union and productivistic clientele to now include the clients of the welfare state and the social movements. *The more universal and generous the welfare state, the broader and less particularistic its clientele and defenders.* Although this solves the organizational and electoral problem of the broad Western European Left and strategically positions it to dominate the unified European Community into the future, it leaves unsolved the more general ideological crisis created by the absence of a clearly agreed on socialist "project."

It also leaves unsolved the more serious problem of governability and legitimacy of democratic politics themselves in an era in which the historic arena for those politics, the nation-state, is facing fundamental challenges. These challenges come from both supra- and transnational organizations and institutions, such as transnational financial institutions and corporations on one hand and revived ethnic nationalism, regionalism, and single-issue particularlism on the other. On one hand, both sets of challenges put in question the nature, efficacy, and even the very legitimacy of the nation-state as the framework in which to make decisions. On the other hand, mass society disintegrates the sense of citizenship, which requires some sense of there being a common identity and therefore the possibility of working for a common good. Those are necessary to provide a basis for accepting some sacrifices for universalistic goals, in order for broad programmatic parties and classes that have society-wide programs and gain wide support to emerge.

The alternative to the notion of a common good or goals shared by the citizens of the polis is social and political fragmentation to parochial localities, ethnic and tribal loyalties, and single-issue groups. This fragmentation produces a political paralysis that makes a democratic politics with clearly defined and broadly accepted goals impossible, and the effect is that the established elites continue to rule through what becomes a permanent government.[8] In turn this breeds cynicism about the efficacy of democratic politics and produces individuals ever more open to manipulation by mass media and mass commodified culture. Such a political culture reduces politics themselves, and certainly the elections, to yet one more commodity to be bought and sold. This is what the danger of an "Americanization" of European politics consists of, and it quite rightly alarms political observers and democratic and leftist politicians throughout the European continent. It reduces democracy itself to a ritual and a commercialized sham.

Democracy and Socialism Are Intertwined but Not Identical

The most basic of the claims of the defenders of the status quo is that any basic societal change is dangerous, undesirable, or quite simply impossible. Therefore, the most fundamental of the claims by the democratic Left and therefore of socialists in general, from the French Revolution onward, has been that it is possible for ordinary men and women to make effective transformation of the societies they live in, in their own interest, and, above all, that they can make those changes democratically. The democratic Left has claimed that it is possible for the objects of history to become its subjects. It is this belief, rather than the belief in state or social ownership of the means of production or confidence in the ability of the state to plan national economies or achieve high industrial growth rates, that is absolutely fundamental to socialism. Therefore, the crisis of confidence in the possibility of democratic social transformation is, for the socialist movement—a movement committed to a fundamental change of the status quo—a more serious problem than similar crises for supporters of the existing social, economic, and political order. The crisis of socialism, therefore, reinforces the confidence of the conservative and liberal defenders of the status quo that this capitalist world is and should be basically unchangeable.

Belief that social transformation, no matter how gradual, is possible and can be achieved democratically is absolutely fundamental to both socialism and any meaningful concept of contemporary democracy. It is fundamental to any substantive prospects for a democracy appropriate for the twenty-first century. The fate of the two is intertwined; it is not identical. I cannot imagine socialism without democracy, but I can certainly imagine a very inadequate and incomplete democracy without socialism. After all, I have lived most of my life in just such a system in the United States of America. Stated differently, democracy is *absolutely* essential to socialism, whereas socialism is needed to round out democracy, to complete *that* project. Without socialism or a very great level of egalitarianism and social justice, genuine democracy will be crippled; it will be a shadow of what it can be. But clearly, democracy itself is at least problematicized if it is argued that even democratically agreed upon change is not possible. What is it *for,* in that case, a cynic might ask. Social stasis, autocracy, or traditional premodern patriarchal rule of notables would do just as well, probably better because there would be a closer fit between the normative claims of the society and its practices. At least it would not raise impossible hopes that cause disturbances.[9]

Many conservative theorists claim that democratic change from capitalism to some other system is not only not desirable, it is essentially not even possible. To this assertion some conservatives add that even democratic control over capitalism—that is, an advanced welfare state—no matter how much popular support it generates, both endangers liberty and is inherently inefficient. Welfare states tend to be popular, and some specific social legislation, like the relatively universal social security, was widely popular in the United States even during the Reagan presidency.

Conservatives therefore found it necessary to bypass these delusions of the public by avoiding or short-circuiting democratic processes and public debate. Thus, since social security was politically untouchable, as were most welfare programs that benefit the middle class, deliberately run-up deficits, coupled with tax cuts, created artificial revenue shortages that were designed to *force* on the Congress drastic cuts in the American welfare state. Because Congress was in the hands of the Democrats, they would have to share in the blame for the cuts in services, which after a decade almost ruined the large American cities and public education. This was clearly a deliberate attempt to engage in social engineering without any popular mandate or support. It was also a cynical attempt to do away with any democratic debate or decision making, as are the repeated attempts to strengthen the presidency.

But, we are now told, there are no real fundamental political, social, or economic issues that could be placed before a democratic public in a modern America, or in the industrialized world for that matter. There are only administrative problems and questions of efficiency.[10] In short, history has come to some kind of stop. And lo, a very popular and influential article, "The End of History" by Francis Fukoyama,[11] claims exactly that. Moreover, it celebrates this world victory of liberal capitalism although in its very heartland, the United States, both liberalism and capitalism are in deep trouble. The political system has produced a stasis and a perpetuity in office of "elected" popular representatives that would have been envied by any of the now departed Communist *nomenklaturas*. Even they would have been somewhat taken aback by our scandalously low levels of voter participation. The electoral ritual, when stripped of substance, is ever less popular. When deprived of genuine political alternatives and effective political decisions, elections in the United States are increasingly seen as an irrelevant confirmation of the incumbents, effectively the party in power.

The economic system is subject to recurrent recessions, whose name dare not be uttered by those supposedly in charge of avoiding just such happenings. It seems that although the economic system is clearly not functioning well, the political system—that is, U.S.-style democracy—must not and should not be expected to fix things. The new orthodoxy demands that the government stay out of the business of attempting to regulate the rougher aspects of an economy. The result of this withdrawal of the government from even the most essential watchdog functions in the economy over the past decade has been wholesale looting of the economy and the public. Our banking scandals cost the public hundreds of billions, which a complacent Congress bills to taxpayers. Deregulation of banks is matched by deregulation of airlines, which has left hundreds of cities without viable air transport and bankrupted dozens of airlines while enriching corporate raiders and gamblers. No new technologies or manufacturing techniques or services begin to create the kind of wealth that manipulation of paper stocks and corporate raids do. No wonder the U.S. economy fails to provide a better life for the broad majority of the population as the gap between the rich and the working population grows and as a massive underclass is created. The legitimacy of a system of "democracy" in which the demos has little genuine access to power is clearly a problem.

Why should those outsiders, who are now being told that they are latecomers to the party where the goodies have already been distributed, accept such rules of the game as legitimate? Clearly, a more vital and enabling concept of democracy is essential. I can imagine no better time to raise that issue than now, when the United States and Western Europe are busy preaching the virtues of democracy to the Eastern European countries and the former Soviet Union, as well as to Africa and rest of third world. *There*, in the former Communist-ruled countries, we are busy trying to make sure genuinely *contested* elections take place, through which things (i.e., the economic and political system) can most assuredly be expected to change as a result of popular will. Sandinistas and Eastern European reform Communists were expected to gamble the fate of their entire systems at election times. No defeatist talk about the Nicaraguan electorate being unprepared to make fundamental decisions under the threat of economic strangulation by the United States, if it decided wrongly, was permitted to interfere with *that* election.

The fact that massive amounts of money from abroad (which is against the law in the United States) were poured into some of the Eastern European elections, reinforced with advisors and clear indications of what the West expected, did not put into question the legitimate right of parties that had won bare pluralities to dismember an entire system of economic and property relations. I can imagine how the very skies would be rent if a *socialist* party after an electoral victory proceeded to attempt to dismantle capitalism! It would be even worse if it announced that it would eliminate all former capitalists from public life.[12] Perhaps some of this fervor for democracy elsewhere and faith in the infallibility of the demos when it makes political choices will rub off on the United States. It would be a very unexpected and good, but quite unanticipated, consequence indeed if it did.

Moving Beyond the Welfare State: Utopia or Illusion?

A contemporary discussion of what could remain of a socialist project, one still politically relevant after the abject debacle of state socialist politocracies in the Soviet Union and Eastern Europe, must specify a time frame that is both imaginable and realistic and a physical location somewhere in the real world. In other words, it must be anchored sometime and somewhere, in some kind of imaginable framework, one that extrapolates from some existing society. Otherwise, we would be engaged in what is a perennial and useful effort to imagine utopias—utopias in both senses of the word, in both historical usages, as the imagined and desirable place and as *noplace*, which is what *utopia* originally meant when Sir Thomas More coined the word in the sixteenth century. Imagining possible utopias is useful, if not indispensable, for socialists and radical democrats because without a boldly imaginative utopian dimension, without thinking about what the desirable society could be and should be, contemporary socialism remains excessively rooted in the present social, political, and economic arrangements.

On the other hand, thinking about noplace, a pure utopia, so to speak, relieves one of the responsibility of asking how one could conceivably get there. Utopias, then, become limited to voluntarily self-selected intentional communities, that is, small communities of self-selected enthusiasts like the utopian socialist or religious communities, communes of Spanish anarchists, Israeli kibbutzim, urban communes of New Left activists in the 1960s, or even the wider and more successful ones such as the contemporary Mondragon cooperatives of the Basques. These may well set up very worthwhile models and relationships among individuals, but they fail to answer the difficult political question of how to transform "outside" society, especially how to do so democratically with the active consent and continued support of the majority in a society that is politically alive with debate and popular participation in the wielding of power. Short of that idea, the support of a majority will do; that is why *representative* as distinct from *direct* democracy was invented. Representative democracy is the only practical form of democracy for prolonged periods in larger polities than the classic Greek *polis* or the voluntary community or cooperative. This is why, in practice, objection to mere representative democracy ends up being objection to democracy itself. More than one single-party tyranny that rejects this inadequate representative or parliamentary democratic model has portrayed itself as a form, usually a new and specific form, of direct democracy. This intellectual and political con game is getting harder to play nowadays but is still the fashion in Cuba, Libya, and some other squalid third world dictatorships. It was a game played to the applause of many Western leftist intellectuals, unfortunately, which is one reason the Left's democratic credentials are sometimes still in doubt. China and the Asian Communist dictatorships no longer even bother with this charade.

This avoids the real problem in thinking about a socialist society or program, and that is how to make such a society possible and desirable for normal, presently existing human beings who have been shaped by the existing capitalist culture and social order, human beings who have not been already transformed by conversion to radically different values. The values implied in egalitarian socialist politics are in direct collision with the presently dominant possessive and competitive individualism; instead, they emphasize community, without which it is difficult to generate cooperation and equality. This is, of course, the central problem of socialist politics for Socialist or Social Democratic parties today: the cultural hegemony of the capitalist order is stronger than it has been at any point since the industrial revolution. All institutions, certainly all mass media, in these societies reinforce the dominant culture and its values. Minor and inconsistently conscious exceptions are found in autonomous social, religious, and class movements. To be sure, Socialist and Social Democratic parties in advanced industrial countries increasingly solve that particular problem by not worrying about any kind of socialist politics whatsoever and doing what they do rather well: defend the welfare state. Although this is a totally worthwhile thing to do in itself, it does leave unanswered the problem of socialist politics in contemporary advanced industrial democracies. Are such politics even feasible, whether or not they are desirable?

Mass literacy and state-controlled education, combined with a highly commercialized mass culture, successfully confront the all but universal retreat of the islands of cultural autonomy that were provided by the organizations and residential concentration of the industrial working class throughout the smokestack era. That autonomy provided by homogeneous working-class neighborhoods, with their pubs, clubs, political organizations, and cultural associations linked to leftist parties and unions, has, for the most part, either vanished or is disintegrating throughout most of Western Europe and North America. Thus, the majority of even the leftist voters in advanced industrial societies today have been socialized to accept a whole range of assumptions of a capitalist civilization about what is possible and desirable as a life goal, how one should live one's own life, and what is the minimum of essential material goods that must be possessed. Traditional solidarities of class, occupation, and workplace are increasingly replaced by possessive individualism.

Leftist politics today end up, far too often, talking about sectoral resentments of segments of the population and the unfairness in distribution of the benefits of increased productivity, rather than raising universalist egalitarian demands and a vision of a radically different organization and goals of production and leisure. The latter is considered unrealistic, but failing to raise such demands destroys the movement within the broad socialist Left and leaves behind the electoral machine and perhaps the trade unions.

That kind of self-restricting "realism" has almost destroyed the Western European socialist *movement*, leaving behind reasonable but dull socialist organizations, parties, and institutions that spend much of their time administering a more humane capitalism within welfare states, a capitalism much modified and humanized by advanced welfare state legislation, egalitarian social policies, increased attention to environment issues, and powerful trade unions. That is the face of most of the advanced contemporary capitalist states, with the exception of the "Anglo-Saxons," the United States and Great Britain, at least at home. The role of that capitalism on a world scale in the face of the growing North–South income gap is discussed in Chapter 4.

Mass socialist politics since the late nineteenth century have been rooted in an autonomous working-class subculture that, whatever its inadequacies, provided an alternative political socialization for generations of socialist, trade unionist, and broadly radical democratic voters and activists. The movement created and controlled its own educational and cultural institutions. Mass state education and commercial culture either has absorbed much of this energy or has replaced it with its own simplified and commodified product. The present urban community is atomized, collective goals are mobilized in the service of the existing order, and the idea that the common good may require sacrifice and effort is replaced by the notions of individual self-fulfillment, as often as not through individual advancement and accumulation of possessions. The process extends to all organizations of citizens in the modern capitalist democracies, so parties, voluntary associations, and unions become goods to be passively consumed and democracy becomes an exercise in consumer choice rather than a process requiring active participation of an informed and responsible citizenry. It is not an organized, active, and informed citizenry that one must imagine a possible socialism for; rather one must think of a possible socialism for the currently existing, real political publics as they are. Democratic socialism is not a reward for good behavior and proper organization and participation; however, organization and participation are tools without which achieving social change democratically is all but impossible.

A high degree of organization is not required to disrupt or even to topple an existing political order, but it is required for constructing an alternative and legitimate order. That is one of the recent lessons from Eastern Europe and even the Soviet Union. However, I am of the opinion that only in societies with an atypically high degree of autonomous self-organization and a thick set of overlapping movements and institutions, formal and informal, does it become possible to think of moving beyond the limits set by the present capitalist civilization. These limits are "set" mostly in the minds of the political public. To be sure, they are considerably more flexible than the traditional Left used to believe. When faced with worse and more dangerous alternatives, very advanced egalitarian and welfare state measures may well be accepted. However, the main ingredient of the intellectual hegemony of the capitalist system is the ability to define what it is "objectively" possible to do in society and the economy; that is, to define the limits of the legitimate debate about policy alternatives.

Therefore, it is a useful thing to try to make the question of what could be a viable socialism in an advanced industrial society more specific: to locate it in time and space, to ask us, for example, to imagine what could, or rather should, lie beyond the reformist Valhalla, the Swedish welfare state. Thus, we are asked to think about a real or almost real place, possibly something like a more advanced Sweden, and that also gives us an implicit time frame, presumably a few decades. My assumption is that the Swedish labor movement will return to political power by the mid-1990s at the latest.

I can begin responding to this question by returning to my earlier point about the present cultural hegemony of the capitalist culture, not merely in advanced capitalist countries but as a world system and a world culture. What can, to some extent, be counterposed to the total hegemony of the dominant world culture over a given society are the independent organizations and social movements that accept at least partially different values. The most massive example of that type of independent voluntary organization, which has, to a limited extent, alternative values to the dominant capitalist ones in the world today, is the Swedish labor movement. *That* is what makes Sweden different and special for me, not the welfare state, not even the fact that Social Democrats have been in power for most of the second half of this century. That can and does change from time to time with democratic elections, which is as it should be. After all, advanced welfare states exist in other Scandinavian countries and in the Netherlands. Germany, France, Belgium, and Italy also have relatively advanced welfare states with a fair degree of control over capital accepted as a minimal norm of civilized behavior. That is increasingly a European norm.

What is still unique about Sweden and makes it *possible* to think of it as a site for a project that could go beyond the welfare state in the imaginable future is neither its generous social provisions nor its high living standard; rather it is the sheer and unique massiveness of its labor movement. It organizes so much higher a percentage of the working population as to be qualitatively different from all other existing social democracies and welfare states. The figure for the trade unions is 85 percent of all employed! That is 90 percent of all production workers. No other country begins to approach these figures. Now, of course, such outlandish figures skew other political statistics, including the proportion of Social Democratic voters who are members of the party, the cooperative movement, the women's organizations, or any other of the many organizations that make up the Swedish labor movement. This special quality of the Swedish labor movement remains relevant even, or especially, in those intervals when the Swedish socialists are out of office (they do on occasion lose elections). In such periods the massiveness of the Swedish labor movement is a guardian of a social democratic political culture, of the interests of the demos, or the welfare state, of the lower third of the income pyramid.

For me it is the degree of organization of that movement that makes it possible to answer other questions about what can be possible in a Sweden. I note that most critics of advanced welfare states who stress their limitations, for example, Robert Heilbroner,[13] do not seem to consider the question of popular organization, and by implication potential popular power, as being of particular importance in posing questions about a hypothetical Sweden.

Such critics are not alone; most egalitarian democrats, particularly in America, seem to have a blind spot when it comes to thinking about mass organizations and their potential effect on political, economic, and social power in modern society. Our sort seem to think that popular or any other kind of power is a messy and unclean sort of thing, best left alone, or at least not mentioned in polite society. For me these are crucial questions in determining what is possible for a decent social democratic government to do. It determines what popularly supported measures it can undertake without being brought down by the invisible but very real power of capital even in an advanced welfare state. That power can be exercised through a myriad of legal and extralegal mechanisms as the briefest reference to attempted reforms by democratically elected leftist governments in this century can attest. *That* very real threat of overthrow and "strike of capital," backed up by the world capitalist order, is established in its most benign form through the world market and in its least benign form through an externally backed civil war and intervention. That threat acts as the real limit on how far one can move beyond the welfare state, not some abstract "objective" economic laws requiring a free market in capital and labor.

The only counterpower that even potentially exists against that constant possible veto of any major move toward greater equality and democracy on the part of a leftist government is massive popular organization of the type the Swedish labor movement possesses. In Sweden, labor has, at least potentially, the moral and organizational hegemony that capital has in the other industrial democracies. It can veto any attacks on the welfare state, and it can block any attempt on the part of capital to sabotage legislation. Imagine a political strike in a country where 85 percent of the work force is organized! Its numbers give it the organizational strength, but its solidaristic wage policies over protracted periods of time, which have reshaped Swedish income distribution in the direction of greater equality and equity, give it its moral weight. Unlike, for example, the Anglo-Saxon unions, Swedish labor did not favor the strategically better-placed and more powerful unions; instead it pushed for increases across the board as a conscious decision to reduce wage differentials between skilled and unskilled and between women and men. That is, they rejected the capitalist competitive norms when determining their strategy. This may at times cost them the support of the more skilled and professionally trained workers; changing values in what is increasingly a capitalist world culture is a daunting task. That is what makes democratic politics a continual struggle.

However, what a labor movement can do in Sweden is also limited by what it can persuade the majority of the electorate to accept. At this time there is a standoff. The proposals to move beyond the welfare state, and there were such proposals during the 1970s, do not yet have a convincing majority. Therefore, quite properly, the Meinder plan, which would effectively have abolished capitalism through wage earner funds, is on a back burner for the time being. I remain convinced that it will be revived and that it is viable, proper, and just. It is important to remember that political moods and consensuses have swung wildly in the past. It is dangerous to reify the present conservative mood and assume that it is carved in a rock; it may change, just as the moods of the late 1960s and early 1970s changed. Political attitudes do not develop in a unilinear and consistent way; at least they have not done so in the past.

Heilbroner's real question is, what would one need beyond the present social policies of a social democratic Sweden for it to be considered as moving toward socialism? My somewhat simplified answer is that to move toward socialism Sweden would have to move in two major directions at the same time. The first is to effectively expand control over the workplace and work life through the development of workplace committees and councils that would involve the vast majority of people in making the day-to-day decisions about their work life, personnel policy, and the overall direction their enterprise or institution should take. Such bodies should control the management and be regarded as the economic counterparts to local self-government and to citizen participation in exerting local power. In short, they would establish a working system of self-government in the economy.

The second would be to abolish the present concentrations of private ownership. Although mixed forms of property ownership—private, public, and cooperative, or mixtures of the three along the lines described by Alex Nove—seem to make overall sense, great concentrations of wealth are clearly incompatible with socialism or, for that matter, with democracy. Very steep progressive taxation, combined with an almost confiscatory inheritance tax, may alleviate this problem in more advanced welfare states, but we are still left with the question of social, economic, and political effect for great concentrations of wealth.

Gross differences in wealth and income are unacceptable from any point of view, either equity or democratic theory. The economic and social benefit of such concentrations for society as a whole is denied by the very existence of the Rockefellers of this world and their international brethren. But even the responsible and aesthetically acceptable superrich represent a problem for any genuine democratic polity. This is for many good and well-known reasons, the most important of which is that wealth tends to translate into political and social power. Democracy cannot exist in any meaningful manner when there are gross disparities in political power among citizens. Today that argument is sufficiently obvious and well established as to make the language of democracy the most effective language in which to express socialist arguments.

Thus, my ultimate argument is that the Swedish welfare state must, at some point in the future, move toward completing the democratic transformation of Swedish society. This would create an egalitarian democratic community of citizens in which social policies develop social and gender equality and economic policies create sufficient equality of power to make democracy itself possible within an advanced modern economy. For me, that is the goal of socialism today, not a utopia—that is to say, noplace—but rather a very specific place: the endless battlefield for real and effective equality and community within the existing advanced capitalist industrial societies.

World Capitalism Is Facing a Major Transformation

Socialism as an idea, as a movement, and as a practical program is in a crisis, as we have stated earlier in this chapter. This crisis is either welcomed or deplored depending on the person's point of view, but there is little argument that something of profound importance is happening to the most important secular movement of our century. However, there are many different aspects of political malaise that pass under the name of the crisis of socialism today. For one thing, it is not at all clear that socialism is in a more fundamental crisis than is either contemporary liberalism or conservativism. What is clear is that the major structural shifts in the societies and economies of the advanced capitalist industrial countries, combined with the prolonged stagnation since the oil shock of the early 1970s, have fundamentally shaken both the post–World War II optimism about the capacity for economic management of national economies and the relative social consensus that characterized the years of stable growth between 1950 and the mid-1970s.

The grotesque caricature of "socialism" that has existed under Communist-ruled dictatorships is in a terminal crisis, with the collapse of Eastern European Communist regimes and the transformation of the Soviet Union. The cold war is over. European unity will create an economic superpower dominated by a social democratic welfare-statist consensus, that is, a form of capitalism that is best described as neocorporatism. Within that European community the major power will be Germany. One of the consequences will be a relative decline in the economic and military importance of the United States, which consequently will have less moral and political authority. This will mean that although capitalism does have some time ahead for itself as a world system, it will be under new and peculiar circumstances. It will be without the familiar cold war, without the United States in its established role as the dominant world power, without a threat, real or imagined, of Soviet expansionism, and without a whole set of other things that were taken for granted and considered essential during the past four and a half decades.

We thus find ourselves today at a historical switching ground, with three new developments that come together, happily or unhappily, at one point in time. The three developments, again, are the collapse of the Communist dictatorships in Eastern Europe, the growing pace of European unification, and the end of the cold war. Each of these three would by itself be a major development; the three together make for a fundamental historic change, and whatever else will be the case after this, the world will not be as we have known it. It will take some time for the magnitude of these changes to sink in. However, the presently existing capitalism of the post–cold war era clearly will not be the capitalism we have know. Capitalism is not just an abstract system, nor is it solely an economic system, whatever that would mean. It is an integrated economic, political, and social system that has an indispensable political dimension.

Capitalism has its institutions and legal systems, armed bodies of men to protect it, a dominant ideology, and certain kinds of political relations on a world scale. It is a world system. More precisely, it is *the* world system. Capitalism is thus not simply the absence of socialism and feudalism. Capitalism is also a system in which the *political* rule of parties committed to the maintenance of capitalism, as it exists in real life, is necessary. This is the case whether the dominant party is nominally procapitalist or prolabor, conservative or social democratic. As it exists, capitalism implies the whole raft of political, economic, and social relations, including the not so minor question of which are the dominant groups, or more crudely put, the ruling class. In that sense capitalism is in very serious trouble.

The Specific Situations Are Not Rosy for Capitalism

Capitalism is in trouble in at least three places: the third world, Western Europe, and Eastern Europe. Let me take them in reverse order, keeping in mind that the fact that capitalism is in trouble is not always good news for democrats and democratic socialists. A very large section of the Eastern European intelligentsia in the opposition and even in the regimes is fascinated by the idea of the market today. However, that "market" has very little to do with the market as it exists in the real world, particularly the real capitalist world. The market, in former Communist states, is a synonym for getting the state and, above all, the party out of controlling the economy and the society and, through those, the politics of their respective countries. The market that is being introduced into those societies without a recent usable tradition of political democracy, without an established culture of political democracy, without developed free trade unions and alternative movements and parties, will result in something I would call the Mexicanization of Eastern Europe. There are many parallels between Mexico and a "Mexicanized" Eastern Europe. Both have to deal with giant superpowers, one in the north, one in the west; both will be mixed economies with a very powerful state sector and a corrupt and quite vital private sector with an elite that includes technocrats, trade unionists, corrupt trade unions, and decent trade unions, as well as the rich, as well as gangsters. I think we will have all of that in Eastern Europe. Whatever it will be, it will not be capitalism as it is described in any civics textbook and certainly not in any book describing free enterprise.

Post-Communist states in Eastern Europe and what had been the Soviet Union will emerge as highly politicized systems, where dominance over the political terrain will still manifest itself in the economy although it will be at least in good part a market economy. It will, *nota bene*, also be a market economy subject to considerable corruption as former members of the *nomenklatura* join foreign investors and the new post-Communist nationalist political elites in the scramble to grab up the more lucrative chunks of the economy at knock-down prices made possible through political connections. Happily, many will also lose their shirts, as always happens in gold rushes. Fates are sometimes just in allocating rewards.

Given the kinds of societies these are, my predictions are that some very grim and serious economic and social issues will emerge in the very near future in the new post-Communist states. The prognosis for the development of decent and democratic outcomes is best for those societies that will have powerful, old-fashioned, garden-variety, economistic trade unions, which are going to struggle to make sure that the burden of transformation of these societies is not borne entirely by the industrial workers and the other employees in those states. Whatever else is reported by Western journalists and analysts, the upheavals in Eastern Europe did not take place in order to abolish the crude and almost universal welfare systems. To the contrary, *improvements* in services, health, education, and pensions, not to speak of living standards, are expected, sooner rather than later, as a result of toppling unpopular authoritarian dictatorships. The proposal to introduce the raw market of what is called a "Thatcherite capitalism" is therefore politically inviable, even if it were morally and economically desirable, without authoritarian repression. Given the collapse of the Communist parties, that authoritarian repression can effectively come only from the Right or from strange new symbioses of former Communist technocrats with national populists. Therefore, the optimistic prognosis for Eastern Europe will be for parliamentary democracies with strong unions and mixed economies with, for historic reasons, a large socially owned or nationalized sector of the economy within that mixture. In other words, a social democratic type of neocorporatism similar to Western European welfare states, with somewhat larger publicly owned sectors. The pessimistic prognosis is for right-wing xenophobic, nationalist-populist, authoritarian neocorporatism with limited pluralism and democracy. Neither represents exactly the victory of capitalism that is being celebrated in the Western press. It should go without saying that neither represents the victory of socialism either.

In Western Europe, capitalism is also facing very peculiar circumstances. There are at least three forces that militate against capitalism as it is popularly understood, particularly in the United States and Great Britain; that is, the free market, the basic purpose of which is profit maximization. That system is, of course, a myth, although a very powerful myth. There are a number of obstacles to such a mythopoetic system dominating a unified European Community. In the first place, powerful trade unions are allied to the Social Democratic parties, which have a plurality in the European parliament and whose votes and prospects for increased political power, against all past predictions, are increasing or at least stable. In the second place, the Catholic church and the Social Christian parties it dominates do not take to naked possessive individualism with any more enthusiasm than do the Social Democrats—as a matter of fact, their formulation, which I find entirely reasonable, is that private property is morally acceptable, provided one understands that society holds a mortgage on it. Presumably, that means a mortgage that can be called in when the private property in question no longer serves socially acceptable means. And the third group, which is not exactly committed to free marketing or capitalism, consists of the Eurocrats, the increasingly influential European bureaucracy in the powerful commissions of the European Community in Brussels. The Eurocrats are economic- and social-interventionist statists, anything but free marketeers.

So the capitalism we will see in Western Europe in the coming decade will be a sort of neocorporatist arrangement, with powerful trade unions, an advanced welfare state, and a great many controls—conscious, politically imposed controls over what can and cannot be done with the movement of capital, where investments should go, and what social policies should be. In other words, a capitalism highly modified and defanged by an organized social democracy that will dominate *both* the individual nation-states and the European Community. This dominance will be, if anything, strengthened if the more successful new democracies in Eastern Europe develop a closer relationship to the European Community. Social democracy will clearly be stronger in a unified Germany. That may take time, but I believe it will be the case for a large number of reasons

This, of course, will not be socialism. This will be a capitalism of a sort, although one that will be almost unrecognizable to the American businessmen and their intellectual cheerleaders. It will be capitalism—I agree here with Robert Heilbroner—however, only in the sense that Sweden is a form of capitalism. But that then tells us something else, that the political, social, and economic terrain that contemporary capitalism represents in real life is an enormously wide one, and the political and social outcomes are not at all predictable. This is especially the case in the advanced parliamentary capitalist democracies of Western Europe. Once you have said a society is capitalist, you have not said very much about it. You are only beginning to describe that society and what can and cannot occur within it.

Contemporary socialism, as manifested in real life by the parties and government that still use that name, may, in advanced capitalist democracies, be doomed to end up being something that is in itself very worthwhile; the endless struggle for continued reform and improvement of the inequities and injustices of the existing capitalist system and the industrial civilization it has created. That, after all, was the view of Edward Bernstein, the first great Socialist revisionist. However, that socialism remains restricted to the definition of what is "realistic" within the definition of what is possible to do or attempt to do—or, without a utopia, what is even imaginable as a goal—in the existing order. The borders of what is possible are not even tested in one's imagination. The transition from feudalism to capitalism took centuries. It is entirely possible that a new postcapitalist social and economic order, a new social formation called socialism, will take centuries to develop. But it will make an enormous difference whether that development occurs in a society in which labor and the socialist parties are hegemonic, where the social and economic differences are diminishing, where social justice is legislated, and where a kind of democratic egalitarian welfare state exists that is more egalitarian than what the Communists have had over the past forty years. The difference in wages between a director of a Swedish factory and a worker, at least in the auto industry, has a ratio of 1 to 3. This is within a developed welfare state where, unlike the Communist regimes, the services are distributed in an egalitarian manner and bribery is unknown. That means the actual social and economic differences are smaller than they were in the Soviet

Union or anywhere in Eastern Europe. So when we say that Sweden is a capitalist society, we are saying something that needs to be qualified over and over again.

The third place in which capitalism clearly is not in very good shape is the third world. Despite the brief celebration of the economic results of the teachings of the Chicago school in Chile, Brazil, Ghana, Ivory Coast, and Argentina, it turns out that the formula that markets and capitalism necessarily bring about democracy is not true. Quite to the contrary, insisting on marketizing those economies, insisting on having them abide by the rules of the International Monetary Fund (IMF) and the World Bank, is an almost sure guarantee that in those societies democracy is endangered. They cannot be democratic and carry out the World Bank's economic cure, which generally includes cutbacks in already miserly social spending, freezing wages, and letting prices find their natural level. The economic burden such a policy imposes on the working population is not one that any popular regime or democratic polity can bear. That is the Achilles heel of the capitalism that has triumphed in the third world. It cannot be democratic.

Capitalism has triumphed in the third world, but it has triumphed in a very peculiar sense. The indispensable symmetrical opposite, the enemy, the Communist bloc, has collapsed. Therefore, its model for developing the third world has also collapsed. What remains of the Soviet Union is no longer a rival of a world capitalist system in the third world. It is difficult to treat somebody as a rival if he comes requesting loans and technological aid. It is extremely difficult to convince anybody now that there is a military threat from the former Soviet bloc. This could be for all kinds of reasons, not necessarily because Yeltsin is peace-loving.

What follows is that the main ideological prop of the postwar social order in the third world, the cold war, is now gone. That then means, to use an old-fashioned term, that the contradictions of the capitalist system itself become the terrain of political struggle. One cannot say anymore (not that it was ever morally valid, but unfortunately it was politically effective), "Yes, yes, we, or our paid thugs, murder nuns and priests. But there is a more dangerous Communist menace." And one cannot keep saying, "Free trade unions are a nice thing, but of course we will postpone that until we defeat communism or pro-Communist insurgency." But now we have defeated communism. Communism, rather, to put it more precisely, has defeated itself. So under those circumstances it means that the internal conflicts—the issues of social justice, trade union rights, public squalor and private wealth—are now being fought over and will be fought over in the next decade. An openly socialist party came within a hairbreadth of winning the first democratic election in Brazil campaigning on those issues.

The capitalists and their apologists are not very good at fighting those issues. That is in part because the love for capitalism as a system in the abstract is really limited to a very small section of the population. What I mean by that is that, for example, most Eastern Europeans I speak to love the market, abstractly. The market they love means a guaranteed job for them and, of course, for their children, their relatives, and their friends, as well as cheap housing, public health, free education, and a pension. Provided they have all of those things, they would love to have a market in which they could get jeans that fit and shoes that are attractive. But that is not really what the market is all about. That is the essential misunderstanding. Most of the free market supporters in Eastern Europe would be utterly shocked at the poverty and social injustices of American society. Poor as most of the Eastern European cities are, you will not find people sleeping in the streets. You will not find them sleeping in the streets in most of Western Europe.

The most obvious visible exception is Great Britain; social brutality and homelessness seem to be a contemporary Anglo-American specialty. However, once one can no longer wield the threat of an expansive dictatorial communism in political debate, a whole host of postponed social domestic issues become truly intolerable. If the whole set of issues on the domestic agenda, let us say in the United States, was postponed to deal with the Soviet menace, to permit the grotesquely huge military buildup, what happens when peace breaks out? What about the enormous cutbacks in military spending that are now politically feasible, not the piddling ones now proposed by the Bush administration and the Democratic Congressional leaders? What then happens to the social and political backlog of issues that are desperately needed? It is not only the Left that feels that America as a society has desperately overdue social agendas that have to be met if this is to be a minimally decent society, even a minimally decent capitalist society. This is why the smarter pundits of the American Right, like Kevin Phillips, predict that the 1990s will be a decade during which the pendulum will swing away from the conservative dominance that characterized the 1980s. He is right; the naked greed of the U.S. economic elites that has been unleashed by the years of Reagan and Bush does not inspire even minimal social cohesion and loyalty. Therefore, that unregulated capitalism the Reagan and Thatcher counterrevolutions created has a very poor prognosis for the future.

The capitalism that survives will be highly regulated. The Asian tigers did not get their development by leaving it to the free market; on the contrary, developmental success stories, just like that of the Western European miracle of postwar reconstruction, are based on sharply limiting capitalism and the market. The Anglo-Saxon ideological model of capitalism, that capitalism has to go hand in hand with the dismembering of the welfare state and a weak trade union movement and an increased gap between the poor and the rich, is archaic. In democratic societies capitalism that survives will be intertwined with an advanced welfare state with powerful trade unions and social movements. But then, the models of democracy inspired by eighteenth-century Whig theories that are dominant in the United States and Great Britain are also backward compared to those of continental Europe, where it is increasingly understood that an advanced welfare state is a part of the social contract on which modern democratic states rest. That is the minimal basis for the socially and politically accepted notions of common good without which democratic societies cannot remain legitimate. Perhaps the United States will prove capable of learning that from the European democracies.

Capitalism is indeed in serious trouble and has not triumphed. So what has triumphed? What has triumphed is the notion that socialism is not something that can be wished into being overnight. What has triumphed is the notion that there may be an extremely long period of social transition during which most countries will be a part of a single world market that is essentially capitalist. But what has not triumphed is all of the ideological and political baggage that goes with that. What has not triumphed is the worldview of the Chicago school, of Milton Friedman, of Margaret Thatcher, the Reaganauts, and the others, that very peculiar inefficient and puritanical version of capitalism that is really a part of Anglo-Saxon exceptionalism.

Organization of Work and Leisure: Key Issues in the 1990s

There are two powerful arguments for a radical assault on the organization of work in modern industrial society. The first is that the huge increases in productivity of the past two decades in the countries of advanced capitalism have simply not been fairly distributed. The wealthy got wealthier, and the workers got unemployed. Instead, a radical cut in the working day, week, and life of people could be financed by a frankly redistributionist wealth tax, rather than increases in income tax, which generally hit the middle- and lower-income groups. So the first argument to be made in a push for redistributive policies is that huge technological increases in productivity now make the traditional organization of work irrational and antisocial because it forces millions on the scrap heap of unemployment while the economic capacities exist to redistribute work and income more justly.

For a radical assault on the hours, days, and years of work to be anything but economic suicide for a specific country, the Social Democratic parties and the trade union movement must make that push internationally, beginning in the unified European Common Market and pushing similar changes at least in the advanced industrial countries for a start. Such a policy would also require more direct aid to the unions in the NICs (newly industrialized countries) like Brazil from the labor movements in the advanced industrial world. The reasons for the internationalization of labor strategy in this regard are even more obvious than in the others, given the ability of multinationals to shift funds and production around the world. That is one more reason why even moderate reformist, labor-based parties must now put the question of control over the export of capital and jobs on the political agenda.

A second argument for a redistributive strategy that is gender-sensitive is that an economy must have a *societal* purpose and, one could add, a moral justification; and surely a set of arrangements that dooms an increasing proportion of the population to marginal and insecure employment so that a small minority can get wealthy, in what is increasingly a "casino economy," cannot be it. Classical capitalism worked morally with the assumption that the massive pursuit of individual, rational, selfish economic goals would produce social good and an advanced technology and economy, which, in turn, improves the lives of all. That is increasingly made mockery of by an economy in which billions are not made by manufacturing or inventing new processes but by moving speculative paper and gambling on real estate.

The further point is that in this moral critique of capitalism and market fetishism Socialists are joined by the Catholic church in most of its recent statements on the economy and the dignity of labor. *Fulfilling, decent, well-paid, socially useful, and respected work is a human right, and it is a right superior to that of the right of capital to make larger profits.* Clearly, when a society cannot, for whatever reason, provide such work, it is obliged to at least provide decent, nonhumiliating support for however long it takes to restructure the economy so that it can provide the closest equivalent of full employment that is feasible. I am quite familiar with the "modern" argument against full employment and can make only two points about it. One is that it is not so new; it was very present indeed in the old classical socialist movement. Marx's son-in-law, Lafargue, even wrote a longish pamphlet titled *Why Work?* For a more modern argument, see John Keane's "Work and the Civilizing Process" in his *Democracy and Civil Society* (1988). The second point is that I believe the argument to be profoundly wrong because a new socialist civilization will not be based on new ways of distributing goods but *also and centrally* on reorganization and democratization of production. It is significant that it is the best-paid, most unionized, and most secure working classes in Europe—the Swedish, Norwegian, West German, and Dutch workers—who have been consistently the most willing to give the largest percentage of GNP that any country gives to third world governments, toward third world development. Their parties and trade unions have been exemplary in solidarity campaigns on behalf of liberation movements and trade unions in the third world. They are also the movements that have been most receptive to measures increasing equality of the sexes and have been the most responsive to ecological demands. They have pursued solidaristic wage-pattern bargaining, which has lowered the pay differentials between skilled and unskilled workers for decades. This collective bargaining strategy has tended automatically to lower the wage differentials between men and women. So one need not be all that pessimistic about the possibility of a decent egalitarian labor movement being able to convince people that they should act on the basis of solidarity and not only economic egotism for prolonged periods of time. However, that is a conscious policy that a political party and a labor movement have to decide to accept and pay the political price for, not something that comes naturally out of one's class location, as primitive Marxists used to think and argue.

Social Democratic Left Will Dominate a Unified Europe

The labor-based Socialist and Social Democratic parties,[14] as well as the former Italian Communists who are now allied to them, already form the single largest and most cohesive organized political group within the European Community Parliament. Despite all of their efforts and protestations to the contrary, the small ecologist Green group will find itself pulled into an alliance with this bloc, that is, if the Greens survive at all as a force separate from the broad Left. This has been a growing trend over the past two decades and was repeatedly confirmed in elections between 1989 and 1991, particularly in elections for the European parliament. Internationalism and transnational organizational ties and cooperation are generally more ideologically congenial to the Left than to the Right. The Right's "internationalism" has more often been expressed in the recent past as Atlanticism or the defense for unrestrained free trade. But the Right is uncomfortable with any kind of internationalism; indeed, *nationalism* and *protectionism* are more congenial to right-wing politics. For reasons already stated, Atlanticism, which was based on placing a primacy on close "special" relations with the United States, does not seem to have too rosy a future. In any case, the Reagan and Bush administrations have successfully educated a whole generation of Social Democratic leaders in Europe about the shortcomings of Atlanticism through their relentless hostility. Therefore, Atlanticism is not a matter of consensus within the Eurocracy or the states of the European Community but rather the property of the parties of the Right and Center. Even these old friends are no longer blindly faithful to the old alliance. Genuine free trade is also a nonstarter for the broad social Left in the European Community. The costs are fearfully obvious. The benefits of free trade are more obscure, except to the transnationals.

No other bloc of parties today operates in an organized manner throughout Western Europe to anywhere near the same extent that the Socialist parties and the allied institutions do. These institutions include the international secretariats of the International Confederations of Free Trade Unions. To be sure, both Socialist parties and the unions also attempt to operate in a global context, not only a European or Eurocentric one. However, the more effective cooperative arrangements for both the parties and the trade unions associated with European social democracy, broadly defined, are to be found in Western Europe. The more global non-European role is at this time often more an expression of intent than a reality, although the Socialist International contains a growing number of non-European parties. Liberal and Conservative parties are more parochial and thus limited to their specific national state, whereas the social Catholic parties, Catholic unions, and mass organizations are all but nonexistent in Northern Europe. The International Union of Socialist Youth, an international of the youth sections of the parties in the Socialist International, played an important role after World War II, in creating the present informal networks that connect a number of the present leaders of the Socialist parties. Many of them first met at international Socialist youth events for which no real parallel exists in nonsocialist parties. Paralleling these Socialist International organizations are the international secretariats of the trade unions, which are assuming more importance in coordinating transnational campaigns and struggles. Although some of these international institutions of the labor and socialist movements are mostly symbolic, symbols are important, and they form a network linking the Social Democratic institutions internationally in a way that has no equivalent in the bourgeois parties. The closest parallel are the Catholic parties and unions.

Even granting that a great deal, if not most, policymaking and policy proposal generation originates within the vast Eurocracy (European Common Market commissions and their bureaucracy) at this time, that does not weaken the dominant role of the pro-welfare-state broad Left and Left Center in the European Economic Community (EEC). This is because that bureaucracy tends to be generally "statist," that is, sympathetic to a broadly interventionist role of the state in the formation and financing of social policy. Such a view willy-nilly places the European bureaucracy in conflict with British conservative and other neo-Darwinian market enthusiasts and on the side of those who argue for a social Europe and for a maximalist view of what the unification of the market in 1992 should include. Whether openly or more discreetly, the Eurocrats tend to support the steady growth of the prerogatives of the bodies of the European Community in respect to the individual member states.

It is important to remember that whereas the Left, particularly the far Left, has had an authentic and vigorous antistatist and anti-institutional tradition of its own, most recent antistatist discourse has been the language of the market-oriented Right. The social movements, as well as the broad Left, have to restore legitimacy to the idea that an active, interventionist democratic state is needed to assure the minima of decent social and civic service that a modern society needs. That is a major field for intellectual and political contestation in the immediate future. The contest will be affected by any future expansion of the EEC.

The expansion of the EEC to include the European Fair Trade Association (EFTA) will strengthen this "natural" majority of leftist labor-based parties within a unified Europe. For one thing, it will bring the strongly Social Democratic and welfare state–oriented Scandinavian bloc, with its powerful trade unions and labor parties, into the EEC. The unification of the Germanies will further strengthen this "left" or social tilt of the EEC after the euphoria of unification fades and the grim economic and social costs of unity begin to be felt. Even the non-Left and vehemently anti-Communist parties in what used to be East Germany accept an advanced welfare state as a given. Roughly a third of the German electorate voted for the Left even under the unfavorable conditions of a momentum in favor of the ruling center-right coalition created by a national euphoria. By April 1991 the German electorate not only began to revert to its more normal voting patterns, it swung sharply against Chancellor Kohl and his Christian Democrats in the critical election in the Rhineland-Palatinate, giving the state *(Land)* to the Social Democrats for the first time since World War II.[15] This also gave the Social Democrats control of the upper house of the German Parliament. In any case, even the Christian Socialists in Germany are, for the most part, also committed to a high degree of social spending and to an advanced welfare state. Their majority represents a neo-corporatist and less confrontational line within modern capitalism, in sharp contrast with the practices of the Anglo-Saxons. Their own term for their capitalist economy is a *social* market economy. Labels are sometimes politically important. The economic and social dislocation that has followed the very rapid integration of the East German economy has produced increasingly sharp political reaction. My guess is that the long-range beneficiaries will be the German Social Democrats.

These are only some of the reasons ideological conservatives like Thatcher had become increasingly and shrilly "little European" by the late 1980s, that is to say, minimalist when it came to the economic and social policy prerogatives of the EEC. It was one of the principal reasons Thatcher had to be removed by her own party: anti-Europeanism is becoming bad politics, left, right, and center in Europe today.[16] Even the traditionally and proudly neutral Swedish Social Democrats have accepted the necessity of entering the Common Market, which in *their* case, given that Sweden has the most advanced welfare state and most powerful union movement in Europe, means a step backward. That step is inevitable to be able to survive in an ever more "internationalist" economic arena dominated by transnational banks, financial institutions, and corporations.

For one thing, the Swedish financial and industrial elites had the constant goad of the growing European Common Market, with its more permissive economic rules, before their eyes. This has made them chafe under the restrictive Social Democratic legislation of Sweden and resent the costs of the more generous welfare state even more than they normally would have. The result is both a more politically confrontational scene at home and, even worse, a constant financial hemorrhaging of the Swedish economy as money poured out into the less restrictive European economy. Because the effective creation of barriers to the export of capital is practically all but impossible, when political costs are figured, the Swedish Social Democrats have been forced to propose a retreat into the Common Market. Their situation dictates a larger arena and market than one that can be provided by a single medium-size state for the further defense of the welfare state and union gains. That arena is the EEC, particularly *tomorrow's* EEC, with its ever-widening set of pan-European regulations and social and economic policies. That will require a lowering of the extraordinarily steep Swedish income taxes to something more in line with Northern European norms. It will also mean taking a few relatively minor steps back in those aspects of Swedish welfare state policy that are too far out in front of the EEC averages. These steps will be minor, but they are sure to be resisted bitterly by the unions. Social politics in Sweden promises to be much more confrontational in the near future. It is the very good fortune of the Swedish Social Democrats that, by narrowly losing the 1991 elections to an unstable coalition of non-Socialist parties, they will reap the political advantages of the fact that a non–Social Democratic government will carry the onus for the unpopular measures that will have to be taken in order to integrate Sweden into the EEC.

Although such standardization and leveling of social and economic policies will temporarily water down the most advanced programs of a few Scandinavian countries, it will also immensely aid the less-developed parties of Europe. Swedish entry into the Common Market will, with their natural Scandinavian allies (Norway is likely to enter the EEC at the same time Sweden does), increase the weight of the "social" bloc in the EEC. That point has been very well understood by the Mediterranean Socialist parties, like those of Greece and Spain, that look to the EEC to provide European minimal standards of social policies, including pensions, minimal wages, and union rights. This will clearly be a leveling upward for the southern members of the EEC. It is only through a massive leveling upward of the less-developed part of the EEC that a solid base of social and, even more important, political unification of the EEC is possible.

Common citizenship and a sense of a commonwealth in a contemporary Europe, increasingly linked by nearly universal literacy and communications, is not possible if economic differences are too stark, if they are perceived to be fundamentally unjust. This general principle will have to be slowly but surely extended, first to the rest of Europe, creating a genuine community from the Atlantic to the Urals, and later even further. Such a Europe could even try to create a new and very different alliance of developed countries to which a nonhegemonistic United States would be welcome. But that alliance would have to have a purpose beyond furthering trade and increasing the wealth of the already rich. A peaceful and democratic EEC cannot indefinitely continue to exist in a world where most humanity is doomed to famine, tyranny, and wars. In sheer self-preservation, if for no better reason, it has to organize to do battle with these scourges of humanity. To join in that battle is to struggle for the creation of the world human community. Such a community can come into being only through prolonged efforts, which must be inspired by values that are, in effect, universalist. Democracy, community, and equality are not bad starters for such values.

6

Conclusion

Between Demos and Ethnos

History does *nothing*, it "possesses *no* immense wealth," it "wages *no* battles." It is man, real living man, that does all that, that possesses and fights; "history" is not a person apart, using man as a means for its *own* particular aims; history is *nothing but* the activity of man pursuing his aims.

—Karl Marx and Friedrich Engels, *The Holy Family*

The Fatalism of Received Political Wisdom

We have completed a decade in which the citizens of advanced industrial democracies have been widely assured that it is not possible for any humanly constructed political and economic arrangements to provide a decent living for most of the people. Although this assertion originated with the Anglo-Saxon conservative duo, Great Britain and the United States, their startlingly reactionary dogmas have dominated the social policy and political debates of the decade throughout the West. Since the late 1980s these views also have been dominant among the intellectual elites and policymakers in the post-Communist states in East-Central Europe and what used to be the Soviet Union.

A minimal state, private property and unrestrained marketization are the foundation of the new paradigm in politics and social policy. Insistence on this paradigm endangers the potential for a democratic transformation of the post-Communist states. Following it creates social and economic strains that fragile new democratic arrangements cannot sustain. Democracy is not long for this world if it comes packaged with insecurity, unemployment, and a drop in real living standards for the majority. Even the celebration of a renewed or restored national identity cannot provide sustained support for a new social order that demands great material sacrifices from the majority and offers great rewards to small minorities.

The conservatives and their new fellow travelers sincerely believe that prosperity has to begin with a wholesale attack on the role of the state in social policy, that dismembering the welfare state, inadequate as it already was in the Anglo-Saxon countries,[1] is the key to massive prosperity. Or put differently, that cutting back on social entitlements for the large majority *and* turning loose and removing restrictions from the rapacious greed of the tiny stratum of speculative gamblers in a casino economy would *ultimately* provide a solid base for prosperity for all. Oddly enough, it did not work out that way. To the contrary, the income differences have increased sharply, the large majority is worse off and more insecure, and only the very rich have gotten richer.[2]

Massive deindustrialization has wiped out decent-paying blue-collar jobs. The economic infrastructure has been permitted to decay, schools have been starved of funds and fail to produce skills that can be useful in a postindustrial economy, and public transport is increasingly squalid. The cities are becoming more unpleasant to live in and, not so strangely, keep losing jobs. Wealth is now made not by inventing or making things and by new manufacturing processes but rather by gambling on real estate, shaky papers, junk bonds, and savings and loan operations.

Was the dismal result of a decade of Thatcherism and Reaganomics fated? Is it the case that economic and social consequences of capitalism at this stage of development are absolutely impervious to political intervention by—yes, let us not shy away from the word—states? Is the economic system so international today that by now no state, not even the United States, can *have* its own economic or industrial policy? These are questions that can be extended further.

Are there *any* policy options whatsoever in Eastern Europe and the former Soviet Union? Can the third world countries be anything but passive observers of world economic trends? *How much room is left for human agency, for free will, in today's political economy*? Just how much can an independent Europe be genuinely independent? In addition to economic fatalism, political institutions and habits seem all but impervious to change.

Can a democratic and egalitarian politics be constructed for our era that is not hopelessly dragged back by the excessive fragmentation of issue constituencies, on one hand, or marginalized by the ruling class's ideological domination of the mass media on the other? In other words, are democratic egalitarian politics possible at all? Or are blind, uncontrollable forces of an ever more integrated world economy out of any human control? Herbert Marcuse was fairly clear on this issue. His answer was that democracy in capitalist states was a sham.[3] Others, with more soothing theories, have argued that the *form* of democratic politics remains possible, provided one does not do anything excessively rash: "democracy" requires that there be a low level of conflict and confrontation.[4] "Rash" means actually making some decisions that might change things in way that would inconvenience the real holders of power in a capitalist society, who are, unsurprisingly, the capitalists. The academically proper way to state the above proposition is that democracy is possible only if no vital interests or passions are at stake. Clearly, if that is so, it rather does stack things in favor of those for whom the existing order is not so bad. *They* can wait for "responsible" incremental reforms indefinitely

Democratic Politics Require Hope and Self-confidence

But what about those whose situation is not so fortunate—the vast majority who were born of the wrong color, gender, ethnic group, or, above all, class to have had it made from the very beginning? What about entire societies and states that are latecomers to the feast? Is it the message of contemporary political wisdom that democracy is a nice sandbox for citizens to play in, if they insist, but that real decisions involving their personal destinies and those of their societies and, above all, their *economies* are made elsewhere? The argument of both neoconservative *and* neoliberal theorists is that these decisions *should be* made elsewhere for the greater good of society, which is here used as a synonym for the existing social order. These are the kinds of questions that will determine if there is a future either for the Left or for democratic politics in the new century.

In an era of unprecedentedly rapid political, technological, and social transformation, the received academic wisdom is fatalistic about the effect of human agency on society and the economy. It is as if *anno mirabilis* 1989 never took place in Eastern Europe. What forces exactly are supposed to have toppled the Communist authoritarian regimes throughout the region—elves?

We are told that even the existing welfare state in America, one of the skimpiest in the industrialized world, is not only too expensive but that it harms the needy. That proposition is linked to assumptions about a future stagnant economy in which decent jobs will become even scarcer. However, that economy was not the result of divine intervention or creation, it was man-made. An economic policy encouraging close to full employment, at decent union wages, would benefit society as a whole. If only a small percentage of people were unemployed or on welfare, it would not matter *economically* how generous benefits were.[5]

A Democratic State Is a Must for Democracy and Social Justice

Antistatism is an issue on which the democratic Left is responsible for much of the ideological and political confusion about democracy, socialism, and capitalism. The confusion lies in the ambivalent attitude the Left has had toward the role of the state in democratic societies. I do not think that it is possible to begin dealing with the problems of capitalism until the notion that a popularly controlled democratic state is a good thing is relegitimated. Abstract and popular antistatism on the Left has generally been trivial, whereas for the conservatives it has successfully served the economic and social political agendas of the Right.

It is not the libertarian Right but real-life political conservatives and reactionaries who set the social agenda. Antistatist rhetoric in America and Europe almost always has been a cover for a consistent, continual use of the state in favor of the rich, the greedy, and the powerful. This antistatism is where possessive individualism becomes the jointly held, common ideology of both the Left and the Right.

This ideology is one of the reasons much of the Left in America really could not ever relate in a sensible way to European social democracy. The criticism was that social democracy was statist, which is the case; it undoubtedly does use the state to deliver services. American leftists are more often than not communitarians. We believe in doing it from the bottom up. So as a consequence, you hear drivel from the Left in the United States like "We like the generous and competent child care the French provide, but we Americans find it unacceptable for ourselves. We want something in which parents can make the basic decisions. Failing that, we would rather not have any child care system." The result of this self-indulgent nonsense is that we do not have any child care at all for most people.

Americans want parents and localities to participate in running the schools—and we have a school system that is the shame of the Western world. We want more individual autonomy to do our own thing. And one effect of that resistance to using state authority for legitimate, democratically determined goals is that most people think of the political processes in America as something nasty, dirty, murky, and dominated by the immigrant workers and ethnic minorities in the cities, who are into collective action for group and individual betterment.

The liberals in the United States still cannot come to terms with the fact that they are not going to have a decent society with political parties that are not responsible to either a party membership or an electorate. It cannot be a matter of brand X versus brand Y with a Ralph Nader to see to it that they compete cleanly; there must be a *content* to politics, not merely a form. We have a great deal to learn about the limits of possible reformist action through state intervention if we are going to live under capitalism, no matter how it is modified by the actions of the democratic state responding to pressures from organized and unorganized labor. The state increasingly becomes the terrain, perhaps the most important terrain in contemporary societies, for class and political struggle.

The Democratic State Is the Framework for a Civil Society

In Eastern Europe the first goal of democratic opposition has to be the creation of a legal order, a *Rechtstaat,* with a judiciary system independent of the state, a richly varied civil society autonomous from the state and the dominant political parties, genuine mass democratic trade unions and a multiparty parliamentary democracy. In other words, Eastern Europe will be forced to move beyond the social movements to *institutionalize* a democratic state and political organizations. Nationalism and anticommunism are not enough.

These are necessary but not sufficient prerequisites for the struggle for genuine democracy, which should include workers' control in the workplaces, and popular, grass-roots participatory authority in the various institutions and authorities of local government. However, these goals are not *counterposed* to the institutionalization of a democratic polity. To the contrary, fighting for these goals requires stable democratic institutions, political parties, and the development of a democratic political culture. A parliamentary democracy with powerful unions, parties and social movements is the optimal terrain on which to work for democratic change. This requires tolerance, a virtue that is rare enough anywhere and positively priceless in Eastern Europe, where common sense argues against pushing political and national differences to the limit, at least until democratic institutions develop some firmness and stability—in other words, legitimacy.

However, what makes good sense in the long or even medium run is all too rarely the same policy that provides most immediate political advantage. Tolerance of differences is essential to building stable democratic regimes. It is the precondition for a democratic civic culture. That means no vengeance, no matter how justified, no witch hunts of former Communist hard-liners, no attempts to illegalize Communist parties, and above all, no hunt for scapegoats for what will be economic and social grim times for most of post-Communist Eastern Europe. Those scapegoats will be, all too often, those who are ethnically different, the minorities and Jews, or intellectuals or political liberals or leftists.

Eastern Europe is populated today with ghosts of chauvinist, populist, and right-wing and corporatist parties. It is important to try to keep those ghosts quiet and buried. Nationalism is the red meat of the organic, "genuine" Heideggerian national community, which is all too easy to mobilize against a mere "cool" legal and rational democratic universalism. It is therefore a continual threat to those who would build a multiparty, democratic, parliamentary legal order. It does not help the prospects for democracy or tolerance that so many of the reformist democratic intellectuals have passionately fallen in love with the idea of the market. For the love of that idea, almost as much suffering may be visited on the population of Eastern Europe as had been for the equally abstract idea of centralized planning. There seems to be no limit to how much suffering can be imposed on the living bodies of existing societies in the name of abstract ideas. That apparently is the original sin of intellectuals. They have thus set themselves up to be blamed for the grim consequences of their present infatuation with yet one more abstraction.[6]

The road to democratization runs through perilous straits in Eastern Europe. It has many enemies. Although few are open enemies of democracy, many are covert. They include what remains of the Communist parties and the bureaucrats in the state and other institutions, populists, nationalists, and technocrats. That is why it is essential to help democratic institutions, trade unions, and civic groups with massive moral, political, and material support from the West. That must supplement generous economic and technological aid to these societies. The EEC and EFTA are already more generous and effective in this task than the United States has been.

Genuine political democracy requires at least minimal commitment to social justice and egalitarianism. Those are essential if there is to be sufficiently wide acceptance that there exists a common polity worth defending. Effective political equality is not consistent with great differences in wealth. Wealth all too easily translates into political power. More to the point, the social solidarity required to make the sacrifices necessary to modernize the Eastern European economies without authoritarianism cannot be generated with an untrammeled, so-called pure market economy. That requires that the social order be considered minimally just and committed to the general good, not just to the maximization of production and profit. But economists love models, and models, in order to be clear, simplify and all too often ignore the social consequences and political costs. There is no such thing outside of economic models and classrooms, as a "purely" economic policy that can be isolated from social and political consequences.

The present world economy, with low growth and stagnation for most of the past decade, has reinforced the assault on progressive social policies. Social Darwinism, economic egotism, and "toughness" became politically fashionable on the right. This was aided by a growing intellectual and programmatic crisis on the left. The attacks on the social programs and on the whole idea that the state has major responsibilities for the welfare of its citizens in the United States and Great Britain have turned out to be a form of self-fulfilling prophecy. As the ideologically inspired budgetary cuts crippled and warped the social programs of the welfare state, the remaining programs became more socially mean and inadequate. The shifts in population created through migration of the work force mean that the poor and badly paid are often members of different ethnic groups and do not generate much solidarity from the larger community. Racism and nationalism weaken the ties of community and solidarity essential to providing a broad political base for a welfare state and income transfers. The development of a separate, transclass youth culture in much of the industrial world has also weakened transgenerational solidarity.

The secularization of mass socialist movements in the present mass societies of Europe has also weakened the solidaristic values that supported an egalitarian welfare state. All of these trends together have diminished the minimal sense of community necessary to maintain a notion of common good that would justify common efforts and sacrifices for a better society for all. As a consequence the remaining social programs became less broadly popular politically and more explicitly limited to the poor and dependent populations.

A Broad New Alliance for Social Justice and Democracy

The historic changes in world Catholicism over the past several decades have strengthened the socially progressive wing of the church. This is most obviously the case with North/South issues but also extends to issues of war and peace, social justice, and democracy. This in turn raises the possibility of a de facto alliance between social democracy and Catholicism. Such an alliance, made much easier to imagine by the collapse of communism as a contending *world* system, could focus on three major areas: a joint concern with North/South issues, accepting that the North has a major responsibility to help the South; a joint agreement on a defense of the right of workers to their own unions and movements; and a joint concern with joining social justice and democracy. Democratic socialists and social Catholics are thus *both* in fundamental conflict with the neoliberal fetishization of the market as the end-all and be-all of social and economic policy.

The Catholic church[7] is no more willing to accept the cult of market as the supreme regulator of what is socially and culturally desirable than are the democratic leftists. The church does not approve the most widespread U.S. ideological export, the celebration of possessive individualism as the ultimate value in a free society. Like the socialists, the church—or more accurately in this case, the churches—believes in collectivities and cooperation, in mutual support and responsibility. These are basically anticapitalist values. This is more important than it may seem on the surface, since the Vatican has been a firm ally of the United States during the years of intense cold war. In many European countries the Catholic hierarchy was a major barrier against the Left, both Communist and non-Communist.

The role of the church in social and economic politics, as an ally of the anti-Communist and antireformist political right wing, is over today. The church has already shifted its stand on the issue of redistributive justice for the impoverished South. It is likely to steadily extend that same reasoning to the poor in the North. Who are the poor? That is a relative question once the most basic needs have been met. However, the policies of the Catholic bishops in the United States, as well as the sense of anger that seeps through the statements on social policy and social justice, is very congenial to American democratic socialists. This shift increasingly makes the church and the churches allies of the democratic labor and socialist movements in a worldwide struggle for greater equality and social justice.

Although sharp differences will remain—above all, on issues of culture and sexuality—the two largest international movements increasingly find themselves allied. That potential alliance bodes well for the likely outcomes of the conflictual social and economic politics of the twenty-first century, or at least it means that the transnationals and the politics of greed will be given a genuine fight.

Nationalism and Populism Are Substitutes for Democracy

What is to bind complex states and communities of the near future into polities that are accepted as legitimate parameters within which to make political decisions? One thing could be a common concept of social justice and citizenship. That is because the very idea of a political community will have to become much wider, as it becomes clear that ethnically homogeneous states are a thing of the past. If it is not to be organic ties of kith and kin, of a common traditional and confessional culture, that bind a polity, what else is it to be? Another could be agreement that the rules of the game are fair and just, that newcomers have access to the game on relatively fair terms; that is to say, that the system is democratic and open to new players.

But can democracy exist at all in the polity if unrestrained plutocracy reigns in the economy? And even if the two theoretically could coexist as separate spheres, so to speak, like the separation of church and state, can the great barons of the economy be prevented from trying to influence the polity? And if they do, what then becomes of fair and just political competition among citizens over choices for the state and society? Even posing the question in this manner requires that one acknowledge that this *very theoretical* division between the economy and the state is precisely what is supposed to be the unique advantage of capitalism *and* that maintaining that division requires the kinds of restraints on the economic behavior of individual wielders of great wealth, on behalf of the stability of the system as whole, that they find obnoxious.

That question is being answered in its own unsatisfactory way by the revived national populists in former Communist states and by Islamic fundamentalism in the Middle East and North Africa. Both have answers that are capable today of mobilizing passionate commitment and massive support,[8] which is why post-Communist populist governments in Eastern Europe are not hastening to sell off nationalized industries to foreign investors but are keeping them nationalized. The Moslem fundamentalists simply reject the very notion of a separation of religion and state or of state and society, let alone religion and the economy.

National populists assert the primacy of the nation, or rather the Nation, the *ethnos* rather than the *demos*, expressing itself through its own state. It is as if all of the Eastern European nationalists had adopted the narrow Zionist definition of the relationship of the people, the political nation, to the state. In point of fact, contemporary Croatian, Slovak, Polish, and Serbian nationalists, much like the Zionists, even insist on "the right of return"—not for the *citizens* of their states, to be sure, but for the members of the chosen dominant nation. In defining the legitimate borders of the nation, all kinds of mutually contradictory arguments are used. God's will as expressed in Scriptures is convenient but applied only to Israel. It is no guide to just boundaries between Serbs and Croats, Ukrainians and Russians, or Kurds and everyone else. The most commonly accepted argument among liberals and democrats is some version of the Wilsonian argument based on self-determination. Unfortunately, in many disputed areas that is hard to establish and even harder to achieve. For example, is it self-determination of the *present* population or of the original population? How far back in the past does one go? If only the status quo is used, is this not rewarding forcible transfers of population? Do the Germans forcibly removed from Sudetenland in Czechoslovakia or from Silesia in Poland have a just claim to return?

Conflicting claims are the norm in much of the world. When convenient, nationalists insist on historical boundaries, meaning those boundaries from the historical past that would support a claim to a disputed territory, rather than those boundaries that reflect the political choices of the present inhabitants. Of course, in those *other* cases, where the historical argument is weak or nonexistent but the ethnic composition of the population is favorable, the plebiscitary argument (it is the will of the people) is used. Where neither historical nor ethnographic arguments exist, the argument of strategic necessity is used. But when all arguments fail, force or forcible defense of a desired status quo is employed. Ultimately, that tends to be the most effective argument, alas.

Ironies abound, and Israel's relationship to the West Bank represents an explicit model for some of the Eastern European nationalists about how to treat areas inhabited by other national groups. This extends even to those nationalists whose predilections for right-wing populism and organic nationalism emphasizing "blood and soil" might, under some circumstances, have been expected to turn to anti-Semitism. The parallel of the right-wing

Zionist attitudes in Yugoslavia with the expressed Serbian attitude toward Kosovo (which, unfortunately for them, happens to be inhabited by as large an Albanian majority as the West Bank's Arab majority) are striking. They are even explicitly recognized by the Serbian nationalists. But then, Serbian right-wing nationalists also regard *both* Israel and Serbia as victims of a worldwide Islamic fundamentalist conspiracy. Neither the Israeli nor the Serbian case has a thing to do with democracy. Some Georgian nationalists go even further: they would give Georgian citizenship only to those who can prove that their ancestors lived there in 1804! Estonian and Latvian nationalists propose to restrict the vote of members of other nationalities, living in those countries since 1945, on crucial questions while giving that vote to their own ethnic nationals who immigrated generations ago. A similar line is taken by the Fiji Islanders and the inhabitants of New Caledonia, that is, that the vote must be restricted to the "original" inhabitants, no matter how long the other citizens of the country have lived there. It is an old, if not necessarily honorable, position that there is a "state people," and all others are there on sufferance with lesser rights.[9]

Nationalists, in both their traditional and populist variants, pose a major challenge, even obstacle, to the transition to democracy in many parts of the world. However, they certainly do mobilize passionate support. Therefore, any effective democratic program must take into account national sentiments and desires for identity and *combine* them with individual citizen rights for all. That is difficult, but ignoring national feelings is impossible. Surely, an adequate alternative to nationalism for democrats cannot just be the cold bureaucratic-rational community of minimal economic common self-interests projected by the Eurocracy in the European Community and the liberals in the United States. *Nor* can it be the social Darwinian jungle of the free marketeers who support the most minimal state, except when it comes to repression, and defend the inspiring proposition that individual pursuit of greed is the supreme road to achieving a decent society.

Nor yet can a democratic community be built within a polity conceptualized merely as a perpetual bargaining ground for mutually hostile ethnic, gender, and single-issue social movements bound by no idea of the common good. Worse, not only is an idea of the common good itself absent, but a part of the bargaining is about past wrongs, which must be paid by those who did not commit or benefit from them. (We can leave out the cases where what is sought is not even retribution but vengeance.) Such a polity may be accepted as a potential paymaster for one's *true* community (ethnic, gender, life-style, generational, etc.), where one bargains for the most that one can get, unbound by any sense of mutual interdependence, but not as the legitimate democratic arena for politics. It is not the organic "passionate" politics of *pays réel*[10] or the abstract alienated politics of *pays légal* or even the mutually antagonistic, fragmented politics of interest groups and social movements that provide a basis for a modern democratic political community and state. Such a state and democratic civil society are possible if there is an overarching idea of the common good, of a purpose for organizing politically. That is provided today by democratic socialist politics at its best; it is also provided by social Christianity or more precisely, social Catholicism.

Democratic socialism posits the possibility of a voluntary fellowship or movement that does not consider the "believers" as part of a hierarchically organized, suprademocratic, transnational institution. In short, it is a more open community with a more limited, less totalizing view of what is *common* and what is private. Catholics, like Islam, unfortunately, have a set of beliefs about rules of individual human behavior, derived from their particular faith, that are not subject to negotiation and modification through democratic debate and are valid *and enforceable* for all, including nonbelievers. Religious ultraorthodox Jews stone *others* when those others desecrate the Sabbath or dress in a way the faithful consider objectionable. There is nothing in the least bit tolerant and pluralistic about this behavior, and the claim to special (i.e., different) treatment is sometimes explicitly stated. "We are *supposed* to be different," states an anonymous Lubavitcher Hasid, responding to proposals for community conciliation and dialogue.[11]

Universalist rules, specifying morality and personal codes of conduct create a problem for all living in states that are not composed exclusively of believers. Contraception, abortion, divorce, civil marriage, veiling women, and religious instruction in public schools are only the best-known examples. But we must not cheat here, socialists and democrats *also have* their own universalist values, which they enforce when they can. These values are often less overarching than those that come from religion, but their impact on individual behavior is not necessarily less immediate. Children have been taken away from parents, mostly foreign workers adhering to differing cultural standards, by social workers, on behalf of the state, for failure to meet the social standards of Swedish society. Traditionalist views on how children should be disciplined or brought up are unacceptable. We democratic socialists also generally support vigorous enforcement of laws preventing child marriage, widow burning, bride dowry killing, child labor, corporal punishment of children, and the abandonment of the old.

Many democrats, of whom I am one, support compulsory *public* schooling up to the age of eighteen for both sexes, something that may clash with religious and national customs *and individual* preference. For that matter, I am against religious schools, except as voluntary after-hours or weekend options. This is because (a) I believe that society has a right to participate in the socialization of its future citizens and that this is not a decision to be left exclusively to the parents, and (b) that when there are private *and* public schools, the public ones will, after time, suffer from fiscal neglect as children of the better-situated are withdrawn into private schools.

One can also argue that proposition when it comes to transportation, medicine, universities, and a variety of other essential services provided to the public. Generally, in capitalist societies, when a two-tier system is provided, the public sector will be starved and abandoned to those who have no choice. Why is it that none but the most ferocious of free-market ideologues argues for a private police force? To be sure, a case could be made, *and is* being made in the United States, to "privatize" the prison system. Why not also probation, the courts, the military, the post office, and the intelligence community? In practice, many of those are already semiprivate or have private equivalents. That is the trouble.

There are those who would march to different drummers and live in "intentional" (i.e., voluntary) communities bound by their own rules. This includes religious communities, communes, psychoanalytic cults, and the like. I simply claim that their right to do so is necessarily limited in a democratic polity. It is especially limited when it comes to rights over others, like their "own" children or spouses. No one owns anyone, even if custom, ancient or newly invented, and religion might grant such power.

But that means that we radical democrats would not accept as equally valid a number of other, mostly non-European codes of behavior. My own personal answer today is as culturocentric as that of an eighteenth-century British conqueror of Bengal. "We hang people who burn women" was his response when informed that widow burning was a local custom sanctified by religious tradition. Quite, except, of course, like most civilized people, I also oppose the death penalty. There are other forms of restraint available to society and a democratic and civilized state.

The broad democratic Left remains the staunchest defender of the welfare state; in this it retains as allies the progressive majority wings of the churches as well as those "technocrats" who realize that broad social programs and entitlements are worth their cost in stability and the creation of a work force needed in the future. The costs of education, retraining, transport, communication, housing, health, and other infrastructural essentials *have* to be carried by the society as a whole and organized through the state. That state should be democratic and decentralized to the maximum, but it cannot retain even minimal effectiveness if it is not seen as an extension of an essentially just society. That is why attacks on the welfare state and social justice are so destructive of community and inimical to a modern economy and society.

Democracy does have a fighting chance in the twenty-first century, but it will have to go beyond matters of procedure and participation, both of which are important, to questions of equality and social justice. Such a democratic world order, not the hegemony of a superpower or of a consortium of the rich, may lead to the beginning of a genuine world human community. The contours of such a community will have to develop through trial and error; it certainly will not be uniform and will vary from region to region, responding to different histories and political cultures. However, this community, if it is to be worthwhile, no matter how heterogeneous, will need certain minimal but firm universalist values at the core: growing equality between occupations, genders, ethnic groups, and regions; universally available decent housing, health, and schools; accessible protection against one's own state and the community; fair access to political participation; the right to identity, both collective, as nations and voluntary organizations, and individual, as citizens; and, not the least, the right to decent creative work.[12] These are some of the minima of a decent society and world community.

Politics of the Possible: An Egalitarian Welfare State

There is today a broad, generational, postmodernist current of irrationality with its roots deep in the seductively brilliant thought of Nietzsche and Heidegger, which is at its core elitist and antidemocratic, even though that thought is often absorbed only in the flattened, simplified version popular among today's students and intellectuals. This is the cloven hoof of earth mother communitarianism, the need for the organic, the authentic feeling and for passion as against the cool "patriarchal" logic of the broad Left. This trend includes the rejection of science as well scientistic fetishism. And, of course, it is permeated by utter contempt for the warp and woof of genuine democracy, for discussion, give and take, compromise, and elected representative bodies.

However, it is clear that the defense and imaginative and intelligent expansion of an egalitarian universal welfare state are not minor issues. For one thing, it is clearly the most broadly popular and acceptable of the current, immediate socialist programs, and it is where their public support is widest. It directly affects the lives of the millions who live today and sets the parameters within which one can develop policies and strategies for going further. Therefore, we must insist that the social welfare state as a principle of organization of modern industrial democracies is part of the democratic social contract, a civic right, *not a field for political bargaining*. An attack on the welfare state is an attack on the legitimacy of the social order itself in a modern democracy.

The second point is that an advanced welfare state must be increasingly egalitarian. It must radically reduce the range of economic and social differences and keep reducing those differences, mostly through a combination of steeply progressive income taxes and massive investments in universally available and distributed social goods—schools, child care, health, culture, housing, leisure, pensions, and the rest—thus sharply reducing the part of income that is made up by salaries. Socialists favor large inheritance taxes as a matter of social principle and equity so that all individuals have a right to make their own lives according to their talents, efforts, and choices. Within such parameters, however, democratic socialists will favor diversity and the minimal of societal interference with personal choice and liberty.

Production of goods, however, is not a personal thing but a supremely social task. Therefore, the goal of a socialist policy is that production basically should be socially owned and democratically controlled and organized, with whatever plurality of forms of social and private property and combinations of market allocation by plan and indicative and macroplanning turns out to be most consistently effective. There are two firm foundations of democratic socialist strategy for moving beyond the welfare state: genuine democracy and popular power, which in turn implies, no matter how unfashionable it may now be, the massive transfer of private control over the economic and financial system from the capitalist minorities to democratic social control.

Despite all of the negative experiences with centrally run and bureaucratically planned economies in Communist party–run states, democratic social control over the economy and the financial system must unavoidably also include the use of a democratically controlled state with a popularly controlled and responsible administration.

The socialist project of moving toward a new human civilization must be informed and permeated by modern feminism and socially responsible, antielitist, and noncultist ecology. A movement has to deal with the mundane reality about how to effectively organize a society and an economy on a day-to-day basis, but also, and perhaps more urgently, it has to answer the question of how we are to live as decent and full human beings. That is why socialism cannot be national or limited to the prosperous North.

However, all oppression does not necessarily create democratic movements, as can be readily proved by any examination of the programs of some of the oppressed national groups. Often, the demand of a painfully oppressed people or group is for revenge or the right to oppress others in turn. A brief look at some of the programs of oppressed groups in the Middle East will make that clear. Muslim fundamentalists are undoubtedly victims of oppression in many countries. They suffer bitter persecution and repression in most Muslim countries, for that matter. They are at least as close to being a social movement as any political grouping in Egypt, Syria, Turkey, or Morocco, for example. They often represent subordinate strata and the urban poor. Yet it is clear that the movement's goals would be to repress others. Oppression does not always generate *progressive and democratic* movements as a response.

That is a regrettable lesson of much of the upheaval in Eastern Europe and the Soviet Union. To the contrary, all too often it results in narrow movements seeking vengeance and special privileges rather than universalist justice. This has been made clear in the post-Communist states, where previously oppressed national groups too often mouth outrageously chauvinistic and undemocratic demands. Their political parties are often national-populist social movements led by charismatic nationalist demagogues, and their social movements are "organic" or communitarian. That is a feature that movements of the Right and Left, traditional and modern, share today. That is why a democratic polity depends on bringing *politics* back in, and that requires political parties and an active, engaged, critical citizenry.

Notes

Preface (pages vii–ix)

1. Garden City, New York: Doubleday, 1951.

2. New York: Random House, 1983.

3. It was conveniently forgotten by Western cold warriors just how much bitter opposition there was under Communist rule in Eastern Europe. Berlin workers' demonstrations in 1951, the Hungarian revolution of 1956, and repeated riots, strikes and revolts in Poland showed how massive and desperate that resistance was. The Prague Spring in 1968 showed how widespread the desire to change and democratize these regimes was even within the ruling Communist parties.

These obvious failures of "totalitarianism" to "totally" submerge all opposition to communist domination were inconvenient to a theory of the invincibility and irreversibility of totalitarian rule. That rule was in practice fragile and needed *external force* in the form of Soviet tanks to stay in power. This need was hardly a sign of the strength of these regimes or their ideology.

1. European Unity, Neocorporatism, and the Post–Cold War World (pages 1–23)

1. There has never been a satisfactory count of the Panamanian casualties resulting from the illegal military adventure in Panama. Thus, the numbers vary from an improbable one hundred or so to an equally unlikely ten thousand. Both numbers completely depersonify the non-U.S. civilian dead. While successfully kidnapping the local dictator who refused to stay bought by the CIA, the United States seems to have replaced him with a venal incompetent, sworn in on a U.S. Army base, who is continuing the time-honored practice of using Panamanian banks to launder drug money. The casualties, as is usual when they are in the third world, were irrelevant and uncounted.

2. This is not to say that decades might be needed to revive the popularity of socialism but simply that great organizing paradigms have faded and revived in the past.

3. On the other hand, numerous parties in the former Soviet Union and Eastern Europe have adopted the social-democratic label and are vying for recognition by the Socialist International. It is also the case that in a number of these countries parties with socialist labels have obtained substantial votes, even without fraud.

4. On corporatism and neocorporatism, see G. Lehmbruch and P. Schmitter, eds., *The Patterns of Corporatist Policy Making* (London: Sage, 1982); E. Kirchner

and K. Schwaiger, *The Role of Interest Groups in the European Community* (London: Farnborough, Gower, 1981); and W. Grant, ed. *The Political Economy of Corporatism* (London: Macmillan, 1985), a very good collection; see especially "Corporatism and the European Community" by J. Sargeant.

5. Harold Draper, *Karl Marx's Theory of Revolution*, vol. 1, p. 323 (New York: Monthly Review Press, 1977). This, incidentally, is a magnificent set of volumes on a topic on which a great deal of uninformed nonsense is written.

6. Ibid., 410.

7. It was this mutual interest in the continued stability of the major class players in advanced industrial societies that drove Herbert Marcuse to look for *outsiders* as potential disruptors. If the working-class parties were indeed major players, outsiders would have to be the students, the *Lumpenproletariat* (today known as the underclass), or racial minorities. Thus, neocorporatist stability led to the development of a theory for a New Left.

8. The very influential work on the peculiarities of American trade unions, Selig Perlman's *Theory of the Labor Movement* (New York: Kelley, 1949), argued that because of the lack of a mass class-based socialist party, the U.S. labor movement was more independent than were European labor organizations of the influence of intellectuals, who would emphasize broad and overarching social and political goals. The result was that the early U.S. labor movement was "workerist" and social Darwinian, at least before the growth of the industrial unions of the Congress of Industrial Organizations (CIO). As a consequence, American labor was "right-wing syndicalist," that is, it was antistatist and preferred to slug it out with the employers. To be sure, labor's antistatism was the result of bitter experiences in real life in which the state repeatedly sided with the employers.

9. I much prefer the term *transnationals* to *multinationals*. The former is more accurate because very few such corporations are *genuinely multi*national in ownership and control; rather, they are national, very often U.S.-owned corporations that operate across national boundaries, manufacturing abroad to use cheap labor and sometimes registered abroad to avoid regulations and taxes. They are thus *trans*national. Old, established types of such firms are the Greek-owned ships of Panamanian registry, managed by Germans and crewed by Yugoslavs and Latin Americans.

10. For example, in the case of Yugoslavia, these remittances have been higher than the earnings of the tourist industry for most of the decade. In 1988, remittances were over $3 billion and account for a large share of the hard-currency bank deposits. Remittances also play a major role in economies of Portugal, Greece, Turkey, Mexico, and many of Caribbean island states. This is a subject that deserves much more attention. It is by no means a new phenomenon.

11. Reliable statistics are very hard to come by, when it comes to immigrant labor in France, or for that matter in the European Community. For one thing, "immigrants" are not a homogeneous mass; some have already obtained citizenship, some are undocumented illegals. A fair guess for the European Community is around 10 to 12 million. At least 3 to 4 million are in France, which thus has a substantial Moslem and African population today. Low population growth throughout Europe makes continued heavy immigration almost certain. Recession may slow such processes, but they cannot stop them, let alone reverse them.

12. This is a very important issue that I discuss at more length in Chapter 7. Some of the debate is summarized in Andre Gorz, *Farewell to the Working Class* (Boston: South End Press, 1982) and in Andre Gorz's article "S(he) who Does Not Work Shall Eat All the Same," *Dissent* (Spring 1987). An interesting critique of

Gorz's views is Varda Burstyn, "Andre Gorz and His Disappearing Proletariat," *Socialist Register* (1982).

13. The New Forum was a democratic socialist–dominated coalition of previously repressed democratic Left oppositionist groups and individuals who wanted a chance to develop an East German democratic socialist model and then negotiate gradual unification. The mass of the electorate were impatient to get into an existing and prosperous West Germany and understandably tired of social and political experiments, especially ones in the name of socialism. That name has to spend some time in purgatory in former Communist-ruled countries.

14. Closer trade links between the major republics of the former Soviet Union and a unified Germany are ever more likely since the chances of political strings being attached to such trade, as in past experiences with the United States, are minimal.

2. The Decline of the United States (pages 28–51)

1. One should not be deceived by brief interludes of military glory like the Persian Gulf adventure, particularly in a world where the utility of sheer military power is increasingly in question. The money markets were certainly not deceived; the dollar rose briefly against other hard currencies immediately after the war but returned to its normal lows soon afterward.

2. These critics would be at least partially right because "capitalism" is too abstract a term. That system comes in many variants, and the U.S. variant is a particularly nasty and uncivilized one, one untamed by an advanced welfare state and a neocorporatist consensus on the rules of the game.

3. See special issue of *The Economist*, Dec. 22, 1990, pp. 29–32, for a brief summary.

4. What is, after all, in a name? Why not African-Americans? Roughly for the same reason I will not speak of European-Americans. One could also argue that "black" is hardly a useful descriptive when it is used in the United States, as often as not, to refer to persons who have considerably more European than African ancestry in their genealogy.

5. To be sure, the former Soviet Union and South Africa have kept the death penalty, but even in these societies, which are not normally considered "advanced industrial democracies," the trend of death sentences is declining. In the United States, with the energetic help of the Supreme Court, death sentences are increasing, and the procedures are being streamlined. One should not have to add that African-Americans are sentenced to death in quite disproportionate numbers for the same crimes that earn their white colleagues lesser punishment. The key variable appears to be the race of the *victim*. Black murder victims almost never elicit death sentences; white ones often do.

6. See Cornel West's moving article on nihilism in the African-American community, in *Dissent* (Spring 1991).

7. See *Wall Street Journal*, April 23, 1991, p. B4.

8. The *New York Times* report of this case of the CEO of the International Telephone Corporation, Rand V. Araskog, on April 26, 1991, seemed indignantly unobjective. The point of this memorable story was that the chief executive of the California retirement system, which owns more than 1.5 million shares of ITT stock, objected, particularly since ITT reported that earnings had increased by 4 percent and 21 percent of the net came from selling of assets. If that is how ITT does busi-

ness, what about the smaller fry? This is a good illustration of how greed is killing the American economy.

9. To be fair, it has also helped create the trade unions that such a system serves. Comparing U.S. trade unions with European unions as to political and social programs is a bit like comparing the United States with advanced Western European welfare states.

10. Karl Marx, "The German Ideology," in *Collected Works* (Moscow, 1966), 75.

11. There have been intriguing reports, difficult to document, about some U.S. funds going through the expectedly circular route, via the CIA and the AFL-CIO man in Europe (Irving Brown) to the Algerian resistance. French conservatives were convinced that this was the case and were properly indignant. They saw it as a U.S. attempt to purchase some future goodwill. I would not be surprised it were true. Yugoslav journalists who were there confirmed the story in private conversations.

12. See David Calleo, *Europe and America: The Future of the Western Alliance* (New York: Basic Books, 1987); and Paul Kennedy, *The Rise and Fall of Great Powers: Economic Change and Military Conflicts 1500–2000* (New York: Random House, 1987).

13. For a very brief outline on the history of socialism in the United States and its varied organizations, parties, and sects, Daniel Bell, "The History of Marxian Socialism in the United States," in *Socialism and American Life*, ed. Drew Egbert and Stow Person (Princeton, N.J.: Princeton University Press, 1952), vol. 1, is still very sound. Also see Irving Howe, *Socialism and America* (San Diego, Calif.: Harcourt, Brace, Jovanovich, 1985).

14. The best summary of the discussion on American exceptionalism is in Seymour Martin Lipset, "Why No Socialism in the United States," in *Radicalism in the Contemporary Age*, ed. Seweryn Bialer (New York: Westview Press, 1977), vol. 1. That volume also has a useful extensive bibliography, "Sources of Radicalism and Revolution: A Survey of the Literature" by William Overholt. The entire issue is treated at greater length in *The Failure of a Dream? Essays in the History of American Socialism*, ed. John Lasslett and Seymour Martin Lipset (New York: Doubleday Anchor Books, 1974). The two important books for the exceptionalism of American labor unions are Selig Perlman, *A Theory of the Labor Movement* (New York: Macmillan, 1928) and *History and Labor in the United States*, ed. John Commons et al. (New York: Macmillan, 1926).

15. Engels also kept up a lively correspondence with German Marxist immigrants, whom he kept urging to get out of their ethnic ghettoes and into mainstream working-class politics.

16. While there are more contemporary monographs on details of American Communist history, I still consider Theodore Draper, *The Roots of American Communism* (New York: Viking, 1957) and *American Communism and Soviet Russia: The Formative Period* (New York: Viking, 1960) to be the soundest overall work. To this could be added the one-volume *The American Communist Party: A Critical History 1919–1957* by Irving Howe and Louis Coser (Boston: Beacon Press, 1957).

17. American Communists achieved their greatest successes under Earl Browder during World War II. An interesting history of the party during the period when it began to approach the role of a mass working-class party is Maurice Isserman, *Which Side Were You On? The American Communist Party during the Second World War* (Middletown, Conn.: Wesleyan University Press, 1982).

18. There are, after all, two open "card-carrying" Socialists in the U.S. Congress, members of the Democratic Socialists of America, both elected and reelected as Democrats. Interestingly, both are black. Congressman Bernie Sanders of Vermont is an open socialist, but is not a public member of any socialist organization. There

are certainly many more who would be open (i.e., "card-carrying") members if red-baiting was not a well-developed political ploy in U.S. politics. After all, if as pallid a figure as Dukakis could be baited for being a member in the American Civil Liberties Union, membership in the American affiliate of the Socialist International does not promise many extra votes today.

19. A fairly broad traditional statement is John McDermott, *The Crisis in the Working Class and Some Arguments for a New Labor Movement* (Boston: South End Press, 1980).

20. David Halle, *America's Working Man* (Chicago: University of Chicago Press, 1984); Pat Walker, ed. *Between Labor and Capital* (Boston: South End Press, 1979); and Stanley Aronowitz, *Working-Class Hero: A New Strategy for Labor* (New York: Adama Press, 1983) discuss the changes in the structure of the American working class and the probable strategic consequences.

21. This primarily means unions like the International Association of Machinists (IAM), United Auto Workers (UAW), Hospital Workers (1199), American Federation of State and Municipal Employees (AFSME), State Employees International Union (SEIU), United Electrical Workers (UE), Communication Workers of America (CWA), Amalgamated Clothing Workers of America (ACWU), International Longshoremen and Warehouse Workers Union (ILWU), and a few others. Some of these unions have a tradition of having had Socialist or Communist leaders.

22. This would include the unions mentioned above, where leftists tend to work as staffers, with the addition of United Mine Workers of America (UMWA); International Brotherhood of Teamsters (IBTU), where particularly bitter rank-and-file struggles against the leadership, led by socialists, have taken place over decades; United Steel Workers of America (USWA), where major insurgent groups have existed in the past; and the United Federation of Teachers (UFT), where entire districts and regions have been in the hands of the opposition.

23. Harrington makes a particularly timely and powerful argument in his *The Next Left: A History of the Future* (New York: Henry Holt, 1986). Particularly see pp. 47–70.

24. CORE, alas, although at the cutting edge of many of integrationalist battles in the South in the 1950s and early 1960s went Black Nationalist in 1966 and declared its white members and leaders unwelcome. I remember this from personal experience.

3. The Future of (Dys)topia (pages 56–75)

1. *Nomenklatura* is the formal system that prescribes the position, obligations, and privileges of the officials engaged in decision-making processes in Communist politocracies. Security and promotion are guaranteed in return for discipline and obedience.

2. For a longer discussion of politiocratic systems, see Bogdan Denitch, *Limits and Possibilities: The Crisis of Yugoslav Socialism and the State Socialist Systems* (Minneapolis: University of Minnesota Press, 1990).

3. The terms used to describe these societies among independent Marxists ranged from "degenerated workers' state" (Leon Trotsky) to "state capitalism," "bureaucratic collectivism," and "postrevolutionary societies."

4. Pedants can validly argue that the Communist seizure of power in Czechoslovakia in 1948 was an exception, in that a genuinely massive Communist party seized pwer in a scenario appropriate to an advanced industrial society. The Czechoslovak party, with the aid of its unions and fronts, did seize power without

direct Soviet armed help. However, the reality of Soviet power in the region demoralized the non-Communist democrats. It also gave enormous confidence to the Communists.

5. I distingush here between third world revolutionary regimes, which have often used Marxist-Leninist rhetoric and symbols but lacked a mass Communist party under whatever name, and genuine Communist party regimes.

6. The well-known Yugoslav democratic dissident Milovan Djilas has long argued that authoritarian Communist regimes cannot evolve toward other democratic forms. His argument is that they can merely decay and thus become less effective in obtaining compliance from the population.

7. The most serious and substantial argument to that effect is by Seymour Matin Lipset in "No Third Way: A Comparative Perspective on the Left," in Daniel Chirot, ed., *Crisis of Leninism and the Decline of the Left: The Revolutions of 1989* (Seattle: University of Washington Press, 1991). This book can be seen as a polemic with that now widespread view.

8. Most observers agree that Yugoslavia is blocked politically and in a mess, perhaps even a terminal one. However, the Yugoslavian economy was in better shape than that of the other Eastern European countries, at least until the fall of 1990, when politics began to catch up with the otherwise fairly decent economic picture.

9. This is very clearly laid out in Tatyana Zaslavskaya, *The Second Socialist Revolution* (Bloomington: Indiana University Press, 1990). The same basic case has been made by a number of other analysts. Zaslavskaya, however, has been a major figure in the reform circle around Gorbachev. This vision of the *aim* of the reforms does not at all conflict with the view of Gorbachev as a reformer from above.

10. Alex Nove's *The Economics of Feasible Socialism* (London: George Allen and Unwin, 1987) is still the best guide to Soviet economics and the problems of economic reforms for the nonspecialist. It is one of the few indispensable books on the subject.

11. This is shown rather clearly in the first empirical study of the ruling Yugoslav Communist elite in *The Opinion-Making Elite of Yugoslavia* by Allen Barton, Bogdan Denitch, and Charles Kadushin (New York: Prager, 1971).

12. Renamed in the spring of 1990 the Socialist party of Serbia. It is still the ruling party, inheriting the money, property, power, and as much of the membership as it could cajole into making the transfer from the old ruling League of Communists, which for the purpose of changing its name merged with its broad front, the Socialist Alliance.

13. "New Philosophers" in Paris, often former New Leftists and Maoists, proclaimed, with the same certainty with which they had denounced "bourgeois" democracy during their radical days, that a vote for as innocuous a leftist as Mitterrand was the first fatal step toward the gulag universe, whose existence they had generally loudly denied during the heyday of its existence.

4. North/South (pages 88–112)

This chapter has benefited from constructive editing and criticism from my assistant, Kimberly Adams, whose help is gratefully acknowledged. I am entirely responsible for both the errors and the political judgments.

1. See the discussion on neocorporatism in Chapter 1. These particular societies are variants of the neo-corporatist model of capitalism, with relatively weak trade unions and relatively strong governments and military.

2. An extensive and now increasingly dated literature exists on nonalignment. Two books are very useful even now: Richard Jackson, *The Nonaligned, the UN and the Superpowers* (New York: Praeger, 1983) and, more specialized, Lars Nord, *Nonalignment and Socialism: Yugoslav Foreign Policy in Theory and Practice* (Stockholm: Raben and Sjogren, 1972). Peter Willet, *The Nonaligned in Havana* (New York: St. Martin's Press, 1981) is a critical work.

3. Let it be noted that many "nonaligned" countries were very "aligned" indeed, that is, allied with one of the two superpowers. Cuba is only the most obvious example.

4. A brief list of essential readings on this topic would have to exclude many of the classic works by Marx, Lenin, Trotsky, Bukharin, and Luxemburg. However, with all of the appropriate caveats, I believe the following works to be both accessible and essential: George Lichteim, *Imperialism* (New York: Praeger 1971); Michael Harrington, *The Vast Majority* (New York: Simon and Schuster, 1977); a collection edited by Richard Fagen, Careen Diana Deer, and Jose Leis Coraggio, *Transition and Development: The Problems of Third World Socialism* (New York: Monthly Review Press, 1986); Wolfgang Mommsen, *Theories of Imperialism* (New York: Random House, 1980 [English edition]). James H. Mittleman, *Out from Underdevelopment* (New York: St. Martin's Press, 1988) is excellent. For more specialized readers, three background volumes are heavy but necessary going: Immanuel Wallerstein, *The Modern World System* (New York: Academic Press, 1974); Arghiri Emmanuel, *Unequal Exchange* (New York: Monthly Review Press, 1972); and Marina and David Ottaway, *Afro-Communism* (New York: Holmes and Meier, 1986), particularly the second edition.

5. For many leftists in U.S. academies, the answer is clearly yes! It is also yes for those who would crudely apply affirmative action criteria as quotas. Alas.

6. A good example of this is in the collection *Class, State and Power in the Third World*, edited by James Petras (Montclair, N.J.: Allenheld, Osmun, 1981). This volume is, in my term, "third worldist," whereas the equally anti-imperialist work by Noam Chomsky, *Turning the Tide: U.S. Intervention in Latin America and the Struggle for Peace* (Boston: South End Press, 1985) is free of that taint. Chomsky does not gild the lily of third world regimes or activists in order to attack the United States.

7. New York: Monthly Review Press, 1957.

8. For Afro-communism, see David and Marina Ottaway, *Afro-Communism* (New York: Holmes & Meier, 1986).

9. One only need refer to the elections in Mexico, Colombia, Romania, Bulgaria, and Serbia and Montenegro to underline this point.

10. The continuation of the regime, as distinct from the fate of one of the two centrist procapitalist political parties, has never been at stake in any elections in the United States in recent years, and genuine opponents of bipartisan domestic or international policies, or of capitalism as a system, have not had much access to the media.

11. Very typical, one could write archetypical, are the works by Andre Gunther Frank, Arghiri Emmanuel, and Immanuel Wallerstein despite their many and important differences from each other. However, it appears that this intellectual fashion is going the way that interest in students as the new revolutionary class and theories of the New Left went. Life has its small mercies.

12. The unequal-exchange argument is discussed in Chapter 4. The sharpest form of that argument is that of Arghiri Emmanuel, *Unequal Exchange*. That point of view, that American *labor*—that is, workers, including black and women workers—consciously participates in the exploitation of the third world fits very well

with the other critiques of productivism and consumerism. That is why it is popular among people who are not necessarily Marxists and do not draw particularly radical conclusions from such an analysis. It merely confirms and legitimates the widespread antilabor and anti-working-class attitudes among younger intellectuals today.

13. An insight into this fact was central to Leon Trotsky's theories about imperialism.

14. Inconveniently for Spanish-speaking Sandinista Nicaraguan nationalists from an intensely Catholic culture, the Mosquito Indians were English-speaking, Protestant, and intermarried with Africans. In many ways, as in the case of Belize, their culture was closer to that of the English-speaking Caribbean states than to Hispanic Latin America. Hispanic Latin America, on the other hand, has often had an ambivalent relationship to its Indian heritage. Ambivalence is understandable in cultures based on colonization and rape.

15. Soviet weapons, incidentally, were not gifts; they were sold, on generous long-range terms perhaps, but sold.

16. A very sensitive discussion of this attitude toward the Soviet models of party and mass organizations is found in Marina and David Ottaway's *Afro-Communism* in which they contrast Benin, Angola, Ethiopia, and Mozambique with "African Socialist" countries such as Tanzania, Algeria, and Tunisia. My own estimation is that *both* "models" are in serious trouble.

17. See Rene Dumont and Marcel Mazoyer, *Development and Socialism* (New York: Praeger, 1972).

18. I had argued that Angola, Mozambique, Guinea-Bissau, and Algeria have better prospects than other decolonialized countries because prolonged revolutionary struggle required mass mobilization.

19. Not very much material is readily available on the Spanish anarchists, which is a pity because an extraordinarily rich tradition of self-help and rural mobilization is lost for activists. The materials are becoming very "academicized" and are hard to obtain. Yet for the third world there are valuable lessons and organizational models in the anarchist experiences. The best general introduction is in Murray Bookchin, *The Spanish Anarchists: The Heroic Years 1868–1936*, Montreal, Black Rose Books, 1976.

5. Democracy for the Twenty-first Century (pages 115–139)

1. This almost always is intended to mean the end of *left-wing* or *reformist* or *committed* ideology; maintenance of status quo does not require either ideology or conscious commitment.

2. Few serious minds believe any longer that one can set "blueprints" and, through "social engineering," bring about a new "utopia of social harmony." Daniel Bell, *The End of Ideology: On Exhaustion of Political Ideas in the Fifties* (New York: Free Press, 1960), 370. Note the date and the loaded terms. Why, for example, a "utopia of social harmony"? Why not a better-run and more socially just society?

3. I find two works on democracy absolutely essential for any well-prepared discussion: Robert Dahl, *Democracy and Its Critics* (New Haven, Conn.: Yale University Press, 1989) and Giuseppe Di Palma, *Transitions to Democracy* (Berkeley: University of California Press, 1989).

4. That frankness is now limited to genuine reactionaries like the Saudi, Kuwaiti, and other Arab oil states, a few remaining monarchies and some academic leftists in advanced countries who are still hung up on "false consciousness" of

everyone who does not agree with them. They *would* be for democracy, after a substantial time to reeducate the victims of capitalist brainwashing. Luckily for democracy, these do not seem to be the waves of the future.

5. That association was popularized by Walter Rostow in his *The Stages of Economic Growth* (Cambridge: Cambridge University Press, 1960), which stressed the notion of progressive stages of growth that accompanied modernization and political development. This was gospel throughout the 1960s and 1970s among the experts and academics. Presumably, at some "stage" of development democracy was also appropriate. That approach was also the most common apologia for the absence of democracy in "progressive" third world dictatorships (i.e., they were not at the right "stage" yet).

6. One minor side effect of this kind of "representation" is that despite the fact that massive majorities in the United States have for decades supported some kind of national health insurance, that reform has been effectively stymied. This makes the United States the only advanced industrial country without that civilizational minimum. Equally large majorities have been in favor of steeper income taxes and against cutting the corporate tax, with equal lack of effect.

7. April 23, 1991.

8. By far the largest single party in both houses of the U.S. Congress is the "incumbent party." The number of politicians assured of all but automatic reelection is the envy of legislators in authoritarian and democratic parliaments. This is why no real electoral reform is possible. The only meaningful democratic electoral reform would have elections publicly financed and completely eliminate private funds in elections.

9. There is a self-serving determinism in the arguments made by political scientists who emphasize the stability of the world order and the economic systems of advanced industrial countries. This was noted a good twenty years ago by Dankward Rustow: "The denial of the primacy of politics and the attempt to explain it away accord well with the widespread acceptance of stability and equilibrium as the central ordering concepts of our social theory. A student of the sociology of knowledge might note that these tendencies have become prominent among American scholars in an era in which their country experienced unprecedented (if uneven) affluence at home and has undertaken unprecedented (if at times self-defeating) commitments to the status quo abroad." *Comparative Politics*, October 1968. Quite right, it was so then, and is so now.

10. That is the major argument of neoconservatives and their journals (*Public Interest, The New Republic, The National Interest*, etc.), that all rational modern capitalist societies are essentially the same and that only nuances of change are possible. These changes are more a matter of administrative priorities and the subject of public debate and political conflict.

11. Francis Fukoyama: "The End of History," *National Interest* (Spring 1989).

12. I have not noticed massive protests in the West or the United States against the proposals to purge former members of the Communist parties in Poland, Czechoslovakia, Hungary, and western republics of Yugoslavia from public office and managerial positions for mere membership (often pro forma) in the Communist party when it was in power.

13. See "From Sweden to Socialism," *Dissent* (Winter 1991): 96.

14. For the purposes of clarity, I will use the terms Social Democratic and Socialist more or less interchangeably when referring to the parties and movements of the Socialist International or the heirs of the Second International. This represents what remained of the more or less unified world socialist workers' movement after the historic split following the Bolshevik Revolution in 1917, out of which

were formed the parties of the Communist International. The Socialist International is now the only significant international organization of the mass left Social Democratic parties.

15. The Socialist vote jumped from 38.7 percent in 1987 to 44.8 percent in 1991, a *huge* jump by standards of West German election precedents. It is clear that much of the swing was a reaction to the hasty way the unification was rushed through. With that vote the Socialists can choose to make a coalition with either the Greens, who got 6.5 percent or the liberal Free Democrats, with their 7 percent. If this remains a pattern, my somewhat too early prediction of a massive turn to social democracy as a result of German unification will belatedly prove to be right. I made this rash prediction in *The End of the Cold War* (Minneapolis: University of Minnesota Press, 1990).

16. Even the traditionally parochial and insular British Labour party and Trade Union Congress has waked up to the progressive and organizationally useful consequences of greater European integration for a relatively weak labor movement and a relatively backward welfare state.

6. Conclusion (pages 143–54)

1. I know that the common wisdom is that Britain, as a result of decades of Labour party governments, has a generous welfare state. That is so *only* compared with the United States, whose social policies are, or should be, a scandal. Compared to Northern and Central Europeans, the British have a paltry welfare state.

2. During the past decade in the United States, incomes have increased for the top 30 percent of the population. The same rough figures hold for Great Britain. This is the reversal of the moderate social democratic vision that in postindustrial societies two-thirds would be well off and one-third would need solidaristic social programs.

3. He did not, however, go to the next step, which his less sophisticated followers often took to argue that Communist Party–run dictatorships were therefore democratic. Marcuse's misfortune was that he was consistently misunderstood and oversimplified.

4. I consider that to be the essential argument in Seymour Martin Lipset's, *The Political Man: The Social Basis of Politics*, expanded ed. (Baltimore: Johns Hopkins Press, 1981).

5. It may, and in the case of ideological conservatives does, matter morally. They seem to think that decent social standards corrupt the morals and fiber of the lower orders. However, attacks on the welfare state outside the Anglo-Saxon powers, the United States and Britain, have done poorly politically and have been generally beaten off, even in countries with fairly high unemployment.

6. In Hungary, national populists have already begun attacking "cosmopolitan" (read Jewish) big-city liberals over that precise issue. Similar national-populist attacks on economic reforms and on pluralistic democracy, with or without anti-Semitic subtexts can be expected in Poland, Romania, and the republic of Serbia in Yugoslavia.

7. The role of the Protestant denominations is more ambivalent. In Latin America many of the fundamentalist religious groups pursue very right-wing social and economic politics. On the other hand, the World Council of Churches has tended to have very progressive stands, particularly where the third world is concerned.

8. Marxists have had real problems understanding the persistence of national-

ism. Tom Bottomore is right when he argues that "Marxists have contributed little in the way of analysis and research into these phenomena, and have indeed tended to ignore or dismiss them as being of minor significance"; see the "Sociology" chapter in *Marx: the First 100 Years*, ed. David McLelland (London: Fontina, 1983), 140. A very good book is *The Difficult Dialogue: Marxism and Nationalism* by Ronald Munck (London: Zed Books, 1986), as is Eric Howbsbawm's instant classic, *Nations and Nationalism: Programme, Myth and Reality* (Cambridge: Cambridge University Press, 1990).

9. For example, the position of Hungarian nationalists throughout the nineteenth century was that the Magyars were the "state people" and all others were only tolerated. To be sure, the Hungarians encouraged others to join the state people by becoming "magyarized," that is, adopting the language and culture of the "state people."

10. French historians made a useful distinction between *pays réel*, or the real country, which is the country of traditions, customs, folklore, local vernacular and customary law, what people feel intensely emotionally attached to, and "pays légal," the legal country, or country of laws, which is the invented formal, legal-rational state, with its laws, official language, and bureaucratic (as against traditional) authority.

11. Johnathan Rieder, "The Crown of Thorns," *The New Republic*, October 14, 1991 p. 28.

12. Note: the *right* not the *obligation*. With the continued growth of technology and productivity, on one hand, and ecologically dictated concepts of limits to material exploitation of nature, on the other, it should be possible within a relatively near future to cut drastically the socially necessary labor in most societies. That will pose other, more interesting problems, but work need not remain a curse or a life sentence for most of humanity.

Index

History of

The Society of The Friendly Sons of Saint Patrick

of Baltimore, Inc.

An Historical Memoir

by

Alan Kemp Dolliver
Historian

Baltimore, Maryland
1962

Published for
THE SOCIETY OF THE FRIENDLY SONS OF
SAINT PATRICK OF BALTIMORE, INC.
by
J. C. O'DONOVAN & CO.
BALTIMORE, MARYLAND

First Edition

Library of Congress Catalog Card Number: 62-15070

Saint Patrick

DEDICATION

TO SAINT PATRICK, APOSTLE OF IRELAND AND REVERED PATRON SAINT OF THIS SOCIETY, WHO BROUGHT TO OUR ANCESTORS THE FAITH AND FORTITUDE WHICH SUSTAINED THEM THROUGH CENTURIES OF OPPRESSION AND WHO INSPIRES US TO GREATER AND GREATER ACHIEVEMENT NOW.

George B. Cavanagh

A HIBERNIAN NOTE TO THE PERHAPS HESITANT READER

"Cid glic fri hailchi
Cid saer ac imirt ghela,
Cid ginn a gord fri quana,
Dorchuala as gorg nat legha."

Ancient Gailic Quatrain

Which translated, means:
"Tho' one be cunning at cold blocks of stone,
Tho' one be a master wright at wielding the axe,
Tho' sweet his voice in singing songs,
I have heard, he is dull who does not read!"

ACKNOWLEDGEMENTS

This work was commissioned by The Board of Officers of The Society of the Friendly Sons of St. Patrick, of Baltimore, as an outgrowth of the informal and private publication of several short pieces having to do with our Patron Saint, and with the early days of the "Friendly Sons" in America.

Any history, of necessity, must be based upon research; the past record must be mined, as it were, and thus, in total must be the "work of many hands."

The moving spirit, pushing for the consummation of this undertaking, was our Founder, George B. Cavanagh.

The ever ready, and efficient cooperation of D. Chester O'Sullivan, Chairman of the Board of Stewards, should always be remembered.

Walter M. McCardell, of the Baltimore Sun, and Publicity Director of the Society, was most helpful in locating and providing various newspaper articles and photographs.

The Board of Officers, themselves, were most helpful with advice and suggestions.

In addition, the Author is most grateful for the assistance rendered by the following:

The Enoch Pratt Free Library, Baltimore, and its most gracious and efficient staff under Margaret Rohr Baugh, Librarian of the History, Travel and Biography Department.

The Maryland Historical Society by its Librarian, Mr. John D. Kilbourne and staff.

The New York Free Library, New York City, by Mr. Gerald McDonald, Librarian of its Department of American History, which vast collection of material on the Irish in America is indispensable to researchers.

The Philadelphia Free Library, by its Chairman of Social Science and History, Mr. Robert Scudder.

And lastly, but by no means least, the kindly general assistance rendered by Mr. Richard C. Murphy, Recording Secretary and Historian of The Society of the Friendly Sons of St. Patrick, New York City.

May our prayers that this book be well received, be answered.

INTRODUCTORY PREFACE

No properly and logically conceived history of any organization and its antecedents should fail to take account of the history, spirit, intentions and achievements of all predecessor organizations, local or national.

Accordingly, in embarking upon this history of the institution of the "FRIENDLY SONS" in Maryland under the title of "The Society of the Friendly Sons of St. Patrick of Baltimore," it seems desirable to touch upon the past and most glorious history of such organizations of Irishmen and Americans of Irish ancestry, particularly so for the benefit of those of the younger generation who, perhaps in the hurly-burly of modern living, have not found the time to acquaint themselves with these remembrances of things past.

Research indicates that the first Irish Society organized for purposes similar to those expressed in the Charter of the Friendly Sons of St. Patrick, Baltimore, was the Charitable Society of Boston, Massachusetts, which was founded in 1737 and which was "A Society instituted for the relief of indigent natives of Ireland and their descendants, and for any and all charitable purposes."

Contrary to popular belief, the original Friendly Sons of St. Patrick in America was not founded in New York City but in Philadelphia, Pennsylvania, on March 17, 1771; thus, the Society actually is older than our American Republic.

The New York Society of the Friendly Sons was founded in 1784, and through the years other Societies of similar name have been founded in Cincinnati, Minneapolis, Washington, D. C., and elsewhere.

The Charitable Irish Society of Boston, which actually

is a "Friendly Sons Society" under another name, continues in existence.

At the first meeting in Philadelphia there were 24 regular and 6 honorary members. Among those honorary members were John Dickenson and Robert Morris, who later were to sign the Declaration of American Independence. History records that all of the members present were prominent men of affairs in Eastern Pennsylvania, successful merchants and professional men.

The first President was Gen. Stephen Moylan, later aide'-de-camp and private secretary to Gen. George Washington. During the course of the American Revolution, in addition to his staff duties, he was Colonel of "Moylan's Dragoons" who were in active combat during much of the Revolution.

After Pulaski, Colonel Moylan became General Moylan, in command of all of the cavalry forces of the Continental Army.

The Society (and all other Societies of similar name and purposes which have endured) has survived for almost two centuries because it was founded upon love, the most constructive and enduring force in this vale of tears, and upon charity, which very probably is the very first of the human virtues.

The original Society was and has been since its founding, non-sectarian.

The original Society took to heart the words of the great Irish poet, that singer of sweet songs to keep the memory of dear old Ireland green, Thomas Moore:

> "Shall I ask the brave soldier who fights by my side,
> In the cause of mankind if our creeds agree?
> Shall I give up the friend I have valued and tried,
> If he kneel not before the same altar as me?"

Thus, the Society, through the years, scrupulously recognized and protected the right of the individual to worship God, the Father and Our Maker, according to the dictates of his own conscience, even though in our hearts we may think him to be misguided or in error; and remembering too, as all true Irish should, that many heroic patriots in the fight for Irish freedom, such as Wolfe Tone and Robert Emmet, were Anglican Catholics.

In 1772 the great seal or medal of the original Society, which it was required that the members wear at all meetings, was adopted and is indicated as follows:

> On the obverse—on the right—HIBERNIA—on the left—AMERICA—in the center LIBERTY—HIBERNIA and AMERICA joining hands with LIBERTY.
>
> HIBERNIA is represented as a female supported by a harp; AMERICA represented by an Indian with a quiver on back and bow slung—underneath, the word UNITE.
>
> On the reverse side—ST. PATRICK trampling on a snake with Cross in hand and clothed in full Pontifical robes.

Present day Friendly Sons may not realize that Pope Pius XI gave the original Society his Apostolic Benediction; nor recall that the Society made substantial contributions to the relief of persecuted Jews in Russia.

It is surely not currently known that the ancient and treasured minute book of the original Society was loaned to the *Grand Lodge, Free and Accepted Masons of Pennsylvania, so that the Masonic Order could proudly display the signature of one of its members who was also a Friendly Son—George Washington.*

Yes, the Society indubitably is Irish, but also indubitably "Friendly."

The Society has a long, continuous and distinguished record for purely philanthropic work, along with its constant recognition of the importance of informing all Americans of the tremendous contribution to the cultural, economic, industrial and political development of America made by Irishmen and those of Irish descent. Although not generally recognized, from 1730 to 1830 no country contributed as much as Ireland to the population of America.

Thomas Jefferson and Benjamin Franklin frequently were guests at the meetings of the Friendly Sons in Philadelphia during their lifetimes and were hearty supporters of the work of the organization. General Anthony Wayne was a member; John Cadwalader, an ancestor of your historian, a Colonel of a Cavalry Troop in the Revolution, also was a member.

The so-called Light Horse Troop of Philadelphia, which fought throughout the Revolution under Washington, was made up largely of the members of the Friendly Sons. One might say there was absolutely no Toryinsm in the Friendly Sons, there being but one black sheep—Capt. Thomas Batt, one of the early members who later went over with King George and accordingly was expelled forthwith from the Society.

Appropriately enough, the first meetings in Philadelphia took place in *Mullen's Tavern.*

In later years, in conjunction with the Hibernian Society of Philadelphia, which had been formed in 1790, the members met at the famous Dooner's in Philadelphia. Dooner's is now no more, having been torn down in 1925 to be replaced by the Federal Reserve Bank of Philadelphia building.

At a meeting of the Friendly Sons on April 24, 1775 an express galloped up and brought the news of the Battle of Lexington. Promptly thereafter, the Society resolved, among other things, as follows:

> "To associate together to defend our lives, our property, and our liberty against British attempts."

The Lexington, one of the first vessels of the hastily organized American Navy, was commanded by Captain John Barry, also a Friendly Son, who is buried in Old St. Mary's Church in Philadelphia, which became a virtual shrine of Irish-American heroes.

Later in the war of 1812, the Commander of the Pennsylvania Navy was Andrew Caldwell, also a Friendly Son.

In 1778, during the occupation of Philadelphia by the British, the meetings of the Society necessarily had to be held in secret, when and as the members could get away from their military service for the purpose.

With the exception of Captain Thomas Batt, before mentioned, all members of the Friendly Sons cast their lot with George Washington, and remained in active service throughout the Revolution.

The difficult crossing of the Delaware River at McKonty's Ferry by Washington's troops, before the successful Battle of Trenton, found the Friendly Sons there in force, as were they also at the Battles of Germantown, the Brandywine, Stony Point. It is also a fact that in the Battles of Long Island (Brooklyn) and Harlem Heights it was the "Maryland Line", which included numerous Irishmen among them, which was most active in saving the day.

It is needless to say that the Friendly Sons suffered with Washington and the others through the bitter winter at Valley Forge. No less than five of Washington's Generals were Irish, namely: Wayne, Montgomery, Sullivan, Knox and Hand—all deeply attached to the spirit and work of the Friendly Sons.

It is an interesting coincidence (Irishmen, will say it is no coincidence) that Charles Thomson, an Irishman and a Friendly Son, was Secretary of the Continental Congress. It was he who *first prepared* the Declaration of Independence *for publication* from Thomas Jefferson's manuscript; John Nixon, also an Irishman, was the *first man to publicly read* the Declaration of Independence; Thomas Dunlap, also an Irishman, *first printed and published* the Declaration; and, finally, out of 57 signers, 14 signers of the Declaration of Independence were Irish.

General George Washington was an Honorary Member of the Friendly Sons, a testimonial which he accepted as a genuine honor with gracious pleasure. On January 1, 1782, a dinner was given to General Washington at which time the ensign of the Society was presented to him. At this dinner, in addition to the members, as guests were Washington's full staff of officers and other men prominent in American public life. In accepting the ensign, George Washington said: "I accept with singular pleasure the ensign of so worthy a Society as that of the Sons of St. Patrick in this city, a Society distinguished for the firm adherence of its members to the glorious cause on which we are embarked. Give me leave to assure you my eyes shall never be cast upon the badge with which I am honored but with grateful remembrance of the polite and affectionate manner in which it was presented."

It is a matter of record that Thomas Jefferson, Alexander Hamilton, Paul Jones, and many other truly great men of the day, respected, honored, and cooperated with the work of the Society. The grandfather of General George G. Meade, hero of Gettysburg, for whom Fort Meade is named, was a Friendly Son.

Hercules Mulligan, a confidential agent (spy) for General Washington, was one of the founders of the New York Society in 1783, which, incidentally was the year that Washington entered New York after the British evacuation.

One of the prime purposes of the formation of the New York Society was the relief of the widows and children of Irish soldiers who had served in the American Revolution.

The famous Glee Club of the New York Society was founded by Victor Herbert. It is interesting to note that while all the Irish songs are merry, yet all their songs are sad too. This represents the true Irish spirit, steeped from centuries of high spirits in spite of opposition, militant patriotism, mixed with gentle melancholy which is the expression of all true souls.

One of the greatest charitable efforts of the Philadelphia, New York and other societies was the relief extended to the victims of the Irish famine of 1847-50.

Tom Moore visited Philadelphia for an extended time

in 1804, and while there is no record that he joined the "Friendly Sons" officially, it is handed down to us that he consorted with them, and attended their meetings, as well he might have.

Here are lines from some of his writings at that time. They are typical of his warm, friendly Irish spirit, and evidence his tribute to Philadelphia and its "Friendly Sons."

"Though few the days; the happy
evenings few,
So warm their heart, so rich with
mind they flew."
"Alone by the Schuylkill a wanderer
rov'd
And bright were its flowery banks
to his eyes."

* * * *

"The stranger is gone—but he will
not forget
When at home he shall talk of the
toil he has known,
To tell with a sigh, what endear-
ments he met,
As he stray'd by the Wave of the
Schuylkill alone."

Moore arrived in "Philly" by mail coach from Baltimore, after a bumpy two day trip. However, he records that this discomfort was soon forgotten after his warm reception in Philadelphia, which was a genuine response to their warm-hearted, generous brother Irishman, who was so gifted in humor, the social graces, poetry and music.

John Wanamaker, who had an Irish ancestor, was an active member; Theodore Roosevelt also found an Irish ancestor and was honored and "de-e-e-lighted" to be a member. Our martyred President Wm. McKinley was an Irishman whose forebearers came from County Antrim; he was a Friendly Son.

In 1887, President Grover Cleveland, at a dinner jointly held by the Society of the Friendly Sons of St. Patrick and the Hibernian Society of Philadelphia, said: "There is no association which has in its Charter or history or traditions, a more valuable certificate of patriotic worth than you have." He then recited the words of Washington, spoken in 1782, and concluded: *"These are priceless words."*

Truly, the Friendly Sons are societies of heroes, some distinguished, some humble, but all true men animated by a spirit of resistance of oppression—would that we had more of that spirit among us today, in an age of constantly encroaching big, dictatorial government and governmental agencies.

As the founders of the original Society died out, its activities declined, although it was still in very active existence prior to the War of 1812. In the meantime, as before mentioned, in 1790, an association and later successor organization, the "Hibernian Society for the Relief of Emigrants" was founded in Philadelphia. This offspring of the original Friendly Sons continued to do active work and, in due course, the original Friendly Sons organization was joined with it. In the original 219 charter members of the Hibernian Society were included almost the entire membership of the Society of Friendly Sons of St. Patrick. The first Chairman was John M. Nesbitt, who was also President of the Friendly Sons.

Thus, from 1771 to 1892, 121 years, these groups worked together to keep alive the memory of dear old Ireland and to attest their devotion both to the glorious cause of American liberty and to the spirit of true charity. In 1898 the old original name name of The Society of the Friendly Sons of Saint Patrick of Philadelphia was restored and continues to the present.

A replica of the Society's medal was presented to President Wm. T. Cosgrave of the Irish Free State on January 28, 1928. Eamon de Valera, President of the Irish Free State, was elected a lifetime honorary member of the New York Society on April 5, 1948. Victor Herbert, the noted composer, was a member and past President of the New York Society.

The New York Society, as before mentioned, was founded in 1784. Its first meetings were held at *Bradford's Coffee House, 2 Water Street, near Wall Street, in New York City.* The first President, and one who continued to be President on and off for many years afterwards, was Daniel McCormick. The New York Society was formally incorporated in the State of New York in 1827.

Prominent members of the New York Society, among others, were Gov. Charles Whitman, Mayor John P. Mitchell, Wilton Lackaye, noted Actor, Augustus Thomas, noted dramatic critic and playwrite and Governor Alfred E. Smith.

In 1915, when Victor Herbert was President, at the annual St. Patrick's Day dinner, most of the melodies played were composed by Mr. Herbert and by his grandfather Samuel Lover, of Ireland.

The Friendly Sons, as might be expected, were active in the Spanish American War. General Joseph Wheeler was an Honorary Member, elected out of the love and respect the Friendly Sons who served under him had for his leadership.

The Friendly Sons has continued to be a patriotic as well as a charitable Society throughout its existence. In 1814, at a meeting of the Society, the membership drank this toast:

> "In the hour of danger, we know no party! We are for the Union, and we drink to the head of the Nation, the President of the United States."

In the spring of 1865, at a meeting of the Society, this same toast was drunk again; it was also drunk again in

1917; and, although there is no specific record of it, there is reason to believe it was repeated in 1942.

Here are some other traditional toasts, one of which has always been drunk in connection with all affairs of the Society:

"To the immortal memory of St. Patrick."

"To the immortal memory of George Washington."

In the days of the great Irish immigration to America, it was the practice of the Irish Societies in Boston, New York, Philadelphia, Baltimore, etc. to meet all ships coming into the harbor and to greet all emigrants with the "Hail of the Friendly Sons" and with inquiries as to needs, if any, and the granting of assistance wherever it was needed.

In later days the original type of charitable work of the Society has not been greatly needed; therefore, most of the charitable work has been transferred to general eleemosynary purposes, not only for the benefit of those of Irish descent, but for all worthy purposes, without regard to race, creed, color, or previous condition of servitude.

THE SOCIETY

OF THE

FRIENDLY SONS

OF

SAINT PATRICK

OF

BALTIMORE, INC.

The history of the Friendly Sons of St. Patrick *of Baltimore,* begins during the winter of 1954-55. At that time a group of Baltimore men of Irish ancestry met togther, at the call of *Judge George B. Cavanagh,* to discuss a matter which had been dear to his heart and which had occupied his mind for a long time previously, namely, the establishment of a Friendly Sons organization in Maryland which would exemplify and carry out the spirit and intentions of the original Societies in Philadelphia, New York and elsewhere.

After considerable discussion it was agreed, among other things, to organize in Baltimore as follows:

> The name of the corporation shall be *"The Society of the Friendly Sons of Saint Patrick of Baltimore."*
>
> The purpose for which this corporation is formed and the business or objects to be carried on and promoted by it are as follows:
>
> This Society is instituted for the assistance and association of natives of Ireland and their descendants.
>
> To promote good will and comaraderie among the members of the Society.
>
> To sponsor social activities with a view toward aiding and furthering religious, educational and charitable causes.

To do all which may be deemed necessary or desirable to further the stated purposes of this organization.

The seal of this Society shall consist of an Irish harp, with the motto: "Erin Go Bragh".

Gentlemen of the age of twenty-one years and over, citizens of the United States of America, being natives or descendants of the natives of Ireland, and of good moral character, shall hereafter be eligible for admission to active membership.

Honorary membership may hereafter be conferred by the Society if all the following requirements and conditions are fulfilled:

The person proposed shall have rendered some conspicuous service to the United States of America, to Ireland, or to the Irish people; or shall have achieved distinction by laudable effort that reflects credit and honor upon the Irish name and People.

The Committee on Charity shall consist of seven members to be appointed by the President, one of whom he shall designate as Chairman. The Almoner shall be a member of his Committee.

And, thereafter, the movement took being and proceeded to action.

Following these informal meetings, a charter membership dinner was held on March 22, 1955; the place: the Park Plaza Hotel, Charles and Madison Streets, Baltimore. The group consisted of 71 inspired men indeed imbued with the spirit of Irish cooperation and charity.

The Invocation was asked by the Rt. Rev. John G. Duggan. Judge George B. Cavanagh was unanimously named *Chairman* of this original group. Present also was *Fred I. Archibald, publisher of the Baltimore News-Post and Sunday American,* who in turn introduced the guest speaker, *Leo W. O'Brien, U. S. Congressman for the District of Albany, N. Y.* Congressman O'Brien gave a most interesting and enlightening talk, relating his personal experience in Washington. He closed by complimenting the group upon their splendid inspiration in connection with the organization of a Baltimore chapter and extending his very best wishes, along with those of the New York Chapter.

Mr. Cavanagh called upon *George P. Mahoney, Congressman George Fallon* and *R. Emmet Bradley,* each of whom expressed his enthusiasm for the formation of a Baltimore Chapter; each pledged his cooperation and support.

After thorough discussion, it was the unanimous sentiment of those present that such an organization would be of inestimable value in promoting good fellowship and in rendering a constructive service to the Baltimore community in connection with charitable, cultural and educational matters. *Mr. Bradley* was thereupon designated *Chairman of the Nominating Committee* for the nomination of officers. In due course, the following men were named to this *Nominating Committee.*

R. Emmet Bradley

George B. Cavanagh
George P. Mahoney
Joseph L. Manning
J. Jerome Butler
Daniel J. Moran
J. Anthony Stack
Edward W. Dougherty
William W. Mahoney
Paul J. Reed, Jr.
Thomas J. McKewen, Jr.
J. Harold Grady
Francis X. Gallagher
Edward R. Brown
William J. O'Donnell
John A. Dunphy
John V. Hennegan
Leroy C. Shaughnessy
J. Neil McCardell

Walter M. McCardell, Jr.

Paul J. Reed, Jr. was named *Chairman of a Committee on By-Laws;* other members of this committee selected were *George B. Cavanagh, J. Harold Grady, Francis X. Gallagher, William J. O'Donnell and William W. Mahoney,* all of whom adorn with distinction, the Baltimore, Maryland bar.

Thereafter, the meeting adjourned. Benediction was asked by Rev. Thomas A. Whelan.

Both the Baltimore News-Post and the Baltimore Sun took due notice of this meeting and published accounts thereof, with photographs.

On February 8, 1956, another dinner was held at the Park Plaza, Mr. Cavanagh in the Chair, for the purpose of formally organizing the Baltimore Chapter of the Society of the Friendly Sons of St. Patrick. Mr. Cavanagh gave a very fine and enlightening talk, sketching the history of the various Friendly Sons Societies in America.

Thereafter, the following officers were nominated, and after discussion, were unanimously elected to serve until their successors were duly nominated and elected:

President	George B. Cavanagh
1st Vice-President	J. Neil McCardell
2nd Vice-President	R. Emmet Bradley
3rd Vice-President	Joseph L. Manning
Recording Secretary	J. Harold Grady
Corresponding Secretary	Francis X. Gallagher
Almoner	William W. Mahoney

President Cavanagh assumed office and called upon Paul J. Reed, Jr. for recommendations as to By-Laws. Mr. Reed presented a set of by-laws for approval and William J. O'Donnell moved for adoption. Upon this motion made, seconded and carried they were unanimously adopted. President Cavanagh then appointed the following additional officers:

Paul J. Reed, Jr.	Counsel
Daniel J. Moran	Historian
Walter M. McCardell, Jr.	Publicity Director
D. Chester O'Sullivan,	Chairman, Board of Stewards

Thomas J. McKewen, Jr.,
Chairman, Committee on Admissions
Thomas R. Kelly,
Chairman, Committee on Charity
George P. Mahoney,
Chairman, Committee on Finance
Rev. Thomas A. Whelan was designated Chaplain

It was decided that *Charter Membership* for the Society be closed, as of March 17, 1956. Arrangements were made to send out formal invitations to those gentlemen of the city known to be qualified for membership and whose civic spirit gave indication that they would be pleased to join in the movement.

It was decided to hold an annual affair on or about St. Patrick's Day of each year; also that the organization should definitely form a unit for participation in an annual St. Patrick's Day parade.

J. Neil McCardell and others gave testimony to the fact of the enthusiastic reception the formation of the Baltimore chapter was receiving.

As a result of energetic activities of the officers, the Baltimore Sun ran a lengthy article upon *St. Patrick, the Apostle of Ireland,* who died March 17 in the year 461 A.D. The Sun writer pointed out that St. Patrick's Day commemorates the date of his *death* rather than that of his birth, which is the popular belief. The heading of this article was:

"More than Legend"
March 17 Commemorates Death of Irish Apostle!

A *regularly stated meeting* of the Society was held on March 8, 1956, President Cavanagh presiding. Mr. Cavanagh reported on the progress of the organization in connection with the first St. Patrick's Day banquet of the new Baltimore chapter. He stated that due to the time element involved, it had not yet been possible to secure a speaker of national reputation; therefore, after discussion, it was decided to have a St. Patrick's Day Luncheon instead of an evening banquet. *Chairman of the Board of Stewards, D. Chester O'Sullivan,* advised that the luncheon would be held in the ballroom of the Southern Hotel, and urged all members to invite all friends who might be potential members. He pointed out, however, that the necessary qualifications for membership were strict, further that no exceptions could be made.

Also, because of the time element, it was decided that the Society would not attempt to be represented as a special unit in the St. Patrick's Day parade this year, but that nevertheless all members were urged to join the parade as individuals in connection with other specific units in the parade as known to them.

IRISHMAN OF THE YEAR PROGRAM. After thorough discussion, it was decided, as a fixed policy of the Organization to, from time to time, honor those of Irish ancestry who, by unique acts of heroism or other achievement and performance worthy of recognition, be selected as "Irishman of the Year", this person to be resident in the general area represented by the Baltimore Society of the Friendly Sons of St. Patrick. It was further decided that those so honored by the Society would be invited to attend the annual luncheon or banquet, as honored guest, and be presented with a certificate or other specific record of the honor so bestowed.

In due course, on March 17, 1956, the gala luncheon was held at the Southern Hotel. The ballroom was filled to overflowing. The enthusiastic gathering was treated to a corned beef and cabbage repast amid traditional St. Patrick's Day decorations. Traditional Irish songs were sung led by Thomas McNulty and Joseph L. Manning. Interesting remarks were made by the *Honorable Herbert R. O'Conor* and by the *Rev. John Sinnott Martin.* Among other things, Father Martin pointed out the truism that Americans of Irish descent seem to become "more Irish than the Irish themselves." He also noted with pleasure, that there were so many sober Irishmen present. Father Martin's thought was that Ireland should be united but that we should not have a *riot* over it, especially not in the U. S. A.

It was the pleasure and privilege of the Organization to grant lifetime honorary membership in the Society to *Senator Herbert R. O'Conor* and *Father Martin,* also to *Paul T. Broderick,* in recognition of the outstanding services these men had rendered to the Baltimore and Maryland community. Immediately after the luncheon the membership hied themselves hence to the St. Patrick's Day parade, which formed at Mt. Vernon Place, and which was later hailed in the local press as a great success.

At this time the Secretary noted for the attention and prayers of the membership the following members now deceased:

John M. Butler	Charles R. McLaughlin
Robert E. Gill	Joseph F. Mannion

William H. O'Neill

Prayers lead by the Chaplain were offered for the repose of their souls.

The *charter membership* as closed on this date, was approved as follows:

Alexander, Sr., Arnold Upton
Allen, Rev. Aloysius I.
Appleby, Jr., Joseph Lamb
Armstrong, Sr., Bernard F.
Arnold, Thomas Gerald
Barry, James Michael
Batterden, John Thomas
Beere, Michael Patrick
Blair, Frank J.
Borgerding, Edward F.
Bradley, R. Emmet
Bradley, Jr., Robert E.
Brennan, George Joseph
Broderick, Paul Timothy
Brough, Edward
Brown, Edward R.
Brown, Jr., John K.
Burke, Edward J.

Burke, John Patrick
Burns, John F.
Butler, J. Jerome
Byrd, Richard D.
Carberry, Francis X. Edward
Carberry, Martin Joseph
Caskey, Joseph F.
Cavanagh, George B.
Cecilian, Brother Gabriel
Clark, Melvin Raymond
Clark, Michael Warren
Coburn, Arthur Lee
Colgan, C. Warren
Coll, Leo Martin
Coniff, Edward J.
Connor, Charles R.
Coughlin, Jr., Patrick J.
Counselman, Charles C.
Counselman, Jr., Charles C.
Cremen, Ambrose Robert
Cremen, Robert Joseph
Croghan, Michael E.
Cullen, Newton Taylor
Cunningham, James T.
Curran, J. Joseph
Dempsey, Thomas F.
Dolan, Frank J.
Dolliver, Alan Kemp
Donnelly, Ambrose J.
Donnelly, Henry Gordon
Donovan, Arthur J.
Doud, Charles C.
Doud, Jr., John H.
Doud, Thomas J.
Dougherty, Edward W.
Dougherty, William F.
Duffy, Patrick Joseph
Dunphy, John A.
Erskine, Alfred H.
Fahey, James F.
Fallon, George H.
Fallon, George Michael
Fannon, Rev. Thomas J.
Feehley, John Pat
Feehly, Joseph Aloysius
Firlie, Raymond J.
Fitzpatrick, Frank Farrelly
Fitzpatrick, William Joseph
Flaherty, Joseph E.
Flanigan, John F.
Flynn, William J.
Fogarty, Edward C.
Fogarty, Raymond C.
Forni, Arthur G.
Forrest, Julian I.
Freeze, Joseph F.
Gallagher, Francis Xavier
Garrity, Jr., Bernard A.
Garrity, George Timothy
Garrity, Timothy H.
Gibson, E. Gordon
Goodhues, Jr., George S.
Gosnell, John Thomas
Grady, Honorable J. Harold
Graham, William S.
Griffin, John Thomas
Griffin, Martin Michael
Gunning, John Joseph
Heagerty, Joseph Michael
Healey, Raymond J.
Hennegan, John Vincent
Hillary, George Donald
Kane, John E.
Kelly, Rev. John P.
Kelly, Jr., Thomas E.
Kenealy, Capt. John B.
Kennedy, Jr., Ambrose J.
Kenny, Robert Joseph
Keough, Gerard G.
Lair, III, Horace Waters
Lauer, Louis Francis
Lee, Jr., Bernard J.

Lucey, Michael J.
McCardell, J. Neil
McCardell, Jr., Walter M.
McCrory, Rev. William T.
McDonnell, James J.
McElroy, Robert J.
McFadden, Lawrence F.
McGlone, Joseph Martin
McHale, Michael James
McIntyre, Edward Leroy
McKenna, Thomas Francis
McKewen, Jr., Thomas J.
McNamara, Donald C.
McNeal, Edward J.
McNerney, Dr. Francis Joseph
Mahoney, George P.
Mahoney, William W.
Haley, Thomas Patrick
Manning, Joseph L.
Mellendick, Joseph Robert
Monohan, II, Hugh J.
Mooney, Sr., Lawrence Roger
Moran, Daniel John
Mullaney, Jr., John W.
Mullen, Raymond Norbert
Murphy, Dennis Patrick
Murphy, Francis R.
Murray, Thomas Oliver Miles
Nagle, Jr., John Charles
Nolan, Jr., Bernard Jerome
Nolan, Jr., John Joseph Patrick
O'Brien, Michael J.
O'Connell, Daniel Michael
O'Connor, Sr., Gerald V.
O'Connor, Jr., John J.
O'Connor, Joseph F.
O'Donnell, James J.
O'Donnell, William Joseph
O'Donovan, Joseph Clennan
O'Dunne, David
O'Hara, James Gibbons
O'Malley, Edward Francis
O'Malley, Patrick F.
O'Malley, Paul Thomas
O'Sullivan, Bernard C.
O'Sullivan, D. Chester
Plumer, Edward F.
Plumber, Francis J.
Price, M. Tilghman
Quinn, Albert William
Quinn, John Martin
Rafferty, Jr., John E.
Reed, Jr., Paul James
Reed, Thomas Mooney
Regan, John Patrick
Reilly, Francis H.
Reynolds, James T.
Rooney, Jr., Irving Joseph
Shaughnessy, Leroy C.
Smith, E. Harry
Smith, Franklin
Stack, Joseph Anthony
Stilson, Sr., John Ira Godfrey
Sullivan, Emmett Joseph
Sullivan, William A.
Tunney, Stephen Richard
Waters, Patrick William
Webb, William P.
Welsh, Charles P.
Welsh, C. Robert
Welsh, Francis X.
Welsh, Jr., Joseph F.
Welsh, Leo M.
Welsh, Paul E.
Whelan, Rev. Thomas A.
Whitford, Edward Ellis
Whitford, William Ellis
Wright, Harry W.
Wyatt, Joseph McD.
Wyatt, Joseph M.

THE TOAST OF THE FRIENDLY SONS

O God of our Fathers, behold us tonight,
Sons of St. Patrick as one in our cause,
Citizens of those who through tyranny's night
Championed for Irishmen, Irishmen's laws.
What do we hear? 'Tis the roll of the drum,
As Washington, Moylan, a brave ghostly band,
From Lexington, Yorktown, Gettysburg came.
Sons of the Saint of the little green land,
Here Loyalty lingers, daughter of God,
Here Virtue and Knowledge and Fortitude meet,
Authority, child of the chastening rod,
And Friendship and Tolerance render them sweet.
May Heaven's own breezes to Ireland's coast,
On invisible waves through the lightening and gale,
Bear our message of hope, our perennial toast:
"The Friendly Sons of St. Patrick,
the Knights of the Grail."

THE HAIL OF THE FRIENDLY SONS

"Shall we who meet and part tonight
Remember not our sires?
Shall we forget their agelong fight
Their Quenchless battle-fires?
They handed us the freedom-flame
That Spreads from sea to sea.
They bade it burn in Ireland's name
Till land and race were free.
And we feel the thrill of their mighty hail,
It comes with the boom of the guns,
A heart and a hand for our fair land,
The Hail of the Friendly Sons."

Words by J. I. Clarke—1906

Music by Victor Herbert—1915-16

Past Presidents, Society of the
Friendly Sons of St. Patrick
of New York.

BRIEF CHRONICLE OF ACTIVITIES FOLLOWING

The First Annual Gala Luncheon of March 17, 1956 to the Close of the Calendar Year 1961

At the regular meeting of June 29, 1956, it was decided, for the purposes of good fellowship, and for the raising of funds for the support of the charitable work of the Society, that an *annual crab feast,* likewise an *annual oyster or bull roast* should be held; subject to prevailing conditions, but if possible, a *crab feast in July or August,* and an *oyster or bull roast* in *December, January or February.*

Thus, the *first annual crab feast* was held in the *Roof Garden of the B. P. O. E. Club,* Fayette Street, Baltimore; 375 enthusiastic members and friends were present, and 10 barrels of crabs, with appropriate beverages, were happily consumed. The Baltimore Sun commented favorably upon the affair.

Vice President Manning, in connection with his regular business affairs as an official of the Maryland Retail Grocers Association, visited Hawaii. On his return, the membership were treated to a most interesting account of his experiences there.

It was officially decided that the *prime object* of the *Society's charity* would be the Home for the Aged of the *"Little Sisters of the Poor",* Valley and Preston Streets, Baltimore.

In *November,* the *first annual oyster roast* was held in the basement and yard of *Calvert Hall College* (Cathedral and Mulberry Streets), as a result of the good offices of *Brother Gabriel Cecilian.* The roast was quite successful, gastronomically and financially, and the membership were grateful for the splendid assistance also, of their wives, sisters and sweethearts.

1957

On March 16, 1957, the following officers were elected:

President	J. NEIL MCCARDELL
1st Vice-President	J. EMMET BRADLEY
2nd Vice-President	JOS. L. MANNING
3rd Vice-President	J. HAROLD GRADY
Almoner	WM. W. MAHONEY
Recording Secretary	JOHN V. HENNEGAN
Corresponding Secretary	E. HARRY SMITH
Treasurer	WM. J. O'DONNELL

His Excellency Archbishop Francis P. Keough, D.D. and Senator John F. Kennedy of Massachusetts, were selected and instituted as Life Members of the Society.

After this meeting, the annual gala *St. Patrick's luncheon* was held at the *Southern Hotel,* Baltimore. The ballroom was filled to capacity. President McCardell presided, and the speaker of the day was *Senator John F. Kennedy,* who was introduced by outgoing President George B. Cavanagh. He gave a most interesting talk on Irish history, culture and the cause of liberty and stated that he was a member of the Boston Society and had been since he was twenty-one.

Gov. Theodore R. McKeldin presented Senator Kennedy with a certificate naming him as "Honorary Citizen of Maryland."

U. S. Congressman George H. Fallon was presented with honorary award as "Irishman of the Year," for outstanding civic services in the State and Nation.

On March 17, 1957, the Society officially participated in the St. Patrick's Day parade; the members were equipped with Kelly Green Hats and genuine Irish Black thorn walking sticks.

The parade assembled at Mt. Vernon Place, proceeded down Cathedral Street to Baltimore Street, to Holiday Street and disbanded at the War Memorial, opposite Baltimore's venerable City Hall. Among the celebrities reviewing the parade were, Archbishop Francis P. Keough, Governor McKeldin and Mayor Thomas J. D'Alesandro, also former U. S. Senator Herbert R. O'Conor.

In July, the annual crab feast was held at the Elks' Club; Jos. L. Manning and Frank L. Smith were in charge. The attendance was at capacity, and the affair was a complete success.

In June, Lord Mayor Briscoe, of Dublin, Ireland was presented with certificate of Honorary Life Membership in the Society.

In September, grants were made as follows:

B. P. O. E. Orphan's Fund—$100
Mercy Hospital Building Fund—$500
Bon Secours Hospital Building Fund—$500
Calvert Hall College Building Fund—$1,000

Prayers were offered for the repose of the soul of our Society Brother John Gately Flynn, who departed this life on September 3rd. On November 10th, following Mass celebrated by Auxiliary Bishop Jerome D. Sebastian at the Cathedral Minor Basilica of the Assumption of the Blessed Virgin Mary, the *first annual Communion Breakfast* was held at the *Southern Hotel.* President McCardell presided and the principal speaker was *Father Francis M. Tobey, S.J.,* Chaplain of the Maryland Penitentiary.

A donation of $500 was made to the *Little Sisters of the Poor.*

1958

The *annual oyster roast* was planned for February 15th at Calvert Hall College.

Leo McCormick gave a very interesting account of his visit to Baltimore, County Cork, Ireland; as a result of this, a successful drive for the clothing needed by the poor of that area was completed. The Society received evidences of appreciation for the splendid cooperation of its members in this connection.

On *March 15th,* the following officers were elected:

President	Joseph L. Manning
1st Vice-President	R. Emmet Bradley
2nd Vice-President	J. Harold Grady
3rd Vice-President	William W. Mahoney
Almoner	Donald C. McNamara
Corresponding Secretary	E. Harry Smith
Recording Secretary	John V. Hennegan
Treasurer	William J. O'Donnell

Chairmen of Committees were appointed as follows:

Board of Stewards	D. Chester O'Sullivan
Admissions Committee,	Thomas J. McKewen, Jr.
Charity Committee	Julian I. Forrest
Finance Committee	George P. Mahoney
Sick Committee	J. Joseph Curran

Following the election, the *third annual gala St. Patrick's luncheon* and celebration took place, at the *Southern Hotel.*

President Manning presided; the principal speaker was *Robert F. Kennedy,* Counsel for the U. S. Senate sub-committee on *Union Labor Practices,* a brother of Senator John F. Kennedy, and graduate of Harvard and the University of Virginia Law School. Mr. Kennedy was presented with the following:

Certificate of Honorary Life Membership, by President Manning

Certificate of Honorary Citizenship of Maryland, by Governor Theodore R. McKeldin

Key to the City of Baltimore, by Mayor D'Alesandro

An Irish Shillelah and a Green Fedora, by J. Neil McCardell

The annual *crab feast* was held at *Cottage Grove Beach, Rock Creek, Anne Arundel County,* on *August 16th;* 700 were in attendance, the weather was fine, a good time was had by all, and the affair was a tremendous financial success as well.

A donation of $1,000 was made to the *Little Sisters of the Poor.*

J. Edward Brown was appointed as *Keeper of the Society Seal.*

In *October,* the Quarterly Meeting was held at *Bernie Lee's Penn Hotel, Towson, Maryland,* where the membership enjoyed a lecture with colored photo slides, on Baltimore and County Cork, *Ireland, by Francis X. Hennessy.*

On Sunday, *November 30th,* the second annual Society Communion Breakfast was held at the Southern Hotel, following full attendance at Mass celebrated by Auxiliary Bishop Sebastian, at the Cathedral Minor Basilica of the Assumption of the Blessed Virgin Mary.

Prayers were said for the repose of the souls of brothers Robert E. Gill and Joseph F. Mannion, who passed away during the year.

On the *Sunday before Christmas,* a *special dinner* for the old folks residing at the *Little Sisters of the Poor,* was given. A Committee of the Membership, led by Jos. L. Manning, served the dinner and entertained afterwards.

1959

The Church of St. John the Evangelist, Eager and Valley Streets, Baltimore, was donated $150 for repainting and decorating the Convent. A number of the members gave their services in this connection, in appreciative memory of school days long gone by.

Contributions continued as follows:

Calvert Hall Building Fund—$1,394.43

On *March 14th,* the following officers were elected:

President	J. HAROLD GRADY
1st Vice-President	R. EMMET BRADLEY
2nd Vice-President	WILLIAM W. MAHONEY
3rd Vice-President	DONALD C. MCNAMARA
Almoner	EDWARD R. BROWN
Recording Secretary	JOHN V. HENNEGAN
Corresponding Secretary,	THOMAS J. MCKEWEN, JR.
Treasurer	WILLIAM J. O'DONNELL

E. Harry Smith was appointed Keeper of the Society Seal.

A modern large screen *television set* was presented to The Home for the Aged of the *Little Sisters of the Poor.*

Following the elections, the *fourth annual gala St. Patrick's luncheon* was held at the *Southern Hotel.* Attendance overflowed capacity into adjoining halls. President Grady presided, and the guest speakers were Auxiliary Bishop Sebastian, Mayor Thos. D'Alesandro and Governor J. Millard Tawes. Principal speaker was *Father J. J. Scanlan, S.J., of Loyola College.* Father Scanlan's fine talk may be summarized as follows:

"My childhood memories of St. Patrick's day are still very green. We had in our parish one of those wonderful Irish pastors, the Reverend Jeremiah Nevin, complete with blackthorn cane that was the dread of all the school children, but of course he never used it for he ruled his parish with a gentle roar and a heart full of priestly charity, and he was known to his fellow-priests by a very wonderful title, 'The Watchdog of the Blessed Sacrament.' And though he is dead and gone these many years, God rest his soul, his parish still bears the unmistakable imprint of his faith and his devotion to the Eucharist. Naturally, in school, St. Patrick's Day was always a great day. It was a patch of green in the deepening purple of the Lenten sea-son, a slight preview of the glory of Easter, and of course there was never any school on that day, but we all were gathered at Mass, and I still remember the lifelike statue of the Great Saint, with mitre and crozier and a few snakes slithering away from his feet, and then we always concluded the Mass with that great roof-raising hymn 'Great and Glorious Saint Patrick.'

"The Irish have always had a great respect for and love of the mind, of learning, of truth. The unfading symbol of this is the famous 'Hedgemaster' — 'Way back in 1812 English travelers, driving through Roscommon, used to note with contempt that, as they went along, they saw many a ditch full of needy scholars, and it is said that eighteenth century travelers were frequently amazed that stableboys could quote their Ovid by heart and that Greek students wandered all over the wild mountains of Kerry.

"This great love of learning was made possible by three things: (1) students who were so mad to learn that they would rather learn than play; (2) parents who were glad to sacrifice themselves, glad to go hungry to bed so long as they could scrape together three shillings and a threepence a quarter so that their sons and daughters might enter into a beautiful world of the mind and escape from the degradation that they had been forced into; (3) masters who lived for their boys and were willing to die for them too.

"No wonder then that it is called the *Isle of Scholars!*

"The Irish brought this love of learning with them to this country, and it was here that many of them got mixed up with, of all people, the Jesuits and even a few, as a matter of fact quite a few, decided to follow that old Gaelic axiom: 'If you can't lick them, join them.'

"And it's reassuring too for me to look around my senior class at Loyola College and see myself surrounded by names like Brady, Byrnes, Callahan, followed by Donohue, Doyle and Farrell, the two Fitzzimmonses, the three Kellys, all the Mc's, McGovern, McGuire and McKenna, the O's,

O'Conor and O'Malley, and obviously a Murphy and a Walsh and there's even another Scanlan besides myself, and that spelt with two a's, as is only right. And I feel that it is no coincidence, and if it be, it is a most blessed one, that today your incoming president and Irishman of the year, and the Democratic candidate for Mayor of Baltimore, J. Harold Grady, is a graduate of Loyola College, class of '38.

"The Irishman is a man of heart, of great heart; he's a great lover, and it was the love in the heart of men like Teddy O'Neill and Tim Toolan for such fair Irish lassies as Kathleen Mavoureen and Molly Malone that led them first to the altar where God's love made them more perfectly one, that led them then to build that 'tumbledown shack in Athlone' that was often not big enough to house all the gossoons that came tumbling out the front door. The Irishman brought with him to America this love of the family, and this was one of his greatest contributions to this country.

"Lack of love is the basic lack in the world whether it be in the lives of individuals, of families, of nations, or the family of nations. We hear lamentations about the American educational system and with justification, but we must never forget that it is not enough to educate the mind unless we also educate the heart. We must grow not only in the comprehension of truth. We must also and even more importantly grow in the practice of love, of charity, and it's an old saying that charity begins at home. Love is taught in the family; it is only love that will build families.

"The home is the most important thing in this world, for what are nations made of except families. Take our own United States. Despite what we hear in campaign oratory, it is not the rockbound coasts of Maine nor the sunkist shores of California, to 'corn' a phrase, nor is it the wheat fields of Kansas nor the Great Lakes nor the Grand Canyon nor ever Wall Street. It is the families of this country, and it is a truism to say that 'as the family goes, so goes the United States.' While we are stressing the importance of national defense against attack from without, let us never forget that far more dangerous is corruption from within, and here is where our Irishman of heart must play his part.

"Our friendly son of Saint Patrick is just that, a friend, with a hand that is the symbol of his strength. He is not just a thinker; he is not just a lover; he is a doer of the deeds that his thinking and loving lead him to perform, and in these deeds he does not hesitate to use the divine gift of his hands.

"This hand can be offered in the handclasp of friendship, and the Irish have had a particular gift for friendship with almost all the strange varieties of the human family.

"But also this hand can be made into a fist against an enemy; it can reach down and pick up a shillelagh in the tradition of 'Two-Shillelagh O'Sullivan'. Not that the Irishman is an angry man (as a matter of fact he is by nature a 'quiet man') unless, of course, there is reason to be angry, and just as the hands of St. Patrick were mostly lifted in benediction, still on occasion he could use his crozier to send scattering the snakes from Ireland's green glens.

"Let us not lose our sense of moral indignation; let us not be afraid to be angry when there is reason, when we see injustice perpetrated, chastity ridiculed, charity violated, loyalty derided. We hope that our hands can do the deeds of peace; but if necessary, these hands can, as they have in the past, do the deeds of war. Please God, these deeds will not be necessary.

"The Irish have a love of beauty and, what is more, they are almost compelled to give voice to their love of beauty. Their critics often scorned the way they wasted their time, for how could people come to any good end who spent so much time on song and poetry. But the Irish realized a divine truth, that Beauty is in a sense the most useless thing in the world and yet, at the same time, one of the world's greatest treasures. They could not just look at a sunrise or a sunset, and be silent like a 'mute and inglorious Milton'. They had to give out with a song, and they sang of the beauties of God's creation from the "Green Glens of Antrim' and the "Mountains of Mourne' to 'The Isle of Innisfree' and the River Shannon and 'Galway Bay'.

"Even the word 'Irish' suggests a smile, and with reason. There were also those Irish jokes involving Pat and Mike and all those stories about the boys in the back room at Irish wakes. There were those touching Irish ballads like that one poignantly entitled, 'Who Threw the Overalls in Mrs. Murphy's Chowder?' They had learned to suffer and still to smile, no mean achievement, and they carried their grand sense of humor with them even to the jaws of death.

"The Irishman was a man who believed intensely in the reality of God and in the intimate reality of God's Providence in his everyday life. In his prayer he was not satisfied to say prayers out of a book; he said the prayers he found welling up from the book of his heart, and he did not merely talk when he prayed, for it is ungentlemanly to monopolize the conversation especially with God, and what Irishman would be ungentlemanly most of all to God? He also listened in his prayer, and God told him many wonderful, consoling things that sustained his faith in the moments of darkness and doubt and uncertainty and that fed his hope when all seemed lost, and his religion was not always a comfortable thing. It was often clad in the rags of poverty, and prostrate within the darkness of Gethsemane, not far from the shadow of Calvary. His faith was not a tranquilizer, but it did help him to bear with tranquility and dignity the cross of his own existence.

"Now who but an Irishman could ever compose a prayer like this one?

> 'May the earth be soft under you when you rest out upon it, tired at the end of a day, and may it rest easy over you

when, at the last, you lay out under it; may it rest so lightly over you, that your soul may be off from under it quickly, and up, and off, and on its way to God.'

"Just as on Christmas every man and woman becomes a child again, so this Tuesday will see that great day when all the world forgets its national problems and becomes Irish as an old hymn to St. Patrick rather amusingly has it:

'Today everyone your daughter is or son and our hearts give your shamrock a sod.'

"Let us put together our Friendly Son of Saint Patrick again, and let us walk through this vale of tears as the men that we are, that strange amalgam that chemists stand in wonder of, that strange creature with a shamrock in his coat lapel that is nothing but

"A MIND, A HEART, AND A HAND: A SONG, A SMILE, AND A PRAYER."

Our new President, J. Harold Grady was selected as *Irishman of the Year,* and presented with the customary certificate thereof.

Sunday, March 15th, witnessed the *St. Patrick's Parade,* bigger, longer and better than ever. Members were out in force, and were enthusiastically greeted all along the way and, as usual, the contingent of the Friendly Sons was the largest.

Honor to *D. Chester O'Sullivan,* Chairman of the Board of Stewards. At this time, Mr. O'Sullivan, as a measure of the great esteem in which he is held by the Society, and as a token of recognition of the outstanding services he has consistently rendered to the Society from its very inception, was presented with a *Certificate of Life Membership* in the Society. Presentation on behalf of the entire membership was made by President Grady.

The *annual crab feast* was held *Saturday, August 15th* at *Cottage Grove Beach;* 800 members, families and friends attended.

The principal hosts of the occasion were Mayor of Baltimore J. Harold Grady, and President of the Society, together with Thomas J. McKewen, Jr., Special Chairman of the Crab Feast Committee. The facilities and surroundings were quite satisfactory and the weather was good. Since a bathing beach adjoined the area of the crab feast, many of those present availed themselves of this opportunity for wholesome exercise and recreation. In short, it could be conservatively stated that the affair was an outstanding artistic, gastronomic and financial success.

In *November,* $1,000 was set aside as a contribution to the *Little Sisters of the Poor.*

An additional $1,000 was set up as special *"Emergency Charity Fund",* to be deposited in the Baltimore Savings & Loan Association.

November 22nd, the third annual *Communion Breakfast* was held at the Southern Hotel following the Mass at the "Old Cathedral", *Cathedral Minor Basilica of the Assumption of Blessed Virgin Mary, Baltimore.*

The principal speaker was *Stephen P. Kennedy, Police Commissioner of the City of New York,* no relation to the brothers, John F. and Robert F. Kennedy, who made an excellent talk on proper and wise enforcement of the laws and proper measures for control of so-called juvenile delinquency.

Prayers were offered for the repose of the souls of brothers Donald J. McCourt, Bernard A. Garrity, Thomas J. McCuigan, Charles R. McLaughlin, Bernard A. Kenny and John M. Butler, who departed this life during the year.

1960

On *March 12, 1960,* at the *annual meeting* of the Society, the following officers were elected:

President . . . . Donald C. McNamara
1st Vice-President . . . . . . William W. Mahoney

2nd Vice-President . . . . George P. Mahoney
3rd Vice-President . . . . . . William J. O'Donnell
Almoner . . . . Edward R. Brown
Keeper of the Seal . . . . Paul T. O'Malley
Corresponding Secretary,
Thomas J. McKewen, Jr.
Recording Secretary . . . . John V. Hennegan
Treasurer . . . . E. Harry Smith

The following officers were appointed:

Historian . . . . Alan K. Dolliver
Counsel . . . . Paul J. Reed, Jr.
Chaplain . . . . Rev. Thomas A. Whalen
Publicity Director . . . . . Walter M. McCardell

Re-appointed as *Chairman of the Board of Stewards* was *D. Chester O'Sullivan*. Chairmen of other committees were appointed as follows:

Admissions Committee . . . . . . James M. Manley
Finance Committee . . . . J. Joseph Curran
Charity Committee . . . . Julian I. Forrest
Sick Committee . . . . Michael J. O'Brien

Thereafter, the membership proceeded to the ballroom of the *Southern Hotel* for the fifth gala *annual corned beef and cabbage luncheon;* approximately 500 members, friends and guests were in attendance. The invocation was pronounced by his Excellency Jerome D. Sebastian, D.D., Auxiliary Bishop of Baltimore. Honored guests were His Excellency, J. Millard Tawes, Governor of Maryland, Rev. J. J. Scanlan, S.J. of Loyola College, Baltimore, the Honorable J. Harold Grady, Mayor of the City of Baltimore and retiring President of the Society.

The President-elect of the Society, Donald C. McNamara was presented to the group by Toastmaster William J.

O'Donnell. Mr. McNamara responded briefly in expressing his appreciation of the honor bestowed upon him by his election and called for the support and cooperation of the members and pledged an active and fruitful administration.

Rev. J. J. Scanlan, S.J., of Loyola was presented with a *Certificate of Honorary Life Membership* in recognition of his outstanding leadership in Irish affairs at home and abroad.

Another specially honored guest was *Martin C. McMahon,* Captain of the Baltimore City Fire Department. Captain McMahon, who was nominated as "Irishman of the Year" for outstanding service to the City of Baltimore and to the Nation, in connection with his development of the successful "mouth to mouth" method of resussitation, now adopted nationally, was presented with the customary framed *Certificate* symbolic of this award.

Captain McMahon responded briefly and appreciatively, but pointedly on accepting the award of "Irishman of the Year". He was warmly applauded, in particular, when he stated that the formula of success for public speakers is as follows:

1. The speaker should stand up, to be *seen*.
2. He should speak up, to be *heard*.
3. But he should *sit down* to be really appreciated.

The principal speaker was the *Honorable Eugene J. McCarthy, United States Senator from Minnesota.* Senator McCarthy gave a stirring address upon the meaning and objectives of liberalism in government.

Chaplain of the Society, Rev. Thomas A. Whalen, as well as all of the officers were in attendance.

Governor Tawes and Mayor Grady spoke briefly and approvingly of the progress and prestige and good work of the Society and commended all those responsible therefor.

Music was provided by the John A. Quinn Orchestra, and the group was entertained with songs by Joseph L. Manning, Thomas J. Doud, and the singing of traditional Irish songs by the entire group. The affair was a tremendous success being limited in size only by the physical facilities available.

On *Sunday, March 13th,* the *annual St. Patrick's Day parade* took place. The Society's unit, as in the past was outstanding in the number of those marching, their general appearance and marching efficiency and was greeted with applause throughout the line of the parade. There were over 300 in the Society's marching group, led by President-elect *Donald C. McNamara* and retiring President *J. Harold Grady.*

Honored guests reviewing the parade with His Excellency Archbishop Francis P. Keough, D.D., were Governor J. Millard Tawes and John J. Sweeney, Jr. of the Ancient Order of Hibernians and Chairman of the Parade Committee.

Julian I. Forrest, Sr,. at the request of the *Mother Superior of the Little Sisters of the Poor* and on the recommendation of the President, took over the responsibility of actively cooperating with the Little Sisters of the Poor in the working out of their problems.

On *Saturday, August 13th,* the *annual crab feast,* heavily attended by more than 800 members and their friends, was held at *Cottage Grove Beach.* The affair was likewise a financial success, swelling the charitable fund considerably. General Chairman, *Paul T. O'Malley* was given a well merited round of applause for his fine effort in this connection.

On *Sunday, November 20th,* the *Fourth Annual Mass and Communion Breakfast,* was held. Mass was heard at *Cathedral Minor Bascilica of the Assumption of the Blessed Virgin Mary,* and the breakfast which followed was at the *Southern Hotel.* Celebrant of the Mass was

Monsignor George L. Hopkins, Chancellor of the Archdiocese of Baltimore. The sermon was by *Rev. Harry O'Meara,* Redemptorist missionary.

The principal speaker at the breakfast was *Col. "Father Mike" Harold F. Donovan,* Supervising Chaplain, 29th Division, Second Army, U. S. A. Father Donovan was educated at Mount St. Mary's College, Emmittsburg, Maryland and subsequently entered the U. S. Army as a Chaplain, was stationed at Camp Ritchie, Md., and thereafter saw service in France. Father Donovan gave a very interesting talk upon his experiences from the time he was first ordained and concluded with his experiences in connection with the military during the war and after. Chairman of the breakfast was President Donald C. McNamara; Toastmaster, J. Harold Grady; invocation and blessings by Brother Gabriel Cecilian and Brother Fidelis Thomas.

At this time, the Society donated $1,000 to the *Little Sisters of the Poor* to be used for the general purposes of that fine organization; in addition, $500 *was donated to the "Little Sisters"* for the specific purpose of providing for the annual Christmas party given by the Society for the benefit of the old folks; $500 *was donated to the Calvert Hall School Building Fund.* These donations were most gratefully received and acknowledged.

On *November 20th,* an *oyster roast was held at the new Calvert Hall College* under the sponsorship of *Brother Gabriel Cecilian* and *Brother Fidelis Thomas,* for the general building fund of the college. Past President J. Neil McCardell was co-chairman and as a result, although this affair was not nominally sponsored by the Society, nevertheless it was heavily supported by the membership. The consensus of opinion was that this roast was one of the largest and finest affairs of this kind yet produced in Baltimore, not only because of the fine physical facilities at the new Calvert Hall College, but respecting the quality of the food, the service and likewise the fine cooperation of the joint sponsors. The Officers and Members of the Society were out in force and took great pride in their contribution to the financial success of the Roast.

Through the efforts of past President George B. Cavanagh, authorization was voted for the formation of a *Glee Club* which would represent the Society on appropriate occasions. Mr. Cavanagh reported that Robert Johnson had been secured as Director and stated that Brian A. Dolliver was actively working with him in the development of this organization.

On *Sunday, December 11th,* which was a blustery, blizzardy day, the Society gave its *annual Christmas Dinner to the old folks of the Little Sisters of the Poor,* 1200 Valley Street, Baltimore. Numerous photos were taken and placed in the archives. The leaders cooperating in the handling of this dinner were President *Donald C. McNamara, Joseph L. Manning, George P. Mahoney,* together with *Mother Superior Marguerite* and *Brothers Gabriel Cecilian and Fidelis Thomas.*

Approximately fifty loyal and dedicated Friendly Sons were in attendance despite the very bad weather. For example, Paul T. O'Malley made it a point to come all the way from Yorktown, Va., a distance of 180 miles in order to be present and serve. Others active in serving the dinner and in entertaining were Julian I. Forrest, Sr., Charles C. Doud, Edward R. Brown, Brian A. Dolliver, Dr. Francis J. McNerney, George B. Cavanagh.

Solos, appropriate to the occasion, were sung by Brian A. Dolliver, Joseph L. Manning, Charles C. Doud, John T. Gosnell and were joined by members of the Glee Club. Instrumental music was furnished by Roy Heineck and his "Frivolous Three", aided by saxaphonist Baker from the "Serenaders", a very fine musical group who could not attend, being stalled outside of town by the snowstorm.

At the conclusion of the dinner for the old folks, Mother Superior Marguerite insisted upon providing dinner for the members of the Society who had donated their services. At this affair, Mr. Manning acted as Chairman and there were brief talks by George P. Mahoney, Donald C. McNamara and Alan K. Dolliver. At the request of the Mother Superior and her assistants, Brian A. Dolliver sang some additional songs a capella.

Our friend, confessor and mentor, Auxiliary Bishop Jerome D. Sebastian, D.D., passed away, a great loss to Baltimore, the church and the members of the Society. Many prayers were offered for the repose of his soul and plans were instituted to establish a suitable Society Memorial to his presence and work among us. Also, prayers were said for the repose of the soul of brother Arthur A. McDermott who departed this life during the year.

1961

On *March 11th,* at the *annual meeting* of the SOCIETY, officers as follows were elected:

President	WILLIAM W. MAHONEY (Director of Public Relations of the City of Baltimore)
1st Vice President	GEORGE P. MAHONEY
2nd Vice President	WILLIAM J. O'DONNELL
3rd Vice President	THOMAS J. MCKEWEN, JR.
Almoner	EDWARD R. BROWN
Corresponding Secretary	PAUL T. O'MALLEY
Recording Secretary	JOHN V. HENNEGAN
Treasurer	E. HARRY SMITH
Keeper of the Seal	THOMAS BRACKEN

After taking office, President-elect Mahoney made the following appointments:

Counsel	PAUL J. REED, JR.
Historian	ALAN K. DOLLIVER
Chaplain	REV. THOMAS A. WHALEN
Chairman, Board of Stewards,	D. CHESTER O'SULLIVAN

Publicity Director	WALTER M. MCCARDELL
Admissions	JAMES M. MANLEY
Finance	J. JOSEPH CURRAN
Charity	JULIAN I. FORREST, SR.
Sick	MARTIN M. GRIFFIN

The *annual luncheon* of the SOCIETY, in memory and tribute to St. Patrick, was held in the grand ballroom of the *Southern Hotel, Baltimore, Maryland, at 12:30 P.M. March* 11, 1961. The ballroom was filled to overflowing. "The wearing of the green" was universally evident. The luncheon consisted of the usual corned beef and cabbage and boiled potatoes, Irish green ice cream and coffee. The invocation and closing prayers were said by *Rt. Rev. Monsignor George L. Hopkins,* Chancellor of the Archdiocese of Baltimore.

Hon. J. Harold Grady, Mayor of the City of Baltimore and past President of the SOCIETY, acted as Toastmaster in the course of which he wittily told many Irish stories. For example: the drunken Irishman on the train who explained his condition by the fact that he was placed in a compartment with "bad" companions"; to wit, teetotalers. It seems that he had to drink all the whiskey himself.

Mr. Grady introduced *George B. Cavanagh,* Chairman of the Nominating Committee, who presented the new slate of Officers as elected. Thereafter, the Toastmaster called upon the new President, William W. Mahoney, who expressed his pleasure and gratitude at being honored by his election as President and pledged his cooperation and requested the cooperation and help of all of the membership in carrying on the splendid effective and efficient work of the SOCIETY during his administration as in the past.

Mr. Grady then called upon Donald C. McNamara, retiring President of the SOCIETY, who thanked the membership for their cooperation and help, and reviewed the activities and accomplishments of the past year, such as the various charitable donations made, the very successful crab feast, which 900 attended, the very successful attendance of the membership at the special Mass at the Cathedral, at which 600 were in attendance, and 400 at the breakfast at the Southern Hotel, which followed; the very successful and well received Christmas dinner given for the old folks at the Little Sisters of the Poor, etc.

Mr. Grady also introduced the Hon. J. Millard Tawes, Governor of Maryland, who extended his greetings and expressed his appreciation for the invitation to be present and break bread with such a fine group of men, and praised the work of the SOCIETY. Attorney General Thomas F. Finan and Congressman George H. Fallon also were introduced and responded briefly. Also introduced was Mr. Joseph J. Duffy, President of the Hibernian Society of Baltimore and Mr. James J. O'Beirne, President of the Baltimore Chapter of the Ancient Order of Hibernians.

Mr. Grady read a telegram received from President John F. Kennedy, expressing his regrets at not being able to be present and noting his appreciation for the fact that he had previously been honored with a life membership in the SOCIETY, referring further to the fact that the first Irish society of similar type to the Friendly Sons of St. Patrick was organized in Boston, his home city, and complimenting the Irish and Irish-Americans for their indomitable spirit of freedom, etc.

Thereafter, Mr. Grady introduced Mr. Joseph L. Manning, past President of the SOCIETY, who introduced the guest speaker of the day, Mr. Ian Stuart. Mr. Stuart, although of Scotch-Irish ancestry, was born in Dublin. His father was born in County Roscommon, and his mother was born in County Mayo. He is a graduate of the University of Dublin, a four-letter man and was very active in rugby football. He is Community Relations Director of Florists Telegraph Delivery Association, Inc.; a recipient of an award for service from the Freedom Association of

Valley Forge, Pennsylvania. Mr. Stuart is the possessor of a delightful Irish brogue (of the educated Irishman). He made a very long talk, items of which might be summarized as follows:

Praised the Irish temperament.

Spoke of his Scotch name.

Told of how at one of the big games between the University of Dublin and the University of Edinburgh, which Dublin won, he was approached by an irate Scotchman later who inquired "what the hell was a man named Stuart doing on the Irish team"—it's not the "luck" of the Irish but the "greatness."

Irish steadfastness for liberty

The Irishman's belief that the best place in all the world to be born is in Ireland

In a world of torment it seems that no one is mad at the Irish.

The ideals of the Irish—their strong religious faith and courage which today is so needed if we are to overcome Godless communism.

The Irish have gained their strength the hard way—through adversity, and that this is good since there is no easy roads to our goal.

The great Irish love for their country even though for various reasons they had to leave it. Quoted Edward Everett Hale's "Breathes there a man with soul so dead who never to himself has said 'this is my own, my native land.' "

The Irish have the longest memories and the shortest tempers.

He is proud of being Irish and recommended a motto for

us all since we have a man in the Presidency whose "mother and father are Irish and he is Irish too"— "what can I do for my country instead of what can I get; what can I give my country instead of what will my country give me."

He spoke of the fact that while the Irish are strongly religious, nevertheless they are tolerant and recalled the fact that in Dublin they elected a Jewish mayor because they thought he was the best qualified man available for the job; and how many of the officials of Southern Ireland are protestants, notwithstanding the fact that 90% of the population in Southern Ireland is Roman Catholic.

Spoke of the beautiful Irish countryside and the beautiful Irish women and expatiated on the glories of the Irish and the Irish race all in a voice electric with emotion, uplifting and inspiring.

Honored guests attending were:

Brother Gabriel Cecilian and Brother Fidelis Thomas, of Calvert Hall

Rev. Roger K. Wooden, of Blessed Sacrament Church

Rev. John F. McGlone, of St. Joseph's Church

Rev. J. Chester Griffith, of St. Bernard's Church

Rev. Nicholas W. Dohony, of St. Patrick's Church

Music was furnished by Jack Quinn's musical organization, and the group was edified by songs by Brian A. Dolliver, Charles C. Doud and Joseph L. Manning.

The ANNUAL PARADE, in celebration of the memory of St. Patrick, our patron Saint, participated in by Irish and allied organizations of Baltimore and Maryland took place on Sunday, March 12th. Our FRIENDLY SONS were prominently represented in greater force than ever before. The weather was bleak, but fair, and large crowds lined the route of the parade, down Cathedral Street from Mt. Vernon Place to Baltimore Street, to Holiday Street, to Lexington Street, and to terminus at the WAR MEMORIAL. More than 50 bands together with Fife and Drum Corps providing stirring marching music for the participants and entertainment for the viewers. The FRIENDLY SONS contingent was headed by President William W. Mahoney, Chairman of the Board of Stewards D. Chester O'Sullivan, Congressman George H. Fallon, and most of our Officers and Committee Chairmen. It appeared that this St. Patrick's Day observance is growing in popularity with the public, along with the growing enthusiasm of the increasing number of units participating and the size and splendor thereof.

On July 18th, a fine "Buffet Supper" with refreshments was served at the Schlitz Brewery Tap Room (Private), 1517 N. Gay Street, Baltimore. Our host was past President Donald C. McNamara, to whom all are indebted for his splendid and most generous hospitality. Following the supper, an informal meeting was held in development of plans and in fixing committee assignments, etc., in connection with the coming CRAB FEAST set down for August 12th. Approximately 70 faithful members of the SOCIETY were present, with the officers and members pledging their support toward the successful operation of the CRAB FEAST as planned. A standing vote of thanks was rendered Donald C. McNamara for this and his many other contributions to the work of the SOCIETY.

The "CRAB FEAST of the Year" in the Baltimore area, was held at Cottage Grove Beach on Rock Creek, Anne Arundel County, on Saturday, August 12th. The joint chairmen of the affair were brothers Paul T. O'Malley and Thomas J. Kewen, Jr., together with cooperating special Committees of the Officers, ably assisted by Bernard J. Lee, Jr., with his fabulous "BASKET OF CHEER"; and Edward C. Fogerty with his lucky "50-50" investment opportunity. The SOCIETY was again favored with fine weather and the crabs, crabcakes, cold cuts, salads, etc., beverages and refreshments were lavish in quantity and deliciously satisfying to the palate. Members, their families, their friends and their friends' families swelled the attendance to a record figure. The outing was deemed by all to be an outstanding success, notwithstanding the fact that the net receipts for charitable purposes of the SOCIETY fell somewhat below those of the previous year.

At the meeting of September 25th, Chairman of the Charity Committee, Julian I. Forrest, Sr., advised the delivery of a $500 donation on behalf of the SOCIETY to the Institution of the Carmelite Nuns at Dulany Valley Road, Baltimore County, and read the letter of appreciation from Prioress Sister Mary Magdeline. Chairman of the Committee on By-Laws, Alan K. Dolliver, reviewed the history of the original By-Laws and proposed on behalf of the Committee, a new revised and codified set thereof. After due discussion, during which all questions at issue were answered and disposed of, it was resolved by a vote of 40-6, that the revised By-Laws be and thereby were adopted.

On Sunday, November 26th, a group of our ardent members of the SOCIETY attended a Mass especially dedicated to the SOCIETY and its present and past departed members, at the CATHEDRAL MINOR BASILICA OF THE ASSUMPTION OF THE BLESSED VIRGIN MARY, Cathedral and Mulberry Streets, Baltimore. Due to serious illness of our friend and patron, the Most Reverend Francis P. Keough, Archbishop of Baltimore, was unable to celebrate the Mass as he had originally planned. In the Archbishops' indisposition, Mass was celebrated by the Archbishop Co-Adjutor of Baltimore, the Most Reverend Lawrence J. Shehan, D.D. All of the officers and almost 400 members of the SOCIETY attended and received Communion. Archbishop Shehan delivered a short but very pointed, inspiring sermon on Christian duties in a world of tension, disorder and crumbling morality.

After the Mass, the group repaired to the Southern Hotel, Light and Redwood Streets, where the usual and proverbial "capacity crowd" enjoyed Communion Breakfast. His Honor, Mayor of Baltimore, J. Harold Grady extended welcome greetings and then turned over direction of the affair as MASTER OF CEREMONIES to President William W. Mahoney. After appropriate amenities, the introduction of those officers and honored guests seated at the head table, the honored guest speaker of the day, Jeremiah J. O'Callaghan was introduced. Mr. O'Callaghan was born in Ireland but came to the U. S. in 1934. He served overseas in World War II as a Captain in the U. S. Army; is a past national president of the Ancient Order of Hibernians in America; is a former Assistant Corporation Counsel, of the City of Jersey City, New Jersey. In 1958, Mr. O'Callaghan was presented with the KNIGHTS OF COLUMBUS GOLD MEDAL as Catholic Man of the Year in recognition of his services on behalf of the Church and it's people; is presently Director of Investigation of the City of Jersey City, New Jersey, and also is in private law practice. Mr. O'Callaghan opened his address with a number of jokes with an Irish twist, but thereafter preached a long, ardent, and philosophical sermon touching upon the history of the Roman Catholic Church and on the duties of true Christian and Catholic men and women. His address was given most respectful attention and at its completion was greeted with standing acclaim. On behalf of the SOCIETY, President Mahoney expressed his thanks and felicitations.

At the meeting of December 12th, President Mahoney announced the appointment of the NOMINATING COMMITTEE as follows:

DONALD C. MCNAMARA, *Chairman*
GEORGE B. CAVANAGH

Thomas J. Doud, Sr.
Philip T. McCusker
Francis J. McGee
Michael J. O'Brien
D. Chester O'Sullivan

Plus alternates as follows:

Julian I. Forrest, Sr.
J. Neil McCardell

Eugene W. Coughlin, presently Director of the U. S. Army Field Band was appointed as Director of the SOCIETY'S newly organized GLEE CLUB, an enterprise which has long been the dream of brothers Charles and Thomas Doud, George B. Cavanagh and others. The recommendation of brothers James Cassidy and Julian I. Forrest, Sr., that the SOCIETY defray the cost of a new door, etc., for the needed rehabilitation of the NUNNERY OF THE CHURCH OF ST. JOHN THE EVANGELIST, Eager and Valley Streets, Baltimore, was approved.

The final event of the SOCIETY'S calendar year took place on Sunday, December 17th, at THE HOME FOR THE AGED OF THE LITTLE SISTERS OF THE POOR, 1200 Valley Street, Baltimore. This was the now ANNUAL DINNER and entertainment given by the SOCIETY to the folks at this fine institution. The Officers, led by President Mahoney and assisted by more than 40 dedicated officers and members of the SOCIETY served the traditional turkey dinner with trimmings and refreshments, and candy and smoking supplies. A high point of the affair was the presentation of a check for $1,000 to Mother Superior Marcella, by President Mahoney and the Officers, on the behalf of the SOCIETY. Entertainment which was joined in by many of our guests was provided by the Lou Becker Trio; the Ferdinand Rupp Hillbilly

Band and Vocal Barber Shop Quartet; the Little Sisters Postulant's Vocal Chorus; Charles and Tom Doud, William Cahill, Brian Dolliver, and the impromptu Friendly Sons Glee Club. Chairman of this happily received affair was Joseph L. Manning, assisted by President William W. Mahoney, Vice President George P. Mahoney, Chairman of the Board of Stewards, D. Chester O'Sullivan and the entire official family of the SOCIETY. Charles Herr of the Baltimore *News-Post* and Walter McCardell, of the Baltimore *Sun* (Publicity Director of the SOCIETY) took many photos for publication and for the archives. At a reciprocal luncheon afterwards, tendered the SOCIETY members present, by the LITTLE SISTERS OF THE POOR, mutual thanks were expressed by Mother Superior Marcella; Assistant Mother Superior Pauline and by Head of the Oblates in charge of Postulant's Training, etc., Susan Garvie, another native of Ireland with a delightful brogue. Brief expressions in response were made by President Mahoney, Vice-President George P. Mahoney, Joseph L. Manning, D. Chester O'Sullivan, William J. O'Donnell, Thomas E. Bracken, Paul J. Reed, Jr., Jeremiah Kennedy, George B. Cavanagh and others. Thanks were expressed to Edward C. Fogarty, Donald and Francis McNamara, "Pat" Roche and Michael O'Brien, for gratefully received food and refreshments donated.

Prayers were said for repose of the souls of brothers Louis F. Lauer, John P. Mannion, and Franklin L. Smith, who passed away during the year.

With great sorrow, Officers and members noted the recent passing of our great friend, spiritual leader and benefactor, the Most Reverend Francis Patrick Keough, D.D., Archbishop of Baltimore. Prayers were said for the repose of his soul and arrangements were made that at least 100 Masses for the Archbishop be later said. Our past President The Honorable J. Harold Grady was requested to represent the SOCIETY at the SOLEMN HIGH PONTIFICAL RE-

QUIEM MASS TO be celebrated at the new Cathedral dedicated to the HOLY MOTHER OF GOD, THE CATHEDRAL OF MARY OUR QUEEN, Charles Street Avenue, Baltimore, under the direction of the APOSTOLIC DELEGATE OF POPE JOHN XXIII, our Holy Father in the U. S. A., Archbishop Egidio Vagnozzi.

> "Through Her we may see Him made sweeter, not dim and Her hand leaves His light, sifted to suit our sight." G. M. Hopkins

In the words of our late and greatly lamented Archbishop Keough himself:

"May all offer a prayer to ALMIGHTY GOD for his noble soul whose cherished wish came to fruition in the erection of that Holy Regal House of God, in this oldest center of Catholicism in the U. S. A., and may his name for all eternity be recorded in the mind and heart of one who alone knows how to reward those who have loved "the beauty of His House." In the name of the Father and of the Son, and of the Holy Spirit. AMEN.

BIOGRAPHICAL NOTE

ON THE SAINT WE VENERATE, ST. PATRICK, THE PATRON SAINT OF IRELAND, WHOSE SAINTLY NAME WE ASSOCIATE IN OUR TITLE

Patrick probably was born in Dunbarton (now Kilpatrick Saints) Scotland, approximately in the year 389 A.D.

He was the son of a deacon, *Calpurnius,* and the grandson of a Presbyter named Politus. His father was a middle class landed proprietor, who was not particularly noted for his piety.

It appears, however, that his mother, *Conchessa,* who was related to *St. Martin of Tours,* was very religious. It seems probable that his saintly character was moulded along such lines through her influence. He doubtless was educated as a Christian, but nevertheless was embued with reverence for the Roman Empire, which then controlled most of the known world.

Unfortunately, or perhaps fortunately, when about 16 years old, he was kidnapped by a band of Irish Marauders under *King Niall Noigiallach* and held in bondage. As a slave, he became a shepherd in the North of Ireland, variously noted by historians as *County Antrim or County Connaught,* probably in the neighborhood of what is now known as *Croagh Patrick.*

His bondage lasted 6 years. During that time, he became subject to great religious emotion and beheld sacred visions which encouraged him to escape. After twenty-eight days of walking in constant danger through wilderness, he reached the eastern Irish coast near Wicklow. There he encountered a vessel which was exporting Irish wolf dogs. The kindly captain took him on and the ship eventually landed on the West coast of Gaul (now France). Patrick, in due course reached the monastery of Lerins on the Mediterranean coast. Now, safe with his own people, he began studying for the priesthood under St. Germain, Bishop of Auxerre, in about 410 A.D.

He had had a dream in which he saw a man named *Victorious* bearing various epistles one of which contained the words, *"The voice of the Irish"*. Patrick's words at this time are handed down to us as follows: "I imagined that I heard the voice of those who were near the Western Sea and they cried out 'we pray thee, holy youth, to come and walk again amongst us as before.' " In his vision was a forest in the neighborhood of *Killala Bay, Ireland.*

And so, against the opposition of his relatives, Patrick resolved on a mission to christianize the Irish. In due course, and after a considerable period of trial and study, Patrick was ordained by *Bishop Armator,* and ascended the sacred altar along with several others who later were associated with him in propagating the faith in Ireland; one of these was an Irishman named *Fith,* and the other was called *Auxilius.* All together, his studies are said to have extended over at least 12 years, since his resolve to become a priest and to advance in the church had been opposed variously by *Bishop Palladius,* and certain other ecclesiastics in Gaul and Britain.

While Christianity had taken some root in Ireland, nevertheless, at the time there existed considerable paganism and heresy.

When in 432 A.D. Patrick was consecrated Bishop as the final choice of *Pope Celestine I,* as *Apostle to Ireland,* he set out for *Eire.* In time, he arrived at the mouth of the *River Vartry,* in *Wicklow County, Leinster.* He immediately proceeded northward to the Eastern part of what is now *Ulster,* passing through *Meath.* A convert chief named *Dichu* granted him a wooden barn which he utilized for the purpose of worship, and there began his exhaustive apostolate.

Patrick's zealous activities eventually brought him into conflict with High-King Loigaire. Patrick challenged the royal authority by lighting the paschal fire on the hill of Slane on the night of Easter Eve, which happened to be the occasion of the pagan festival at *Tara* during which no fire was supposed to be kindled until the royal fire had been lit. A number of trials by fire and skill between Patrick and the King ensued, but finally Patrick was victorious; the King, although unwilling to accept Christianity, nevertheless took Patrick, now Bishop Patrick, under his protection. Patrick pleased God by his holy and tireless zeal.

Patrick travelled all over Ireland, establishing monasteries and churches but most of his work is more clearly identified with the *North of Ireland* rather than the South. His work in the South was more as organizer than as propagator. He was successful over great opposition by the heathen ruling chiefs. Twelve times he was captured, tortured and imprisoned, but in the end, Divine Grace and the Gospel could not be resisted. Hardened heathen Irish clans fell, one by one, before the *Cross of Christianity.*

In 441 A.D. he made a journey for the purpose of an audience with the Pope and after several years, brought back with him valuable Christian relics. On his return, he founded the *Church and Monastery at Armagh,* on land granted him by *King Daire,* which *See* was intended by him to be especially connected with the supreme Roman ecclesiastical authority. In all, for 33 years, Patrick spent himself in his divine mission. *Tara, Dublin and Munster* became household words. Monasteries dotted the land of Eire; hundreds of native Irish priests were ordained. The sanctification and security of an entire nation had become a stupendous fact. God was indeed pleased!

Patrick died approximately 461 A.D. *St. Brigid's* shroud was his pall, and *St. Tassach* administered the last sacraments. Some time before his death, he had resigned as *Bishop of Armagh.* His place was taken by his disciple

Benignus and thereafter, he retired to *Saul-Dalaradia* in Ireland, where he spent the remainder of his life in religious contemplation. His burial place is not absolutely certain, but tradition puts it at *Saul.*

While there is not a great amount of original documentation concerning Patrick's life, it is still possible to form a very clear conception of his personality.

Patrick pleased God by his *personal* holiness, by his *private piety,* and his own deeply spiritual life. He prayed incessantly, at *Crough Pat Mountain,* as his Master Jesus, the Christ had prayed at *Mt. Olivet.* He blessed himself constantly, he did penance, and he lived simply. He ate and drank little. God granted him miraculous gifts, which he practiced at *Tara Hill,* in *Limerick, Sangril* and *Munster.* He bore persecution, ill-will and opposition with equanimity and forbearance, but with a grand sense of Irish wit. He was a great and sublime writer! His hymn, known as the *"Breastplate of St. Patrick,"* is a masterpiece; also his *"Blessing From the Hill at Tipperary".*

In addition to the qualities which go to form a man of exceptional ability, he possessed a great enthusiasm which enabled him to surmount all difficulties. His great and enduring accomplishment was that he brought Ireland in touch with Western Europe and more particularly, with Rome. In addition to christianizing the whole of Ireland, he introduced Latin into Ireland as the language of the church.

Through Patrick's work, Ireland became the nursery for the church in Northern Europe. Learning was preserved against the barbarians in her monasteries. Missionaries poured into England, France, Switzerland and Germany from Patrick's converted island, as they now do into Africa, Asia and the South Seas.

Thanks to Patrick, Ireland became the world cradle of scholarship, refinement and knowledge. Thanks to Patrick, Ireland became the *"Isle of Saints",* a firm fortress of the faith that the Irish people have never deserted, a people of dignity, grace and wit, laughter and holiness, even in the face of physical, moral, political, economic and social persecution.

It is small wonder then, that the Holy, Roman, Catholic and Apostolic Church, in the collect of the *Mass for St. Patrick, Bishop and Confessor,* which is celebrated on March 17th, the day of his death in approximately 461 A.D., is the following:

"Oh God, who didst deign to send Blessed Patrick Thy Confessor and Bishop to preach thy glory to the nations, grant, through his merits and intercession, that those commands which Thou dost set before us we may by Thy mercy be able to fulfill. Through our Lord Jesus Christ, Amen."

"Behold, a great priest, who in his days, pleased God and was found just."

"Dominus vobiscum"!

LEGENDS ABOUT SAINT PATRICK

No March 17th in Ireland would be complete without this "Come All Ye":

"St. Patrick Was a Gentleman!"

St. Patrick was a gintleman, he came
 of dacent people
In Dublin town he built a church,
 and on it put a steeple.
His father was a Callaghan, his
 mother was a Brady,
His aunt was an O'Shaughnessy, and
 his uncle was a Grady.

No wonder that our Irish boys should
 be so free and frisky,
For St. Patrick taught them first
 the joys of tippling the whisky.
No wonder that the Saint himself to
 taste it should be willing,
For his mother *kept a shebeen shop*
 in the town of Enniskillin.

The Wicklow hills are very high, so's
 the Hill of Howth, sir,
But there's a hill much higher still,
 aye, higher than them both, sir.
'Twas on the top of this high hill
 St. Patrick preached his sarmint
Which drove the frogs into the bogs
 and bothered all the varmint.

There's not a mile in Ireland's isle,
where the dirty varmint musters,
Where'er he put his dear forefoot, he
murdered them in clusters:
The toads went hop, the frogs went
pop, slap-haste into the water,
And the snakes committed suicide to
save themselves from slaughter.

As we have said, when Patrick first began his missionary work there, the Irish were very antagonistic. Hence this story.

"One time Patrick met a *friendly man.* "God save you", says Patrick— and "the same again to you", says the friendly man, but if I might make so bold as to ask, sir, what does be ailing you? "You've a face on ye as long as a wet week". "Sure", sighs Patrick, "it's two days now since I had bit, bite or sup. I don't mind the hunger now, but oh, there's the death of a thirst on me". "That's easy fixed", said the *friendly* man, and he fetched him a stone jug of water. Patrick took it in his two hands, put his head back, and gratefully drank. "Ah, tis the water of life", he said, "drink you, now".

The *friendly* man did, and got the start of his life when he tasted it. "Tis *uisge beatha* (water of life), indeed", cried he, for the water has been turned to *usgue baugh* or whisky.

And, no matter what you say, this tale clearly proves that whisky was both invented and named by our Saint.

That's why the drinking of "Patrick's Pot" is an indispensable part of all St. Patrick's Day Celebrations (and others) in Ireland.

And the Snakes, now. Did St. Patrick really banish them? Scholars try to tell us that there *never* were snakes in Ireland. Sure, leave it to the "Scholars" and they'll destroy St. Patrick entirely, they will. So he did banish the snakes.

And the Shamrock, which Patrick used as a symbol of the Blessed Trinity. That's why, ever since, the Shamrock has been the symbol of both St. Patrick and of Ireland.

The *Green,* indeed, was first worn by Patrick, and the "Wearing of the Green" stems from that circumstance. The legend is that Patrick converted the High King in this way. He had two huts built, one of *dry* wood and one of *green;* then after sending his servant into the dry wood hut, blessed him—and had both huts set on fire; but, the *green* wood burned mightily while the *dry* wood remained untouched, and Patrick's servant stepped out unhurt. The green of the wood that burned was worn by Patrick in memory of that miracle.

Then there is the charming conversation between St. Brigid and Patrick. Brigid's day is Feb. 1, and she said, thinking of the farmers in a land of rain, "Every second day from my day onward shall be fine." Patrick added, "And *every* day from my day onward shall be fine."

For the farm year begins in February, and the potatoes should be set by March 17 which is regarded as the halfway mark of planting time. It is the day on which the rivers are opened, the cattle pastures changed, the seaweed collected in the neap tide. And, according to an old proverb in Irish, "No straighter is the salmon in the middle of the stream than is *Patrick's Day* in the middle of spring."

March is the month of bitter winds, too. "March borrowed three days from April to finish skinning the cow," the people say, *but it is noteworthy that Patrick's Day is almost always dry and fair.*

Small wonder, then, that Patrick's position is unique. Other countries pay scant attention to their Saints—who notices St. George's Day in England, or St. Denis' in France? —while in *Ireland March 17 is both a holy day and holiday.*

In former years, the butt or the jaunting car would be newly painted, and in it the whole family—in new clothes if possible, but, if not, with new green ribbons and shawls

—used to go to mass. Children were excited weeks ahead of time over their "Patrick's crosses," which they made themselves. These were really brightly colored circles of cloth, with or without crosses, made with rude compasses—or fingers used as compasses—and dyed with home dyes. Grass juice made the green; the yolk of an egg, the yellow; madder and lichen and seaweed gave red, brown and purple. In the center of each was a cockade of ribbon and shamrock. These are manufactured and bought now, but, whether as a cockade or plain, everyone in Ireland wears the green on Patrick's Day.

The parade, which in Dublin, as in New York, has these days become a matter of mass organization, used to be a local event in every village. The men and boys would meet at a crossroad and, headed by a drum, a tin whistle and a green banner, march a tour of the area. This was independent of the games which were always played, and still are; it's a great day for football or hurley.

Dances always crown the evening, and then there is the matter of "drowning the shamrock." Whisky, as we have seen, has a venerable history on the seventeenth, but, contrary to popular opinion, drowning the shamrock does *not* mean getting drunk. *It is the special ceremony of putting into the last drink of the night the shamrock which has been worn during the day.* When the glass is emptied, the shamrock is taken out and thrown over the left shoulder. For sure, as the old Irishman said, *"It was the first drop that kilt me; the last was harmless."*

Feast and faith, Patrick's Day has come down the centuries unchanged.

THE SOCIETY OF THE FRIENDLY SONS OF SAINT PATRICK OF BALTIMORE, INC.

BY-LAWS

ARTICLE I

Name and Seal of the Society

SEC. 1. The name of the Society is "The Society of the Friendly Sons of Saint Patrick of Baltimore, Inc."

SEC. 2. The seal of this Society shall consist of an Irish Harp, with the motto: "Erin Go Bragh."

ARTICLE II

Membership

SEC. 1. There shall be two classes of membership: (1) Active, and (2) Honorary. *The number of active members shall be limited to Five Hundred.*

SEC. 2. Gentlemen of the age of twenty-one years and over, citizens of the United States of America, being natives or descendants of the natives of Ireland, and of good moral character, shall hereafter be eligible for admission to active membership.

Active Members

SEC. 3. The initiation fee shall be five dollars. The annual dues shall be three dollars and payable on Saint Patrick's day in each year for the year then ensuing.

SEC. 4. An application for active membership shall be in writing, setting forth the name, age and business, profession or occupation of the applicant, the facts showing him to be a native or a descendant of a native of Ireland, his places of residence and of business, profession or occupation and such other facts as the Committee on Admissions shall prescribe as indicative of his eligibility for membership and shall be signed by the applicant. Such application shall bear the signatures of two members, one as proposer and the other as seconder, and shall be filed with the Recording Secretary who shall refer it to the Committee on Admissions. The Recording Secretary shall send to the members, with the notice of the next stated meeting, a list of all applications since the notice of the last stated meeting.

SEC. 5. The Committee on Admissions shall consider each application and may require from the applicant such additional written or oral statements as the Committee deems desirable. THE COMMITTEE, IN ITS JUDGMENT, SHALL HAVE THE FINAL AND EXCLUSIVE RIGHT TO REJECT ANY APPLICANT.

If the Committee acts favorably upon the application, it shall so report to the Society at a stated meeting at which there shall be a vacancy to be filled in the roster of active members and the Society shall proceed to vote on the election of such applicant.

SEC. 6. Each new active member shall qualify by paying the initiation fee of five dollars and dues of three dollars within thirty days following notification of his election. *Failure to so qualify shall invalidate his election. If such new member be elected at the December or March stated meetings, such dues shall be in payment of the dues for the year commencing the following Saint Patrick's Day.*

SEC. 7. *An active member who shall be in arrears for dues for the period of two years or a member who shall be indebted to the Society for a sum exceeding the amount of dues for one year, unless the Committee on Admissions determine otherwise, shall forfeit his membership and his name shall be erased from the roster of the Society following written notice from the Recording Secretary.* A member whose name has been so removed shall be obligated to pay all dues and other indebtedness incurred to the date of such removal before he can be reinstated.

Honorary Members

SEC. 8. Honorary membership may hereafter be conferred by the Society if all the following requirements and conditions be fulfilled, *provided there shall be strict observance of and compliance with the qualifications hereinafter set forth.*

(a) *The person proposed shall have rendered some conspicuous service (EXCLUDING PARTISAN POLITICAL SERVICE), to the United States of America, to Ireland, to the Irish people or to the Community, or shall have achieved distinction by laudable effort that reflects honor and credit upon the Irish name or people, and*

(b) The proposal shall be in writing signed by at least three members in good standing, and set forth the qualifications of the person proposed. It shall be filed with the *Recording Secretary* who shall refer it to the *Committee on Admissions,* and

(c) *The Committee on Admissions shall inquire into* the merits of the proposal and if the Committee acts favorably upon *the proposal, it shall so report in writing to the Society at the* next stated meeting. *Notice of the proposal* and of the Committee's report shall be mailed to the members prior to the meeting at which the Committee presents its report. Upon the vote of ¾ *of the members present and entitled to vote at a stated meeting,* the gentleman proposed shall be enrolled as an honorary member and shall be exempt from initiation fees and annual dues. He shall not be entitled to vote or hold office.

ARTICLE III

Officers and Their Election

Sec. 1. The elected officers of the Society shall be: President, First Vice-President, Second Vice-President, Third Vice-President, Treasurer, Recording Secretary, Corresponding Secretary, and Almoner. The President shall *appoint* the following officers: Counsel, Historian, Public Relations Director, Chaplain and Keeper of the Seal.

Sec. 2. (a) *The following officers shall be elected annually at the stated meeting in March from the members entitled to vote: President, First Vice-President, Second Vice-President, Third Vice-President, Treasurer, Recording Secretary, Corresponding Secretary, and Almoner.*

(b) The Counsel, Historian, Public Relations Director, Chaplain and Keeper of the Seal shall be appointed by the President immediately after taking office.

Sec. 3. *The President of the Society, at the stated meeting in December in each year, shall appoint a Nominating Committee of* seven members, one of whom he shall designate as Chairman.

This Committee shall nominate:

(a) *Members for the elective offices to be voted for at the stated meeting in March and*

(b) In the event of the death, resignation or removal of an officer, other than the President or First Vice-President, Second Vice-President, Third Vice-President, a member for the vacant office to be voted for at a meeting of the Society to serve for the unexpired term.

(c) The *NOMINATING COMMITTEE* shall deliver its list of nominees to the *CORRESPONDING SECRETARY* in time for him to mail each member a copy thereof *NOT LESS THAN FIFTEEN DAYS* prior to the stated meeting in *MARCH* or *FIFTEEN DAYS* prior to the meeting at which a vacancy is to be filled.

SEC. 4. *Nominations of candidates, other* than those nominated by the *Nominating Committee, shall be signed by not less than twenty members and be delivered to the Corresponding Secretary in time for him to mail to each member the names of such candidates not less than FIFTEEN DAYS prior to the stated meeting in MARCH, or FIFTEEN DAYS prior to the meeting at which a vacancy is to be filled.*

SEC. 5. Election of officers shall be by *ballot or by a showing of hands of those present* at the meeting at which the election is held. No nominee may be voted for at any such meeting unless nominated as provided in Section 3 or 4, of this Article III.

SEC. 6. In the event of the death, resignation or removal of any officer, other than the President and the Vice-Presidents, the President may, pending the election to fill the vacancy thus caused, designate a member to perform the duties of the vacant office.

SEC. 7. In the event of the temporary absence or disability of an officer, other than the President and First Vice-President, the President may designate a member to perform the duties of such officer temporarily.

ARTICLE IV

Duties of Officers

President

SEC. 1. The President shall preside at all meetings and functions of the Society and shall perform all other duties specifically developed upon him by these by-laws. He shall co-jointly with the Treasurer, be empowered to disburse or withdraw all funds of the Society.

Vice-President

Sec. 2. In the event of the death, resignation or removal of the President, the First Vice-President shall succeed to that office and the Second Vice-President shall succeed to the office of First Vice-President and the Third Vice-President shall succeed to the office of Second Vice-President.

The duties of the President shall, in his temporary absence, devolve on the First Vice-President, and, in the event of his inability to act, on the Second Vice-President, and in case of his inability to act, on the Third Vice-President.

Treasurer

Sec. 3. The Treasurer shall keep the moneys and securities of the Society, withdraw said securities from their place or places of deposit and purchase and sell securities, all as provided in Sections 3 and 4, of Article VII. He shall pay all obligations of the Society as provided in these bylaws and make payments of moneys appropriated and of contributions directed by the Society or Committee on Charity.

The Treasurer shall keep suitable books of account and record therein all receipts and disbursements.

The Treasurer shall render at each stated meeting a report of the finances of the Society, setting forth all receipts and disbursements since the preceding stated meeting, and the credit balance of each fund as it then appears. After the accounts of the Treasurer have been audited by the Committee on Accounts, as provided in Section 8 of Article VI, at the fiscal year, the Treasurer *shall prepare and report* to the members an annual financial report at the stated meeting in *March*. This report shall set forth the cash balance and the market value of all securities in any account; also a statement of receipts and disbursements applicable to said funds during the preceding fiscal year.

The above provisions do not apply to the moneys dispensed by the Almoner or his report.

The Treasurer and President shall be required to indemnify the Society by a surety bond in the amount of one thousand dollars ($1,000.00) for the faithful performance of their duties in connection with the custody of the funds of the Society, the cost of which shall be borne by the Society.

Recording Secretary

Sec. 4. The Recording Secretary shall have the custody of all membership and statistical records and journals of the Society; attend and act as Secretary at all meetings of the Society, the Board of Officers, the Committee on Admissions and the Committee on Charity, and keep a record of the proceedings of such meetings.

All payments on account of initiation and membership fees and dues shall be made to the Recording Secretary.

The Recording Secretary shall at all times maintain a list of the membership and an accurate account, of all moneys of the Society received by him and shall at least once in each month and on the last day of each fiscal year transmit to the Treasurer all initiation fees, dues and other moneys paid to him for the account of the Society.

The Recording Secretary shall promptly forward to each new member, notice of his election and to all members who are in good standing annual membership cards.

Corresponding Secretary

Sec. 5. The Corresponding Secretary shall receive and answer all written communications and mail to the members notices of stated or special meetings and other notices required by these by-laws.

The Corresponding Secretary shall act as Secretary to the Board of Stewards, issue all tickets for the *anniversary dinner or luncheon* (checks for which shall be made to the order of the Society), guest tickets for the stated meetings and other functions of the Society. He shall keep accurate records of any moneys received by him and transmit same to the Treasurer from time to time and the balance of such money, if any, on the last day of each fiscal year.

The Corresponding Secretary shall at the conclusion of the Anniversary Dinner or Luncheon or other functions of the Society, submit to the Board of Officers a complete account of all moneys received by him and transmitted to the Treasurer.

Almoner

SEC. 6. The Almoner shall dispense the moneys appropriated by the Society to his use for any designated cause. He shall report to the Society at each stated meeting the amounts received and disbursed by him since the last stated meeting.

Chaplain

SEC. 7. The Chaplain shall open and close all meetings of the Society with prayer.

Historian

SEC. 8. The Historian shall assemble and record data or documents and endeavor to ascertain facts relating in any way to the activities or accomplishments of the Society or its members. The Historian shall have charge of the preparation of such a history. Upon the completion of a history, or a part thereof, he shall submit it to the Board of Officers for review. After the approval of a history, or a part thereof, by the Board of Officers, that Board when authorized by the Society, shall have the same printed and published.

The Board of Officers may direct the Treasurer to set aside each year from the income of the Society, such amount as that Board determines to be applied to the expenses in connection with the preparation, printing and publication of a history or a part thereof.

Counsel

SEC. 9. The Counsel shall be the legal representative of the Society and its advisor.

Public Relations Officer

SEC. 10. The Public Relations Officer shall represent the Society in all matters of public relations, advertisement, promotions, etc.

The Keeper of the Seal

SEC. 11. The Keeper of the Seal shall be the custodian of the Official Seal of the Society.

ARTICLE V

Board of Officers

SEC. 1. The *Board of Officers* shall consist of the President, First Vice-President, Second Vice-President, Third Vice-President, Treasurer, Recording Secretary, Corresponding Secretary, Almoner, Chairman of Board of Stewards, Historian, Counsel, Public Relations Director and Keeper of the Seal. *The President shall be Chairman of this Board.*

SEC. 2. Except as provided in these by-laws, the Board of Officers shall manage and control the property, affairs and concerns of the Society and may incur any necessary or proper expenses in connection therewith.

The Board shall approve the payment of all obligations of the Society, except as provided in these by-laws.

SEC. 3. The past Presidents of the Society shall be entitled to attend the meetings of the Board of Officers in an advisory capacity but shall have no vote.

ARTICLE VI

Board of Stewards and Committees

SEC. 1. There shall be constituted in the manner hereinafter provided, a *"Board of Stewards"*, and the following *standing Committees: "Committee on Admission", "Committee on Charity", "Committee on Accounts and Finance"*, and *"Committee on Illness and Death"*.

Board of Stewards

SEC. 2. *The Board of Stewards of this Society shall consist of seven members to be appointed by the President, one of whom he shall designate as Chairman. Any officer may be appointed a member of the Board of Stewards.*

SEC. 3. *The SOCIETY shall hold an Annual Meeting, and, unless the Board of Stewards determines otherwise, shall thereafter hold an ANNIVERSARY DINNER OR LUNCHEON, ON OR BEFORE SAINT PATRICK'S DAY; PROVIDED, HOWEVER, IF SAINT PATRICK'S DAY falls on a SUNDAY then in such case, the ANNIVERSARY DINNER OR LUNCHEON shall be held on the PRECEDING DAY.*

The Board of Stewards shall fix the price of tickets, arrange the toasts and select guests of the Society for the Anniversary Dinner or Luncheon and otherwise supervise the Dinner or Luncheon.

SEC. 4. *The Board of Stewards shall arrange for and*

supervise all other social functions or gatherings of the Society.

SEC. 5. *The Board of Stewards shall regulate the admittance of guests to the meetings of the Society.*

Committee on Admissions

SEC. 6. The Committee on Admissions shall consist of seven members to be appointed by the President, one of whom he shall designate as Chairman. The President and Recording Secretary shall be members of this Committee.

The Committee shall have the powers and perform the duties devolved upon it under and set forth in these by-laws.

Committee on Charity

SEC. 7. The *Committee on Charity* shall consist of the *Almoner* and six *additional* members to be appointed by the President, one of whom the President shall designate as Chairman.

The Society may, at a stated meeting, appropriate moneys to be disbursed for charitable purposes to such institutions, organizations or individuals as this Committee may recommend, and shall be disbursed by the Treasurer.

Committee on Accounts and Finance

SEC. 8. The Committee on Accounts and Finance shall consist of five members to be appointed by the President, one of whom he shall designate as Chairman. No officer shall be a member of this Committee.

This Committee shall audit the accounts of the Treasurer and Secretaries and it may examine the proceedings of the Board of Officers, Board of Stewards and the Committees with respect to finances. In connection with such audit the Committee shall receive reasonable compensation as approved by such Committee and shall be paid by the Society. The accountant may be a member of the Committee.

The reports of the Committee shall be submitted to the Board of Officers.

This Committee shall keep informed as to the securities held in the permanent fund. The Committee shall, on or before the first days of *September and March,* in each year, and at such other times as such Committee deems advisable, report to the Board of Officers its recommendations as to retaining, selling and purchasing securities in or for the permanent fund.

Committee on Illness and Death

SEC. 9. The Committee on Illness and Death shall consist of seven members appointed by the President, one of whom he shall designate as Chairman.

SEC. 10. This Committee shall keep the Society informed concerning members who are sick, incapacitated or who have died.

This Committee with the advice and consent of the President and Chairman of the Board of Stewards shall arrange for the sending of Flowers, etc. for the sick or deceased members and shall render such material assistance as may be desirable.

ARTICLE VII

Funds of the Society

SEC. 1. The *fiscal year of the Society* shall be from *Saint Patrick's Day* in one year to *Saint Patrick's Day* next ensuing.

SEC. 2. The moneys in the permanent and income funds shall be deposited in such bank or trust company in the City of Baltimore as the President and the Treasurer shall designate.

SEC. 3. All checks of the Society shall be signed both by the President and the Treasurer.

ARTICLE VIII

Stated Meetings of the Society

SEC. 1. *THE SOCIETY shall hold four stated meetings in each year, as follows: in JUNE, SEPTEMBER, DECEMBER AND MARCH, ON A DAY THEREOF DETERMINED BY THE BOARD OF OFFICERS:* the *meeting held in MARCH shall be designated as the ANNUAL MEETING OF THE SOCIETY.*

SEC. 2. Thirty members shall be necessary to constitute a quorum at any stated meeting of the Society.

SEC. 3. At each meeting the order of business shall be as follows:

1. Opening Prayer
2. Roll Call of Officers
3. Reading Minutes of the Last Meeting
4. Reports of Officers and Committees
5. Election of Officers
6. Unfinished Business
7. New Business
8. Closing Prayer

ARTICLE IX

Special Meetings of the Society

SEC. 1. The President shall call *special meetings* of the Society when, in his judgment, they are necessary. It shall be the duty of the President to call special meetings at the request of the Board of Officers or the Committee on Charity, or upon a request signed by thirty members of the Society. Requests for special meetings shall be in writing, fully setting forth the purposes thereof. At least five days written notice by mail shall be given to the members of a special meeting and the purpose thereof shall be stated in the notice of the meetings.

SEC. 2. At special meetings thirty members shall be necessary to constitute a quorum.

SEC. 3. Special meetings shall be confined to the transaction of such business as is indicated in the notice of the meeting.

ARTICLE X

Amendments to By-Laws

SEC. 1. Suspension, repeal or amendments of any of the by-laws of this Society shall be considered only when the proposal for such suspension, repeal or amendment shall have been submitted in writing at a previous stated meeting and a copy of such proposal shall have been incorporated in the notice of such meeting at which action upon the proposal is to be taken.

SEC. 2. At any meeting where consideration is given to the adoption of any proposal for the suspension, repeal or amendment of any provision of these by-laws, a resolution or motion for the adoption of any such proposal shall require a vote of the majority of the members present and entitled to vote.

MISCELLANEOUS

SEC. 1. A member may resign from the Society by tendering his resignation in writing and having the same accepted.

SEC. 2. Any member who commits or performs any act prejudicial to the best interest of the Society may, after a hearing before the Board of Officers, and on the recommendation of such Board, be expelled by the Society at a stated meeting at which the report of that Board is considered.

SEC. 3. At a stated or special meeting of the Society, the election of an officer or the adoption of a resolution or carrying of a motion shall require the following vote of the members present and entitled to vote, viz:

(a) A *majority,* for the election of an *officer;*

(b) *two-thirds,* on any question involving *finances* or relating to the funds of the Society; and

(c) a *majority,* for the adoption or carrying of any other resolution or motion, except as provided in these by-laws.

SEC. 4. The adoption of a resolution or carrying of a motion at a meeting of any Board or Committee shall require a majority vote of the members of the representative Board or Committee.

SEC. 5. Parliamentary Procedure — Robert's Rules of Order shall govern meetings of the Society, its Board and Committees.

MEMBERSHIP LIST

January 31, 1962

Ahlers, John Clarke
Arnold, Francis Patrick
Aycock, James Melcher

Banahan, Harry John
Bangs, E. Donald
Bannan, Leo J.
Batterden, Charles T.
Bennett, Edward L.
Birrane, Sr., Edward J.
Birrane, Jr., Edward J.
Blatchley, Robert Leo
Boland, Joseph R. P.
Borrell, Richard T.
Bowers, Jr., William Joseph
Bowersox, Gerald O'Donnell
Bowling, Rev. George T.
Bracken, Thomas E.
Bradley, J. Murray
Brennan, Joseph T., II
Brett, John Michael
Broderick, Rev. Gerard W.
Broderick, Paul Timothy
Brune, John Joseph
Bullock, Joseph E.
Burke, Leo John
Burke, Thomas J.
Burns, Edward Pat
Burns, Robert J.
Burns, William Charles
Byrnes, Jr., James B.

Cadden, James Joseph
Cahill, Jr., William Walsh
Cain, Sr., William F.
Cain, Jr., William F.
Campbell, James William
Carey, Gerald Delaney
Carney, James Fitzgerald
Casey, J. William
Cashen, J. Frank
Chadwick, Gerald B.
Clarke, John Joseph
Coffman, William Brennan
Cohee, Edward Elmer
Coldewy, George E.
Cole, Charles (James) A.
Cole, James Arthur
Condon, Robert Emmett
Coniff, Edward J.
Conklin, Jerome Walter
Connell, Philip Patrick
Connell, Thomas Donald
Conniff, James P.
Connolly, James P., Sr.
Connor, Joseph Carroll
Conroy, John Dillon
Conroy, John Ralph
Cooney, William L.
Coppinger, Thomas Joseph
Corbett, Sr., Stephen V.
Corrigan, George Thomas
Coughlin, John Patrick
Cox, James Hugh
Cowan, William Thomas
Cross, Alfred E.
Crump, Maurice Joseph
Curran, James W.
Curran, John Francis
Curran, Jr., John Joseph
Curran, Martin Edward
Cusack, James Edmund

Danaher, John Carter

Dempsey, Bernard Joseph
Denny, James Patrick
Dohony, John Joseph
Dolliver, James Brian Alan
Donnelly, Edward John
Donnelly, Thomas Edward
Doud, John H., III
Doud, Thomas J., Jr.
Dougherty, Michael J.
Downey, Vincent R.
Duffy, John Michael
Duffy, Patrick Joseph
Duffy, M.D., William C.
Dugan, Francis Xavier
Dugan, Raymond Francis
Duggan, James F.
Dundore, Harry Ross

Edelen, Richard L.
Ellicott, J. Thomas
Erskine, Joseph J.
Evering, George C.

Fallon, Sr., Edward J.
Feeley, John James
Ferciot, Jr., Thomas N.
Finan, Thomas B.
Finnegan, James F.
Finnerty, Joseph Gregory
Finnesey, H. Lee
Finnesey, Lee Rennels
Fish, John E.
Fitzpatrick, Cyril deS.
Fitzpatrick, James Edw.
Flanagan, Carroll James
Flanigan, Jr., Dr. Edward A.
Flanigan, Gerald Joseph
Flanigan, Richard Joseph
Flannagan, William Scott
Flynn, Francis Xavier
Flynn, Thomas Shea
Fogarty, William Lawrence
Foley, Gardner P. H.
Forrest, Jr., Julian I.
Frantz, Harry J.

Gahagan, J. (James) Paul
Gallagher, Francis Xavier
Gallagher, George H.
Garrity, John Patrick
Gately, William John
Gibbons, Paul C.
Gillece, F. Earl
Gillern, Jr., Edward Michael
Gilmartin, John Bryan
Goonan, Joseph A.
Gorges, James H.
Greeley, Melvin J.
Griffin, John Joseph
Grogan, Thomas Patrick
Guerin, Richard J.
Gunning, Joseph P.

Hackett, John Daniel
Hambleton, Richard Nicolai
Hanly, James Joseph Patrick
Harris, Joseph Xavier
Hart, Francis Clinton
Hartnett, Jr., James Thomas
Hayes, Kenneth Matthew
Healy, Joseph C.
Hennegan, John G.
Hennessy, Francis Xavier
Hepburn, George R.
Hession, William J.
Hickey, John J.
Hines, John Jos.
Hogan, Frank Thomas
Hogan, Jr., John Francis, Dr.
Hogan, Jr., Richard G.
Holmes, Jr., Joseph Walter
Horigan, Frank Charles
Hourihan, Daniel Joseph
Hughes, William

Hyland, Bernard William
Hyle, Jr., Walter Dewey

Jenkins, Patrick Paul
Johnson, Edward McKenna

Kahl, Eugene Francis
Kane, James LeRoy
Kavanagh, John J.
Kearney, Charles Edward
Kearney, James Gibbons
Keary, Hugh Francis
Kehoe, James F.
Kelly, Arthur C.
Kelly, Edward J.
Kelly, Frank Patrick
Kelly, John Francis
Kelly, Thomas J.
Kelly, William Howard
Kelly, William Worrell
Kennedy, III, Edward John
Kennedy, Jerome McDonald
Kennedy, John Dailey
Kenney, Rev. Joseph Arthur
Kenny, John Berchman
Keogh, Jr., Gerard George
Kernan, Jerome Hayes
Kilduff, Jr., John E.
Kirby, Carroll G.
Kirby, G. Gordon
Kirby, Raymond Aloysius
Knott, Thomas

Lacy, James J., Jr.
LeCates, Robert H.
Lentz, David Charles, Jr.
Loome, John Francis
Lottes, Jr., Charles H.
Lottes, John Joseph
Loughran, Jr., Jerome A.
Lurz, George Anthony
Lynch, Joseph John

McCabe, Lawrence W. T.
McCarron, Edward Francis
McCollom, Robert James
McCormick, Leo H.
McCourt, Edward J.
McCrory, Rev. William T.
McCusker, Philip Tracy
McDonnell, John Richard
McEvoy, Joseph L.
McGarry, John Edmund
McGee, Francis Joseph
McGrain, Thomas J.
McGuire, John Albert
McGuirk, Harry J.
McHugh, George T.
McHugh, John Francis
McKenna, William Carroll
McKew, Thomas Joseph
McKewen, John L.
McLaughlin, James Gibbons
McLaughlin, Leonard L.
McLernon, Elmer Compton
McLernon, James
McMahon, Edward Eugene
McNally, Dr. Brendan I.
McNamara, Francis David
McNamara, James M.
McNicholas, Jr., Edward O.
McQuaid, Lawrence Edward
Maguire, David B.
Mahoney, James Leonard
Mahrer, Joseph Albert
Mairs, Jr., Matthew
Mallonee, Jr., O. Thomas
Manley, James Martin
Manley, Michael J.
Manning, Michael F. J.
Manning, Richard C.
Martin, Carl O.
Martin, J. William
Meagher, Jr., Charles C.
Meehan, James Edward

Michels, Dr. Joseph T.
Miller, Thomas H.
Millman, Gerard Lawrence
Mitchell, Lisle J.
Moan, John Foley
Monaghan, Edward John
Monaghan, Jerome E.
Monmonier, Rev. Charles B.
Mooney, Edward A.
Mooney, Kevin Xavier
Mooney, Roger Patrick
Mooney, Thomas J., III
Mooney, Jr., Thomas Joseph
Moran, Charles E. J.
Moran, Jerome S.
Moran, Patrick Joseph
Morris, William
Mullen, Thomas F.
Mulvey, Jr., John Vincent
Muntain, Charles Thomas
Murphy, Earl Herbert
Murphy, Frank E.
Murphy, James Berkeley, Sr.
Murphy, James W.
Murphy, John M.
Murphy, Jr., John Martin
Murphy, Lawrence Anthony
Murphy, William J.
Murphy, William L.
Murray, Albert Vincent
Murray, John Paul
Murray, Jr., John Paul
Murray, Raymond I.

Nelligan, Anthony F.
Nevin, Paul John
Nugent, Thomas C.

O'Brien, Walter F.
O'Connell, Jack Edward
O'Connor, Dr., John A.
O'Connor, Jr., John A.
O'Connor, John Joseph
O'Doherty, Gabriel Gerard
O'Ferrall, III, Alfred J.
O'Ferrall, John Patrick
O'Loughlin, William Donald
O'Malley, Edward Patrick
O'Malley, Patrick Paul
O'Malley, Vincent Jerry
O'Meara, James E.
O'Meara, Joseph Paul
O'Shaughnessy, Thomas F.
O'Shaughnessy, Woodrow W.
O'Toole, Daniel John
O'Toole, Edward T.

Palm, James Spaniol
Perkinson, John W.
Phelan, William Rowe

Ragan, James Jerome
Rau, William J.
Reeve, Jr., Donald H.
Regan, James A.
Reilly, William Graham
Reynolds, Sr., Joseph M.
Riesett, Frank N.
Roche, Patrick John
Rogers, William C.
Russell, Charles Ralph

Sauter, Albert Emory
Scott, Jr., William Lantz
Scott, William Richard
Silk, James J.
Simmons, Carroll V.
Sloan, John L.
Smith, Albert E.
Smith, J. Frank
Smith, Michael Paul
Snair, Jr., John L.
Spurrier, Anselm H.
Spurrier, John William

Stafford, James Joseph
Steadman, John F. P. V.
Stewart, Thomas Michael
Sullivan, Jr., Francis Joseph
Sullivan, John William
Sullivan, Joseph Francis
Sullivan, Joseph Patrick
Sullivan, William A., Jr.
Svrjcek, Jr., James Joseph

Thomas, F.S.C., Bro. Fidelis
Thommen, Harry O.
Toohey, James William
Tweedy, James Robert

Voelkel, Robert Emmett

Wade, Thomas Carroll
Walsh, Joseph A.
Walsh, William
Ward, Gerald A.
Welsh, James Joseph Jr.
Werneth, Paul J.
Whitaker, John C.
White, James R.
White, III, John J.
White, John M.
Wooden, Jr., William Francis